Patriotic Ayatollahs

Patriotic Ayatollahs

Nationalism in Post-Saddam Iraq

Caroleen Marji Sayej

Cornell University Press
Ithaca and London

Cornell University Press gratefully acknowledges receipt of grants from the Office of the Dean of Faculty and the Department of Government and International Relations at Connecticut College, which aided in the publication of this book.

First published 2018 by Cornell University Press

Printed in the United States of America

Library of Congress Cataloging-in-Publication Data

Names: Sayej, Caroleen Marji, 1975– author.
Title: Patriotic ayatollahs : nationalism in post-Saddam Iraq / Caroleen Marji Sayej.
Description: Ithaca : Cornell University Press, 2018. | Includes bibliographical references and index.
Identifiers: LCCN 2017028911 (print) | LCCN 2017030831 (ebook) | ISBN 9781501714856 (pdf) | ISBN 9781501714764 (epub/mobi) | ISBN 9781501715211 (cloth : alk. paper)
Subjects: LCSH: Iraq—Politics and government—2003– | Ulama—Political activity—Iraq—History—21st century. | Islam and politics—Iraq—History—21st century. | Nationalism—Iraq—History—21st century.
Classification: LCC DS79.769 (ebook) | LCC DS79.769. S29 2018 (print) | DDC 956.7044/3—dc23
LC record available at https://lccn.loc.gov/2017028911

To my daughters, Noor and Rania
And my partner in life, Wael
And for the people of Iraq, may they gain security and freedom

CONTENTS

PREFACE

This book has been brewing in my brain for more than fifteen years. I first became fascinated with the political role of ayatollahs when I taught my inaugural class on Iran at New York University in 2002. Since then, I have taught different iterations of that course on the graduate and under-graduate levels in which we explored the creation of an ostensibly Islamic state, the tensions within the clerical class about the direction of the regime, lay versus clerical interpretations of Islam, and a host of other intriguing topics. What most caught my attention was that several journalists—most of them women—had been able to travel to the city of Qom and interview Iranians to ask them questions about politics, gender, and life. Famous re-porters such as Robin Wright, Elaine Sciolino, Geneive Abdo, and Jona-than Lyons gained access to the highest-ranking clerics and uncovered the complicated and strained relationships that evolved after the 1979 revo-lution. Memorably, in her book *Persian Mirrors,* Sciolino related the tale of her plane ride from Paris to Tehran with Ayatollah Ruhollah Khomeini as he returned from exile. She was the first woman and the first journalist to interview him. From her vantage point, even Khomeini had no master plan for the future or blueprint for an Islamic state. In her travels to the city of Qom, she spoke with students of the grand ayatollahs and reported that the culture of the clerical system was democratic and therefore would never let the supreme leader rule in peace. The clerical class was increasingly marginalized as Khomeini consolidated his power in Tehran.

Nevertheless, that view of democratic ayatollahs stuck with me after the 2003 invasion of Iraq. Had I attempted to write this book then, it would have been very different and incomplete at that. Admittedly, I was viewing Iraq somewhat in terms of Iran, as most analysts did, but Iraq was even more complex than Iran. After the fall of the Taliban in Afghanistan, Iran had a monopoly on self-declared "Islamic statehood," and this subject occupied the bulk of the energies of US foreign policy analysts focused on the Middle East. Yet Iraq was not Iran. I had the time to reflect on Iraq's complexities. There was the US-led invasion of 2003 and the subsequent decade-long occupation. Iraq also had a multi-ethnic and multi-religious makeup. Its religious class had a different historical experience with the state. There was so much to be explored in how these complexities would play out in the post-2003 political milieu.

I had a chance to explore the role of the ayatollahs during the research for my first coedited book project, *The Iraq Papers*. In that volume I only scratched the surface. Beginning in 2011, I began to pay close attention to the role of the four grand ayatollahs in Najaf. I began collecting fatwas, speeches, *bayans,* and all other written statements and directives by the grand ayatollahs as the state-building project unfolded. I wanted to document the ways in which they were able to shape the narratives surrounding nationalism, democracy, sectarianism, and other prevalent themes of the day. Given the ayatollahs' prominence in society, I sought to document the ways in which they reinvented themselves as political actors and public intellectuals in the new state. I wanted to catalog the areas in which they would intervene to shape policy and the topics that were much more difficult to penetrate, such as the self-fulfilling prophecy of sectarian conflict. Regardless of the outcomes, the ayatollahs' ability to flood the public sphere with poignant and prominent political discourses served an important purpose. Their narratives, because they were repeated often and were sourced to reputable moral guides in society, helped to cultivate a sense of nationalism and political identity that served as a counter to the prevailing sectarian narratives emanating from those who wanted to derail the democracy project in Iraq. Narratives, when repeated often, take on truth value, and the ayatollahs served an important purpose in directing the conversation and redirecting it when it went off track. In the end, these ayatollahs, revered for their moral authority, used their informal political power to mold the political process in the direction of an Iraq-centric democracy.

With that in mind, the accounts in this book are neither comprehensive nor exhaustive. I followed the data, and the majority of the data pointed to Ayatollah Ali al-Husseini al-Sistani, the most widely followed Shiite cleric in the world. He worked alongside the state to ensure that the democratic project unfolded during the early years after the invasion. He was also the go-to figure for the media, although he almost never granted reporters an audience, and he was the chosen arbiter for the United Nations. I use fatwas, speeches, and *bayans* from the other three grand ayatollahs of Najaf as a check on the viewpoints of Sistani and also to give the reader a glimpse of the broader political culture of Iraq. At the same time, there are many thematic issues that could have been raised in this text, such as the debates between the grand ayatollahs and the lower-ranking clerics who may fill their seats in the decades to come. While of interest to scholars and students of Shiism, this theme was not particularly prominent in the state-building story I wanted to reconstruct about Iraq, with the grand ayatollahs at its center. By following the data, I developed chapters in the book that built on the most pressing discussions that were happening among the ayatollahs and between the clerics and their followers, the state, and the broader international community.

In reconstructing the stories and themes, I used a variety of sources and methods. For example, I relied heavily on fatwas and statements by Sistani, in Arabic. Most of the translations are my free translations of the texts. I also checked these against some English translations from newspapers or statements given by the clerics to the media that had been translated into English. I relied on English translations only when I looked up the context of a historical event from Arabic news sources on LexisNexis and found additional sources such as those from the Associated Press to corroborate information. The fatwas, communiqués, and directives given by the grand ayatollahs are sometimes short and were provided without context. To reconstruct a particular event, I often had to piece together the story by reading the proclamations of the ayatollahs around that time period, studying the political event in question, and reading additional materials (usually in Arabic newspapers). Often the stories needed to be reconstructed like a jigsaw puzzle.

In addition to the works of Sistani, I used books written by Ayatollahs Muhammad Saeed al-Hakim, Muhammad Baqir al-Hakim, and Muhammad Ishaq al-Fayyad, in Arabic. For sections of these texts, I worked with translators and a translation center for the sake of time and efficiency. Notably, while there has been considerable media attention given to Sistani's fatwas, there has been no previous scholarly attention given to the writings of any of the other senior clerics of Iraq.

This book is ultimately a story about how the grand ayatollahs repositioned themselves from apolitical to political actors after the fall of Saddam Hussein. Yet they were far from copying the Iranian model of the rule of jurisprudence. As Sciolino observed, Khomeini himself had no idea what he would implement or how he would do so when he returned to Iran. That same uncertainty clouded Iraq except that the details of the political process there would take place without the grand ayatollahs at the forefront. They would serve only as guides and allow Iraq's electorate and public officials to make their own choices. The complex relationship between religion and state would unfold in Iraq, as it did in Iran, with the grand ayatollahs wedged in the middle of the debates, though not necessarily perched at the top of the process. This understudied aspect of Iraqi politics challenges simplistic narratives about Iraq and sheds light on crucial issues pertaining to democracy, sectarianism, and the new political role of the grand ayatollahs, all from their unique vantage point. Even for an unstable country with dim prospects for democracy, this study is timeless because it covers an aspect of the Iraqi political system that is foundational and enduring—how crucial religious actors in the informal public sphere negotiated and shaped political discourses and concrete political outcomes in the post-Saddam era.

As the expression goes, it takes a village. This project is not the result of my solitary efforts. Rather, it is the product of critical thinking, engaging conversations, and great relationships that I have cultivated with others over the years. It is with great pride and humility that I recognize the individuals, institutions, and processes that helped lead me down this path.

The idea for this book developed out of a series of excellent encounters with my former department chair at Long Island University, John

Ehrenberg. After reading an early draft of an article, he called to tell me that I had an outline for a book. Over the course of the last decade, John has been my perpetual mentor, interlocutor, and friend. I am deeply grateful for his advice, his willingness to read endless drafts of the manuscript, and his belief in me. I also wish to thank my former colleagues at LIU, Jose Ramon Sanchez and J. Patrice McSherry, for helping to plant the seeds of this project from our previous collaboration on *The Iraq Papers*. Students I have taught over the years have also helped me to refine and revisit my ideas semester after semester. I thank them for the engagement.

Over the past few decades, I have benefited from the guidance of excellent mentors and professors at New York University during graduate school and beyond. There is a special place reserved in my heart for the late Youssef Cohen for his years of support. I cherish all the great conversations we shared over lunches. I also give thanks to John P. Entelis for planting the Middle East bug in me during my undergraduate years at Fordham University. Relationships with colleagues and peers have helped me to reach this point. These people have provided me with advice, read my proposal and then portions of the book, offered moral support, and referred me to people and places. I appreciate the generous support of Marisa Abrajano, Syed Ali, Feryal Cherif, Sheetal Chhabria, the late Sharin Chiorazzo, Joan Chrisler, Maria Cruz-Saco, Nathalie Etoke, Noel Garrett, Afshan Jafar, Arang Keshavarzian, David K. Kim, Andrew Lopez, Nina Papathanasopoulou, Asli Peker, Shira Robinson, Sufia Uddin, and Hani Zubida. Two people have been indispensable to the book-writing process: I am forever indebted to Michael Gasper and Eileen Kane for their friendship and support every step of the way. I am also fortunate to be in the company of great colleagues in the Department of Government and International Relations at Connecticut College. I give special thanks to Tristan Borer for her support as my department chair and Sharon Moody for her administrative assistance over the years. I am grateful to the wonderful staff at the college for all their help in processing my requests, especially Amanda Barnes and Mary Ellen Deschenes in the dean's office.

I thank Dean Abby van Slyck for her crucial support. I also wish to acknowledge grants that helped support various aspects of this project. Early in my years at Connecticut College, I benefited from two summer awards to travel and conduct research provided by the Judith Opatrny Fund. Over the course of writing this book, I was also awarded generous funding from the college's Research Matters Funds, the R. F. Johnson Faculty Development Fund, and the Hodgkins Untenured Faculty Fund. This support allowed me to make use of the very able translators Zied Adarbeh and Nadeen Rashdan. Nadeen in particular went above and beyond my requests and acted as a "fixer," negotiator, and arbiter for me across the region. She was able to sift through Islamic bookstores and seek out sources for me in Jordan, Lebanon, and Iraq. She also helped me in my transactions with the Diamond Translation Center in Jordan. The library staff, especially Emily Aylward at Interlibrary Loan, helped me obtain other hard-to-find texts in Arabic.

I wish to thank Pamela Haag in helping me launch this project. However, this book would not have come to fruition without the editorial guidance of Chris Toensing. His ability to finesse the text kept me motivated to move forward. I am grateful to Roger Haydon at Cornell University Press for his early and consistent support of my project and for acquiring my book. I also thank the anonymous readers for Cornell University Press, who helped me to clarify and refine my thinking. I am solely responsible for all the opinions and errors contained in this text.

Writing this book has been humbling and rewarding. I would not have been able to do it without the support of family and friends. During the crucial stages, I spent time away from my precious girls, Noor (age seven) and Rania (age three). They have been my biggest supporters, always asking me how many pages I've written on a given day. My husband, Wael, has been my rock and my anchor. He always reminds me to reach higher and higher. He has spent countless hours entertaining the girls and creating a sense of normalcy in our home during high-stress times. I thank my parents, Khawla and Suleiman Marji, for believing in me as I chose my career path. Their loving encouragement has been an inspiration. I thank my siblings, Jackleen, Marlene, and Michael, for listening to my endless lectures about the Middle East and for engaging in debates with me about the most controversial of topics. I thank everyone in our family who helped us with our children as I worked long hours over the weekends to crank out the writing. We used countless babysitters and mothers' helpers, especially Lavinia Castillo and Christina Perez, to help us get through long days of work. Special thanks go to Elise Roen and Lucy Buccilli for playing with my girls with such grace and affection. My in-laws, Nariman and the late Nabih Sayej, were always gushing about my accomplishments. No doubt my father-in-law would have been so happy to share in this moment with us. Last, I owe special thanks to my friends who sustained me through this time. Tom and Terry Bavier read drafts of the manuscript with excitement and anticipation. We have the most wonderful neighborhood of friends who entertained us during our famous Friday happy hour gatherings. My dear friends Nirupa Sekaran and Amani Abulhasan allowed me to escape to another world outside of academia.

Abbreviations

AMS	Association of Muslim Scholars
CMC	Council of Muslim Clerics
CPA	Coalition Provisional Authority
IGC	Iraqi Governing Council
INA	Iraqi National Alliance
INC	Iraqi National Congress
ISCI	Supreme Islamic Iraqi Council
ISIS	Islamic State in Iraq and Syria
KRG	Kurdistan Regional Government
ORHA	Office for Reconstruction and Humanitarian Assistance
PMF	Popular Mobilization Forces
SCIRI	Supreme Council for the Islamic Revolution in Iraq
TAL	Transitional Administrative Law
UIA	United Iraqi Alliance
UPM	United Patriotic Movement

A Note on Arabic Transliteration

In transcribing Arabic into English, I have kept the general reader in mind. The text follows a modified version of the Arabic transliteration system according to the *International Journal of Middle East Studies* (*IJMES*). I have eliminated all diacriticals and long-vowel markers except for the ayn (') and hamza (') in cases where the words commonly appear with diacritical marks. Therefore, I use the words *Quran, Shiites,* and *Ba'ath* according to common usage. Words appear in the plural form by the addition of an *s* to the singular, except in cases where the plural form has been standardized. Except on first mention, the article *al* has been omitted from the last names of individuals. Accordingly, Ali al-Sistani appears as Sistani throughout the text. Names with common English spellings, such as those widely cited in Western media, are preserved as such (for example, Hosni Mubarak and Saddam Hussein).

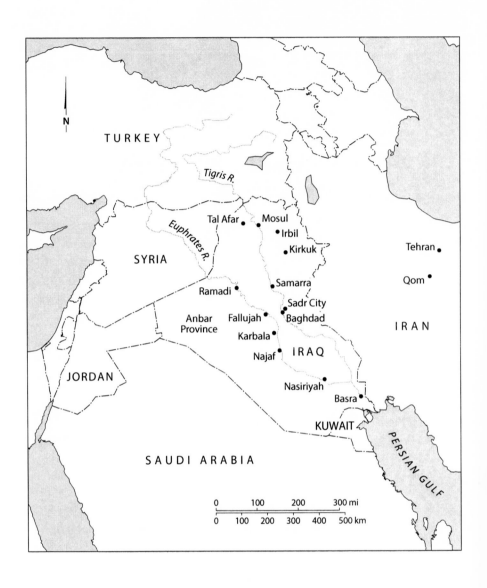

PATRIOTIC AYATOLLAHS

INTRODUCTION

The Making and Unmaking of Iraq

Kanan Makiya, an Iraqi-born academic who spent decades of his life in opposition to Saddam Hussein's regime, gained international recognition for his efforts to lobby the United States to intervene in Iraq, first in 1990 and again in 2003. Prior to 2003, he was most famous for *The Republic of Fear,* which he wrote under the pseudonym Samir al-Khalil to avoid endangering the lives of his family members still in Iraq.[1] In this book, Makiya painted a picture of Saddam's Iraq as a totalitarian state. Throughout the subsequent decade, with Iraq expelled from Kuwait but Saddam still in power, he documented the regime's crimes and advised members of the US-sponsored Iraqi opposition in exile. As the George W. Bush administration prepared to invade Iraq in 2002, Makiya was a prominent voice making the case that regime change was "the right thing to do" in order to rescue the Iraqi people from tyranny and suffering.[2] On the day that Baghdad fell, Makiya was with President Bush in the Oval Office. The oft-repeated phrase that Iraqis would greet the American invaders with "sweets and flowers" is attributed to him.

Makiya resurfaced in 2016 with a novel, *The Rope*, in which he sought to explore the "larger meanings and deeper truths" about what went wrong after the 2003 invasion. The novel, whose title is a reference to the hanging of Saddam Hussein, in 2006, is an indictment of the country's Shiite leaders—former exiles and (some of them) close friends of Makiya during his days in opposition to Saddam, who returned to Iraq and, in his view, drove the country to the edge of collapse with their corruption and ineptitude. Makiya says he has no regrets for supporting the war because his advocacy was based on "Saddam's crimes, not his weapons" of mass destruction, the illicit arsenal the Bush administration alleged was in Iraq but was never found. He is apologetic, though, for "bestowing legitimacy on a group of men who have proved themselves incapable of ruling Iraq." As he explains, "The Americans handed the reins of power to the Arab Shiite leaders, and my books and political activity helped in convincing them to do so." In another moment of introspection and lament, Makiya says it was naive of him to believe that "the Shiites, who had never ruled Iraq and whose culture embraces a deep sense of victimhood, could rise above their history and share power with Iraq's minority Sunni Arabs and Kurds." He refers to 2003 as a moment of political triumph that was "contrary to their entire history." He expresses disappointment in himself for thinking that Shiites would behave with more magnanimity, like Martin Luther King Jr., Nelson Mandela, or Gandhi.[3]

His partial regrets notwithstanding, Makiya continues to describe Iraq's politics much in the simplistic way characteristic of advocates for the invasion. First, he reproduces the framing of Shiites as a monolithic community. The causes of the disaster after the invasion are reduced to the country's "Shiite leaders," who could not escape a "culture of victimhood." His story has no nuance. We do not know to which Shiites he is referring, and he does not describe the conditions under which a handful of Shiites were selected to "rule" the country, as he puts it. He includes no discussion of why these politicians "rule" in a sectarian and corrupt manner, beyond the assumption that they are chained to their history. Makiya's language is itself sectarian. He sees the competing groups in Iraq as Sunnis, Shiites, and Kurds, not as Iraqis. He does not entertain the possibility that flawed political structures, not inherent "sectarian" differences, could be at the core of Iraq's stalled path to democracy.

In *Patriotic Ayatollahs*, I take up the task of examining those political structures, as seen from the vantage point of an oddly understudied set of actors, the four grand ayatollahs of Najaf. These senior Shiite clerics, the best known of whom is Ayatollah Ali al-Husseini al-Sistani, consistently advanced a nonsectarian view of Iraq. In the early days of the war and the state-building project that followed, Sistani was asked whether Shiites should have a special place in the government. His position, which we can now reflect on as visionary, was that "Shiites want what all Iraqis want, the right to self-determination." Their position was "not special," he argued, and no different from the rest of the population. From March 2003 onward, Sistani stated that he represented the interest of not only Shiites but also all Iraqis in the promotion of an Iraq-centric democracy. His political involvement, to the extent that he was able, would ensure that the pan-Iraqi model he laid forth, rather than sectarian categories, would frame the discussion in inclusive political terms. Moreover, he warned that any divisions among Iraqis, either through verbal manipulation or the formation of institutions, would open the way for others to "blame" Shiites for the course of events. After all, the Shiites were the majority. To that end, Sistani and the three other grand ayatollahs of Najaf made it their business, from the early days of the invasion, to engage in a visible, sustained, and interactive discourse about the state-building process. Although it might seem natural for the grand ayatollahs to be more concerned about the Shiites as their own constituents, that was not the case, as we will see. Their vision, contrary to that of Makiya, was an Iraq-centric one, and they foresaw the dangers of sectarianism and warned their followers.

In their political discourse, the grand ayatollahs paid special attention to correcting misinformation about Iraqi history and society, suggesting courses of action that would pave the way for an inclusive form of government and highlighting the causes and consequences of the sectarian fighting that eventually became commonplace. This intervention was important because, following narratives like Makiya's, observers could easily conclude that the conflict in Iraq originated in inherent sectarian differences. Moreover, the sectarian framing implies that the obstacles to Iraqi democracy could be reduced to the inability of Shiites to share power with minorities because of their history of "victimhood." In vivid and powerful ways, the role of the ayatollahs illustrates that the sectarian narrative is inaccurate.

Through an analysis of their writings, fatwas, decrees, pronouncements, and speeches from 2003 to 2016, a period when the ayatollahs
were consistently politically engaged, I explain their interaction with the
state on important issues such as the role of competing social groups,
the debate within Shiism about clerical quietism as opposed to activism,
their ideas about how democracy should be implemented in Iraq, and the
causes and consequences of the sectarian conflict engulfing Iraq. My analysis demonstrates that rather than confining themselves to their religious
duties, as they had done for decades prior to 2003, the ayatollahs have
come to the forefront as public intellectuals and crucial informal political
actors. Rather than beginning with their religious principles and applying
them to the political context, the ayatollahs are keenly aware of the political milieu, and their recommendations are shaped by it.

This book showcases the powerful discourses of the senior Shiite clerics
and how they oriented a state under reconstruction, especially during a
period of brutal and sustained violence. Their importance lies in their ability to affect the state's course of action. With a single fatwa in June 2003,
Ayatollah Sistani arguably jump-started an electoral process. Had it not
been for his intervention, Iraqis might have been excluded from state
building in the early years after Saddam fell. Sistani made it absolutely
necessary that the constitution be written by an elected body so that the
process rested on the notion of popular sovereignty. This study evaluates
not only the moments in which the ayatollahs were effective in pursuing
policy outcomes but also the ones in which they were not. As we will see,
their efficacy was variously a reflection of self-imposed limits, their own
strategic interests, and the hard political realities of war-torn Iraq.

Over the years, and through interaction with the political system, the
ayatollahs matured alongside the system itself. *Patriotic Ayatollahs* offers
a window into the evolution of their thought during a crucial time—the
power vacuum in 2003—that created the opportunity for a multiplicity
of new social actors to emerge. The men in clerical garb, in a surprise to
US policy makers, journalists, and commentators at the time, were at the
forefront of progressive politics in the country. Rather than co-opting
the state, as the clergy serving the majority, or encouraging sectarian violence, they were central in keeping the state-building project on track—to
the extent possible, given the fact that they were not part of the formal
process.

But this study is not about outcomes per se. Its goal is not to measure the volume of fatwas and keep score of which were effective and which were not. It is about the fact that discourse matters regardless of outcomes. Discourse tells us something about the political culture in which people operate. There is interpretive value in the ideas that flood the public sphere and are reproduced over and again, creating new patterns of interaction and new political symbols. The ayatollahs helped to set the parameters for debate—to frame that debate.

As defined by David Snow and Robert Benford, framing is "an active, process-defined phenomenon that implies agency and contention at the level of reality construction."[4] These authors understand the discursive process to have a strategic function because language can be molded to suit the needs of the relevant actors. In post-Saddam Iraq, Sistani and others engaged in the discursive battle over the new symbols of the state. They were intentional in the manipulation of language at moments of contention. Language was an important way in which groups competed in Iraq beyond traditional measurements, such as formal access to power. The ayatollahs emerged on the scene very early on because the architects of the new state project, US policy makers and the former exiles who were their Iraqi proxies, wrote about Iraq in sectarian terms and envisioned a state based on these assumptions. The ayatollahs, through powerful speeches and statements, were able to grant legitimacy to a counter-narrative.

Ariel Ahram summarized the power of discourse best: "[F]rames condense expansive and elaborate ideological positions into evocative symbols, providing interpretations of the world that place blame and suggest courses of action."[5] Drawing on such logic, the ayatollahs made the historical connection between British imperialism and the US invasion to make sense of the new social conditions in Iraq. Whenever they were asked their opinion about how long the occupation should last, for example, they usually responded with long narratives about colonialism and pledged that Iraq's government would be "legitimate" only when it was "free from outside interference." They also made connections between Iraq and other occupied territories, or, more fundamentally, they mocked the question itself as absurd. The same was true during the period of sectarian violence that peaked in 2006–2007. Each ayatollah approached the crisis from a different discursive angle. For example, Sistani was careful not to use the word "sectarianism" at first because he knew that, because of his popularity, it would be repeated in the media, which would render him partly responsible for its reproduction. He also wanted to set the record straight that Iraqis had a long history of peaceful communal coexistence and that, without "foreign meddling," there could be coexistence once more. Sistani's narrative was also replete with details of the connection between the sectarian conflict and the high levels of government corruption. His warnings, after US involvement waned, focused on poor Iraqi leadership. Ayatollah Muhammad Saeed al-Hakim preferred to point out, somewhat more abstractly, that multi-ethnic and multireligious nation-states were the norm and not the exception in the modern era. Ayatollah Bashir Hussein al-Najafi urged people not to be provoked into a civil war. He issued a series of statements that sought to deflect blame from Sunnis and instead redirect attention to US forces for the "lawlessness" throughout Iraq.[6] Ayatollah Muhammad Ishaq al-Fayyad labeled those who engaged in violence as "terrorists" and called for swift punishment. Sistani showed more restraint, using the term "terrorist" only to refer to ISIS, having stopped at "deviant" for Abu Musab al-Zarqawi, the leader of al-Qaeda in Iraq. Najafi, who reached for a wider audience, called on all Iraqis to stand firm against those who undermined Iraqi sovereignty because the fight against terrorism was a fight "on behalf of the whole world." Thus did the discourse of the ayatollahs, in Ahram's terms, reflect their "interpretations of the world" that "place blame and suggest courses of action." Moreover, these frames had the "power to imbue or deny legitimacy to specific political action."[7]

Ayatollahs have a special ability to frame public discourse in Iraq, where Shiites make up 60 percent of the population. The ayatollahs are the highest-ranking clerics in Shiism and reach their position through a rigorous process of peer review, issuing fatwas, and the number and quality of students and followers each cleric maintains. Shiites are expected to follow the guidance of a particular living ayatollah for advice in spiritual matters and in their everyday lives. In Najaf the four grand ayatollahs regularly issue fatwas that have been shown to shape voter turnout and sometimes policy.[8]

Religious authority in Shiism, in the hierarchical sense, is located in the *marja'iyya*. This term refers to the collective of supreme juridical authorities who possess the exclusive authority to interpret Islamic law. The *marja'iyya* is composed of senior jurists, currently the four grand

ayatollahs, who preside over the *hawza,* the seminaries of Najaf. The individual *marja' al-taqlid,* or ayatollah, reaches this position through the
study of jurisprudence, extensive economic networks, and social popularity. Part of his success is also based on his ability to collect tithes from
worshippers. This financial obligation of the Shiite faithful gives the clerical establishment its own source of funding with which to run the seminaries independent of government control. The seminaries of Najaf were
able to retain their identity over the centuries because of their ability to
maintain their political and financial independence. They relied on private
donations and the obligatory religious tax, unlike the Sunni madrasas,
which began receiving government funds. The seminaries' independence
guaranteed their intellectual freedom and the mobility to operate outside
of the domain of the Ottoman state.[9] This economic relationship creates
a bond between the cleric and followers, and can determine the scope of
the seminary's appeal. The more payments an ayatollah collects, the richer
the seminary and the greater its influence. The relationship translates into
political power. Followers also seek advice on political matters from the
ayatollah to whom they adhere. The ayatollah, in tune with the needs of
his constituents, is always aware of the social and political issues of his
time. For example, Sistani has a daily habit of reading prominent Iraqi and
Iranian newspapers. He listens to BBC radio broadcasts. He tries to get
firsthand information about regional and world issues from his trusted advisers. He also consults with the three other grand ayatollahs of Najaf, although his decisions on major political and social issues are deemed final.[10]

Today, as before 2003, Sistani has the largest following of any Shiite
ayatollah, extending beyond Iraq's borders. There is no method of tracking the numbers of adherents of any particular ayatollah because these
decisions are personal and the networks are transnational. A Shiite in
Kuwait can follow an ayatollah from Lebanon; a Shiite in Pakistan can
follow an ayatollah from Iraq. Estimates are made by the collection of
religious taxes and the organization of Shiite pilgrimages. By these counts,
nearly 80 percent of all Shiites follow Sistani.[11] It is a remarkable fact
given that during Saddam's rule, Sistani was under house arrest and was
prevented from teaching for well over a decade. His seminary was all but
defunct.

A parallel element was in play, that events in Iran would have an effect
on Iraq. Sistani was able to rise in the ranks not only in comparison to the

three other ayatollahs of Iraq; he was also able to reserve an important place for himself and for the holy city of Najaf because of the declining influence of the Khomeini effect. After the death of Ayatollah Khomeni in 1989, few clerics were willing to follow his interpretation of statehood. His targeting of the clerics of Qom, Iran, and the creation of the special court for clergy forced him to hastily elevate Ali Khameini, Iran's current supreme leader, from a mid-ranking *mujtahid* (doctor of Islamic law) to an ayatollah, against convention. Clerics were divided on whether they should follow him, and average Shiites have struggled to recognize him as a preeminent religious scholar. As Sistani criticized the Iranian model and distanced himself from it, his credibility and followers increased. This narrative of an Iraq-centric state not hewing to the Iranian model would serve as the backbone of Sistani's philosophy in the post-Saddam era.

Consistent with Sistani's popularity and presence, he receives particular attention in this study. He is the main but not exclusive ayatollah at the forefront of interaction, first with US policy makers and then with Iraqi politicians. I highlight his writings and actions, and when the data allow, I check them against other grand ayatollahs to make more-general observations about political-religious culture in Iraq. Sistani has also been very influential as the go-to figure in Western media. This makes him in some regards a special case but, in other regards, an indicative and representative case of the broader culture in which he participates.

As will be seen in the pages to follow, the connection between an ayatollah and his followers is complex. The fatwa is technically supposed to be binding on followers, but it does not always work that way. It is more common that an ayatollah issues a fatwa and it is left to followers to determine its applicability to specific cases. If an ayatollah determines that alcohol is forbidden, to take a common example, the burden falls on the follower to ensure that all liquids consumed are nonalcoholic. A sense of personal responsibility attaches. To take another example from contemporary Iraqi politics, on June 3, 2012, Grand Ayatollah Kazem al-Husseini al-Haeri, based in Qom, Iran, issued a fatwa that forbade voting for secular candidates. Haeri declared that his fatwa was binding on all his followers and applied not only to the upcoming Iraqi elections but also to all Iraqi government institutions. But a prominent Iraqi follower of Haeri, the populist cleric Muqtada al-Sadr, rejected the fatwa because it was "impossible to separate between secularists and Islamists." Sadr said he would look instead to guidance from Ayatollah Sistani or Ayatollah Fayyad on this issue because "these authorities issue fatwas for the benefit of Iraq, not other countries."[12]

In general, however, the fatwas related to the electoral process in post-Saddam Iraq were much more effective than those that called for an end to sectarian fighting. The disparity is in part caused by the stakes. Fatwas that called for calm amid a civil war were less likely to be effective than fatwas making voting an obligation for all or fatwas that called for a boycott of the political process until legitimate elections were conducted. The efficacy of the fatwa must also be understood in the context of its historical origins and intended purpose, as well as consideration of how that purpose has changed in the contemporary era.

In the sixteenth century, Shiite jurists had established a new concept that transformed the relationship between community leaders and worshippers. Worshippers should either reach the highest level of *ijtihad* (independent reasoning) or follow a person who had attained such a level of education. This was the theory of *taqlid* (emulation). Ordinary Shiites regarded the cleric in their locality who had reached the highest level of Shiite jurisprudence as their *marja' al-taqlid* (source of emulation). Primarily, the jurists gained followers for their legal interpretations, and they collected religious taxes on behalf of the Hidden Twelfth Imam, who it was believed would return one day to rule over the community. The arrangement was highly personal and varied in its particulars from place to place. Mehdi Khalaji, in tracing the evolution of the *marja'iyya,* argues that a transformation took place beginning in the 1830s, when modern communications and transportation allowed local Shiite leaders to become transnational. Universal patronage networks were forged that allowed ayatollahs to extend representation and influence in major cities across the globe.[13]

Prior to the rise of the nation-state, the clerics of Najaf also had active political roles that were on display in sessions called *majalis* or *dawawin.* These sessions often featured lively debates on the pertinent political and social issues of the time. The sessions also had an important function in resolving social conflicts, and they were the base from which important political events were planned.

In the late nineteenth century, their political role played out on a larger stage, as the ayatollahs took action to resist Western colonial encroachment on Muslim lands and the corruption of Muslim political leaders. A case in point was Ayatollah Hasan al-Shirazi's 1891 fatwa that forbade the use of tobacco. This ruling came in response to the Qajar shah's decision in 1890 to grant the British commercial concessions that included exclusive rights to Iran's tobacco industry. The Qajar government had granted countless concessions to the British and the Russians as the foreign presence grew in Iran. Local merchants were increasingly vulnerable to European competition. The tobacco concession was especially sensitive because the crop was homegrown, widely consumed in Iran, and of a special, highly desired variety. The merchant class led mass protests based on a nationalist platform. Shirazi's subsequent fatwa, calling for a boycott of tobacco, united the merchants and the religious class in an attempt to limit the power of the shah and protect national interests from foreign domination. The overwhelming public support for the tobacco boycott cut across lines of class and level of education.

By the dawn of the twentieth century, the political power of the clerics posed a serious challenge to the authorities in both Iran and Iraq. Ayatollahs were key players in Iran's 1905 Constitutional Revolution and in the 1920 revolt against the British in Iraq.[14] The role of the ayatollah had been transformed: No longer simply a jurist settling legal disputes and giving opinions on questions of personal comportment, the *marja'* was now also regarded as a guide in political and social life.

Ironically, the same technological change that made possible a national and transnational political role for the ayatollahs also undercut their unquestioned authority among their followers. Today's followers obey the opinions of their ayatollahs selectively, as Sadr chose to do regarding the 2012 Iraqi elections. They also exercise considerable agency in shaping ties with their religious community leaders.[15] Followers are attracted to religio-political organizations outside of the realm of the *marja'iyya*. In Iraq after 2003, new forms of authority have emerged parallel to the ayatollahs, sometimes mounting an explicit challenge to their authority and legitimacy.

Mehdi Khalaji argues that *maraji'* (ayatollahs) have lost their monopoly over religious institutions and that influential clerics who are not *maraji'*, along with radical lay Islamists, will be able to run religious institutions without the *maraji'* as intermediaries. As new forms of authority emerge, he views the *maraji'* as the "main representatives of conservative Islam." He also predicts that when the religious discourse of the *maraji'* becomes less attractive to the upper and middle classes and the young, they will seek to invent their own religiosity. From his vantage point, the *maraji'* would likely remain models for the Shiites who adhere to an "unreformed version of Shiite jurisprudence."[16] Although there will be greater room for religious interpretation without the ayatollahs as the main intermediaries, the post-2003 milieu demonstrates that the grand ayatollahs are very much aware of this possibility. In turn, they are engaging in a rigorous process of self-exploration. They are updating their institution to account for the needs of this population in the hopes that they may retain their followers and continue to recruit new ones. In fact, their political activism in Iraq from 2003 to 2016 and their use of their religious institution in modern terms, especially as they embraced a secular state structure and affirmed their commitment to Iraqi nationalism, are testaments to their awareness of the changing tide and their desire to take part in it.

Sistani and the other grand ayatollahs have accordingly felt a sense of great urgency. Their struggle to maintain their status is rooted in the onslaught of Saddam Hussein's regime against Shiite institutions and the rise of Qom as a center of Shiite learning under the patronage of Iran. Only a few hundred students were in Najaf at the time of the US invasion. The ayatollahs knew they needed to remake the institution of the *hawza* to appeal to young Shiites seeking a religious education suited to the modern world. Their political message also had to be attractive to and inclusive of the many Iraqis who were not Shiites.

The limits of the ayatollahs' impact after 2003 owed largely to historical circumstances, but also to a conscious choice. From the very start, the ayatollahs determined they would act as "guides"—and guides only—in stark contrast to the Khomeinist model of *velayat-e faqih* (rule of the jurisprudent), which placed the ayatollahs at the center of formal politics and, indeed, the nitty-gritty of government. The ayatollahs never intended to establish a relationship with their followers akin to the relationship between ruler and ruled.

This book makes an important distinction between formal and informal politics. A good deal of the existing literature in Middle East studies is focused on formal politics, the domain of potentates, presidents, parliaments, and armies. But a growing body of work is broadening the definition of political participation in order to capture the impact of important political acts that would otherwise go unnoticed. This newer literature looks at such actors as labor unions, women's groups, and civil society organizations. In recent years, scholars have argued that the formal and informal worlds, which were long studied separately, should instead be bridged. The informal institutions have not been sufficiently studied, and it is increasingly clear that they have an impact on the state in such domains as forging coalitions and mediating conflict. Informal action is in fact the most common form of political participation in the Middle East, given the authoritarian regimes that have long dominated the region. As Quintan Wiktorowicz and Suha Taji Farouki observe, political participation in the Middle East involves the "symbiotic struggles over the rules that guide everyday life" and makes "politics and governance much broader than the state."[17] Surprisingly, the ayatollahs of Iraq are absent from this literature, but they have been very important informal political actors. Analysis of their role is in fact "critical to a comprehensive understanding of state-society relations" in today's Iraq, a post-authoritarian setting in which we may expect a strong residual effect of the authoritarian political culture upon the political landscape.[18]

In the aftermath of Saddam's downfall, the US occupation cast a long shadow over the ayatollahs' possible courses of action. The ayatollahs did not launch an armed insurgency or foment a coup. The clerics did not in fact want to join the formal political system that was emerging. They had no program of revolution, Islamic or otherwise, and no intention to carve out a place for themselves in the new state structure.

Throughout the state-building process, the ayatollahs instead played a crucial informal role. The ayatollahs became political after decades of quietism. They were able to forge "self-help networks" that served the function of providing information, they supplied the "channels to oppose the authorities," or, at a minimum, they "constituted sources of solidarity."[19] They called for protests and appealed to international bodies to gain leverage over state leaders when domestic pressures were inadequate. They tried to maximize the ability of the populace to influence political outcomes. They acted as mediators between Iraqi political factions. With their discourse, Iraqi ayatollahs worked to "imagine the nation," making important contributions to the formation of collective identity in Iraq.

Their goal was to compete over the language and symbols used in the framing of the new state structure. But by remaining outside the state themselves, they maintained an edge over politicians, who had to face constant criticism in the press and the formal accountability mechanism of elections. Because of the nature of the Shiite hierarchical institution, the ayatollahs were more closely linked to society than to the state, and they were careful never to cross that line.

Indeed, what is remarkable about the case of the ayatollahs is that their power is derived from their ability to organize both alongside the state and in dialogue with the state. Their power is sustained precisely because they chose not to be part of the state-building process. By hovering around the system, untangled in the minutiae of government and unbound by the demands of coalition partners, the ayatollahs can pick and choose when and how to intervene.

The ayatollahs, representing a generation of uniquely authoritative clerics trained in Najaf, were from a hierarchical institution and possessed an ability to deliver traditional guidance to their followers, adding to the richness of political discussion after the fall of Saddam Hussein. Yet they displayed a fluidity and fluency in political discourse that rendered them thoroughly "modern" and in step with contemporary developments.

Despite many setbacks, the ayatollahs were able to generate a new language about Iraqi national development that referenced the colonial past and promoted an Iraq-centric identity as the model best attuned to themes of Iraqi history. The ayatollahs, in their pronouncements, demonstrated clarity in language and pragmatism in their delivery of their message, first to reach US policy makers and then to reach the various factions working to implement US plans in Iraq. In their efforts to generate a rich body of rulings on a range of issues, from elections to sectarian fighting, they displayed pragmatism and a keen adaptability to conditions ranging from military occupation by the world's sole superpower to the threat of national dismemberment at the hands of ISIS. They encouraged dialogue, fought for transparency and against corruption, and championed coexistence among religious sects.

The ayatollahs' engagement was not abstract intellectual work—it was pragmatic and highly strategic political thinking. Their interaction with the state laid the foundation for an important discussion about voting and electoral democracy, state legitimacy, and international recognition through the United Nations. This book demonstrates that, contrary to Western notions, religious actors can act as agents of social change, rising above the social constructions of sectarianism that emerge out of colonialism. In post-2003 Iraq, the grand ayatollahs of Najaf were no purveyors of centuries-old hatreds, as mythology about Iraq has come to presuppose, but perhaps the key public intellectuals of their time.

1

THE AYATOLLAHS AND THE STRUGGLE TO MAINTAIN LEGITIMACY IN THE NEW PUBLIC SPHERE

Post-2003 Iraq was new terrain for the ayatollahs of Najaf and for everyone else. Saddam Hussein's authoritarian state had been torn down, and the new political order had no systematic suppression of opposition. The ayatollahs soon realized that their traditional monopoly over religious interpretation and other guidance for the Shiites of Iraq was gone as well. The power vacuum created a space for new social actors to challenge their status and position. The challenges to the ayatollahs' standing—intellectual, social, and material—came from several directions.

One challenge came from Sunni Islamists, ranging from efforts to form a Sunni *marja'iyya* to the sectarian terror of al-Qaeda in Mesopotamia and, eventually, to ISIS. But the greatest challenge came from the rise of lay Shiite groups, which offered Shiites an alternative to the traditional clerical model and appealed especially to the urban poor. The most important of these groups formed under the leadership of Muqtada al-Sadr. Sadr offered a new vision for Shiite leadership outside of the *hawza*. He was able to gain a large following, and his demands often exceeded or contradicted those of the ayatollahs, thereby questioning, at least implicitly, the relevance of the centuries-old institution.

In response to this existential threat, the ayatollahs worked to maintain their position as the most legitimate religious voices at the grassroots level. They also worked to pull the center of gravity away from Sunni Islamists, some of whom were using the same language as the ayatollahs and thereby undermining their authority. It was a battle for the minds of the people, a new discourse to compete for the street.

As will be made clear in this and subsequent chapters, the clerics did not attempt to impose preexisting religious ideas upon reality. Over and again, their religious ideas were derived from political expediency or rational calculations. The ayatollahs had to adapt to a rapidly changing context, and they were able to do so, not in spite of but because of the organization of the *hawza* and its institutional legacy. Today, as in 2003, the ayatollahs are realistic, shrewd, and in touch with the needs of the populace. Like politicians accountable to the citizenry, the clerics are constantly adjusting to the needs of their constituents.

That the ayatollahs in post-2003 Iraq would face the biggest challenge to their legitimacy from *within* the Shiite community was unexpected. The story of Iraq is normally presented as pitting Sunnis against Shiites, and it was thought that this supposedly timeless divide would structure Iraqi politics after the fall of Saddam as well. The United States believed it could reengineer those politics to calibrate the communal balance of power properly. It was consciously to empower the Shiite majority (along with the Kurds) against the Sunni Arabs that US policy makers implemented such policies as debaathification. But events did not unfold the way the United States expected.

To understand why not, it is important to begin with the history of how Shiites were situated within the state in the early twentieth century. Contrary to the sectarian framing that guided US thinking, the marginal status of the Shiites was historically constructed through the discourse of Arabism. They were usually depicted as outsiders because they were "Persians," not because of doctrinal differences with Sunnis.

Shiism has always been the smaller of the two main branches of Islam, with its adherents making up less than 15 percent of the Muslim population worldwide. As a result, historically, Shiite scholars (outside of Iran) were rarely allied with the structures of state power. When Muslim empires came under direct Western influence, as in the case of the Ottomans, Shiite scholars managed to operate below the Europeans' radar. The Westerners' lack of interest also contributed to the survival of the scholars' precolonial position after the Ottoman Empire broke up. The Shiites' minority status and independence from imperial power allowed them to develop authority structures that could endure, with or without state sponsorship. The divergent paths in Shiism between Iraq and Iran in the twentieth century are reflective of the different characteristics of religion and society between the two countries in the centuries prior to modern state formation, characteristics that were later institutionalized. These patterns of ritual, organization, and cultural practices would explain why the clerics of Iraq did not go on to play a prominent role in national politics. The Iranian population became largely Shiite following the adoption of Shiism as the state religion in 1501, which aided the process of widespread clerical support up through the twentieth century. Particular religious practices, tied to the clerical class, were institutionalized and rooted in the culture, such as the role of the bazaar class. The rise of modern nation-states, along different paths, weakened the clergy in both Iran and Iraq. In Iraq, Sunni leaders managed to eradicate much of the power of the traditional shrine cities of Najaf and Karbala as centers of learning, and the madrasas lost their economic independence and came under government control.[1] Lacking political clout, religious scholars adopted the role of community leaders, a role they would assume once again in Iraq after the 2003 invasion.

During Ottoman times, the ayatollahs of Iraq established an institution whose scholarly activities, ideas, and, most importantly, authority were the centerpiece of Shiite religious life. The institution was financially self-sufficient, for it, rather than the state, was responsible for the collection of religious taxes and duties. This arrangement, coupled with a newly established relationship with members of the community, gave the clerical class a great deal of power at the grassroots. It was a connection that the Sunni *ulama* (Muslim jurists) could not claim or cultivate because they were allied with the state, upon which their economic survival depended. Their close ties to the state made them vulnerable and prone to self-censorship. In most of the new states created after the fall of the Ottoman Empire, the Sunni *ulama* became government employees.

It was not only the survival of the *hawza* that mattered. Yitzhak Nakash points out that the structure of the *hawza* was anchored in a relationship of reciprocity between clerics and followers. This relationship, Nakash observes, had much in common with modern democracy: It was "the freedom of ordinary people to play a prominent role in deciding who is to have religious authority—an authority that, in turn, can be used to check the executive and hold rulers accountable."[2] For a century prior to the US invasion of Iraq, Shiite clerics had indeed led many of the movements that advocated constitutionalism and parliamentary rule.[3] Not only was the traditional institution able to engage modern discussions on statehood; it was at the center of the discourse as well. This structure, unique to Shiism, lent itself as well to the participatory politics that emerged in Iraq after 2003.

From the inception of the Iraqi state, Shiites were in many respects outsiders, yet this outsider status was framed from the perspective of nationality, not religion. Over the decades, from the monarchy through the regime of Saddam Hussein, the rulers of Iraq repeatedly questioned the Arabness of the Shiites, often associating them instead with Persian culture and Iran. It was a means of discrediting the Shiites and justifying their exclusion from the state.[4]

The modern Iraqi state was founded under British tutelage after the implosion of the Ottoman Empire in the wake of World War I. As part of the war effort on the Middle Eastern front, the British encouraged Sharif Hussein of Mecca to declare the Arab revolt of 1916. The majority of those who revolted were Sunni Arab officers in the Ottoman army. By contrast, Iraqi Shiites took pride in their position as leaders of a "jihad" for Muslim unity (with the Sunni Ottomans) against the British. In April 1915 the Shiites joined Ottoman forces in a battle over a small town called Shu'ayba, southeast of Basra, in an attempt to recapture that province from the British. Even with a formidable force of soldiers and volunteers, the offensive failed. Yet the battle was to become an important symbol of Muslim unity in Shiite memory as clerics issued edicts in defense of Islam, with vivid stories about the martyrs and heroes who defended Iraq against British occupation.[5]

The Arab revolt of 1916 failed to secure independence from the rule of the Ottoman Turks. The 1920 revolt in Iraq was a reaction to British occupation of Iraq following the San Remo Conference in April 1920, which awarded Great Britain the mandate for Iraq. Mass demonstrations began in Baghdad and spread to tribal Shiite regions. Iraqis wanted independence from British rule and the creation of an Arab government. Despite the various stories about the revolt, agreement exists regarding the role of Shiite clerics in inciting the tribes. The clerics were concerned with British policies in Iran and Iraq that posed a danger to their influence in the shrine cities. The leading clerics of the day, Shirazi, Isfahani, and Ismail Sadr, wanted to establish an Islamic government in Iraq, free from foreign influence. However, they did not have overwhelming support from the majority of Shiites, some of whom were interested in governance along the lines of the Syrian model. However, many Sunnis and Shiites converged in their protest against British policies that targeted tribes, which motivated their participation in the revolt. The city of Najaf, and by extension the clerics, were instrumental in leading the revolt. The British would put down the revolt and establish a Sunni monarchy. Subsequent generations of Sunni politicians would seek to reduce the power of the clerics and their institutions.[6]

From the early days of state formation, Shiite groups developed a dual impulse toward fierce nationalism and Muslim unity. It was an intellectual legacy that would be transmitted through the decades. A pattern of "Shiite memory" aggregated from various historians, poets, preachers, and others records the 1920 revolt as a powerful instance of Iraqi unity. This memory emphasizes the kindling of anti-British sentiments throughout Baghdad and other mixed Shiite-Sunni cities, the main concern being an Iraq free of foreign control.[7]

The myth of Shiites as the enemy was constructed to consolidate the control of the Sunni Arab elites to whom the British turned to help govern Iraq in the wake of the 1920 revolt. In 1921, at the behest of T. E. Lawrence, the British imported Sharif Hussein's third son, Faysal, to assume the royal throne. The British hailed Faysal as a "pan-Arab" hero, but he was scarcely known in Iraq. For his part, the new king expressed disdain for the people of Iraq because of the "deep divisions within society."[8] More than 60 percent of this society was made up of Shiite Arabs.

With no real popular mandate, the new state resorted to classic colonial divide-and-rule tactics. Over and again, both under the British and after formal independence in 1932, the Iraqi state would attempt to define Shiites as Persians. For example, the 1924 Iraqi Nationality Law distinguished between Iraqis who held Ottoman nationality before 1924 and those who held Iranian nationality. Arab Shiites had commonly used

Iranian nationality to escape taxation or conscription into the Ottoman army. Now, only Iraqis who had held Ottoman nationality before 1924 were to be classified as "indigenous" (*asliyyun*), regardless of where they had been born and raised. Shiites were thus systematically barred from state office, and many were denied Iraqi nationality based on this and other laws. Article 41 of the 1964 constitution went on to mandate that the president must be an individual born to parents of Ottoman nationality who had resided in Iraq since 1900. This allowed the government to weed out those who carried Iranian nationality at the time that the nationality law went into effect.[9]

State discrimination against Shiites took on a more virulent form after the Ba'athists came to power for the second time in 1968. Even though Shiites had helped to found the party, Saddam Hussein slowly purged the upper Ba'athist echelons until they were composed mainly of Sunnis.

The Ba'athists took seriously the "manipulation of consent."[10] This is the process whereby elites try to instill beliefs, values, and attributes that might legitimate the subordinate position of groups in society. In authoritarian settings, this involves various techniques of ideological control to explain why groups might remain quiescent in the face of authoritarianism. In the case of Iraq, the Ba'athists sought to lump the Shiites together in a category hostile to the state and its program. In the eyes of the state and many of its intellectuals, Shiites were part of the *shu'ubiyya,* a movement that appeared within Islam in the eighth century. (The term *shu'ub* simply means "peoples.") This movement was composed mainly of Persians and Aramaeans of Iraq who protested the special place reserved for Arabs in that era's Islamic institutions and instead demanded equality for all Muslims. Arab scholars of the time were alarmed, and they disparaged the movement as traitorous. While the term *shu'ubiyya* fell out of use by the fifteenth century, the Ba'ath Party revived it to enforce its interpretation of Arab nationalism.[11] Ba'athists regularly used the word *shu'ubi* to slander their opponents—including, early on, Iraqi communists, the majority of whom were Shiites. Crucially, all were viewed as enemies of Arabism, not enemies of Sunnism. Abd al-Karim Qasim, the nationalist colonel who ruled Iraq from 1958 to 1963, was put to death by the Ba'athists on this charge.

Beginning in the 1950s, lay Shiite thinkers, advised by dissident clerics in Najaf, began trying to build mass movements to compete with

Ba'athism, communism, and other secular ideologies. The most important of these groupings was the Islamic Call, or Da'wa. Da'wa rose in prominence throughout the 1970s, but then it splintered and became predominantly lay in its composition by the 1990s. These lay Shiite movements, because they had ideologies grounded in Islam, came in for special venom from the state, which alleged that they were inciting sectarianism. In instances when Shiites protested against discrimination on the part of the government, these grievances were labeled *ta'ifiyya* (sectarian). This term took on a very specific meaning after Iran's 1979 revolution: It referred to those who allegedly placed their Shiite sectarian identity above their loyalty to Iraq and the Arab cause, a choice that was tantamount to treason.[12] The term *shu'ubiyya* was used at different times to describe non-Muslim Arabs. But *ta'ifis* were always and exclusively Shiites. Ofra Bengio outlines the extensive use of verbal manipulation by the Ba'ath regime over time to explain authoritarian regime survival through the lens of the discourse literature. She argues that *ta'ifiyya* used to be a neutral term for ethnic groups. Under the Ba'ath Party, it took on increasingly derogatory undertones. It was used as a reference to Shiites to describe them as tribal fanatics often engaging in civil strife. Following the 1977 riots in Najaf and Karbala, the term was used to determine loyalty to the state. In 1991 Saddam Hussein implemented a law that prohibited the establishment of "sectarian" parties. This was in reaction to the Sha'ban uprisings in the South and a fear that Shiites would look to neighboring Iran for political guidance. Language manipulation was linked to policy.[13] Bengio demonstrates that the regime's discourse was an attempt to use political idiom to create a monolithic polity.

The language used to brand Shiites as outsiders, taken alongside measures such as the Nationality Law, must be viewed through the lens of authoritarian regime survival. The historical context suggests that the key divides in Iraq were not intrinsic, ancient differences between sects. While history does indeed demonstrate that state discrimination against Shiites in Iraq began with the empowerment of the Sunnis in the 1920s, this discrimination was not inspired by sectarianism per se. It was the policy of secular Sunni rulers and was a function of their determination to remain in power.

And there was an important exception to the pattern of discrimination whose outcome is also revealing. On the eve of the Iran-Iraq war, Saddam permitted Shiite authors to publish their works on the historical role of the community in the early twentieth century.[14] It was a response to the existential fear that the Shiites in the South would support Iran in the war. Despite years of repression, however, the Shiites did not rebel: They were Iraqis and always had been, despite what the Nationality Law of 1924 endeavored to decree.

After the 2003 invasion, policy makers and journalists were keen to see how political Islam would interact with the new Iraqi state. Elsewhere in the region, Muslim social and political actors had made claims to authority, expressed in Islamic idiom, to address the relation between politics and religion, and the matter of how ordinary Muslims might reconcile their traditions with political modernization. The pilgrimages to the Iraqi shrine cities after Saddam's fall, the enthusiastic performances of Shiite ritual, the proximity of Shiite Islamist parties to the US occupation authorities—all these signs seemed to portend the same phenomenon in Iraq.

Frederic Volpi and Bryan S. Turner note that these questions have preoccupied scholars of Islam and the social sciences for decades. To make sense of this moment in history, they contend that we are in a "post-Durkheimian order," where institutionalized religious hierarchies are no longer the drivers of the increase in individuated forms of religiosity. It is not the privatization of religion, for the religiosity is highly visible and public, but rather a personalization of the process. This form of extreme individual subjectivity, they argue, happened in Christianity as a consequence of Western modernization. In comparing Christianity and Islam, the authors build on the argument made by Charles Taylor, who made the case that the origins of individualized religiosity could be traced to the atmosphere that had been created by wealthy Western democracies in the twentieth century. Consumerism and affluence, on the one hand, and the increased human rights culture, on the other, reduced the relevance of traditional forms of solidarity and interaction in Christianity.[15] That same process is now unfolding in Iraq.

The ayatollahs must now compete with new religious actors who do not seek legitimacy through an institutionalized religious hierarchy. These actors claim to speak for Islam and issue fatwas, breaking from the tradition in which only established religious scholars, who followed specific criteria and attained proper community consensus, could issue legal judgments. They assert a person's ability to make his or her own choices about religion. It is by far the biggest challenge the ayatollahs have ever faced.[16]

No previous threat—not even the wrath of Saddam Hussein—had questioned the clerics' basic legitimacy or practice.

For the ayatollahs, the threat to legitimacy in this new nonhierarchical context was much greater than anything imaginable in the Sunni tradition. The Sunni system is decentralized, with four schools of jurisprudence and no requirement of peer recognition or followers. By contrast, the ayatollahs' institution *is* hierarchical by definition. The *hawza*, composed of the schools of the highest-ranking ayatollahs, survives and fatwas remain valid as long as the ayatollah is alive. The whole system is contingent upon the relationship between the ayatollah and his followers, and his promotion is based on that reciprocity. The erosion of hierarchy, then, meant that the ayatollahs faced an existential crisis.[17]

In this new atmosphere, new Shiite Islamist groups formed, some with radical populist orientations. The most important such movement was formed by Muqtada al-Sadr, the son of Ayatollah Muhammad Sadiq al-Sadr, a cousin of Da'wa's founding cleric, Muhammad Baqir al-Sadr. Muhammad Baqir and Muhammad Sadiq were killed by the regime in 1980 and 1999, respectively. This pedigree afforded Muqtada al-Sadr some protection from the clerical establishment as he commenced his activism in post-Saddam Iraq.

Sadr was in his thirties and many years away from ayatollah status in the immediate aftermath of the invasion. But he had an alternative vision for Iraq that did not include the ayatollahs as its leaders. In fact, he worked to supplant the ayatollahs, declaring that his opinions were as binding as those of the high-ranking clerics. In the post-Saddam atmosphere, he was able to offer a "lay" interpretation of Islam—much like Jalal Al-e Ahmad and Ali Shariati did in Iran before the revolution. Although Ayatollah Khomeini is normally associated with the 1979 revolution in Iran, the ideology of the revolution was much more complex. Ahmad coined the term *gharbzadegi* ("westoxification"), the expression that redirected Muslims to find roots in their own cultures. Shariati, who had an "Islamic" political awakening, sought liberation from colonialism through Islam.[18] He wanted to rework religious activism outside of the framework of Shiite religious schools and their hierarchical structure. His awakening was as much a political as a religious one.

In the 1990s, Muhammad Sadiq al-Sadr had condemned Ayatollah Ali al-Sistani as a "silent jurisprudent," in contrast to a "speaking jurisprudent," one who heeded the religious duty to speak out against tyranny. In 2003 Muqtada had this legacy and the Sadr name behind him. He used charisma, not scholarship, to gain followers. He was willing to step in politically when the Najaf ayatollahs preferred to be quiet; he had never gone into exile like other lay groups under Saddam's rule.

In a deliberate attempt to gain the limelight, Sadr singled out Sistani for criticism. He threw down the gauntlet right away. In May 2003, although he was not a *mujtahid,* much less an ayatollah, Sadr issued a fatwa that allowed theft and looting as long as the perpetrators made a donation in the amount of one-fifth of the booty to his office. He thereby secured a source of funding.

Within the first year of the US occupation, Sadr had attracted thousands of followers who wore all black and carried larger-than-life portraits of their leader. He had broad support among the Shiite poor, deploying his disciples to the streets of Baghdad's Shiite slums to hand out bread, water, and oranges. Leaders in the Shiite district of Baghdad that had been known as Saddam City decided to rename the city Sadr City after his slain father. Sadr also formed a militia called the Mahdi Army, estimated in the tens of thousands, and established his own religious courts and prisons. These steps comported with his early vision for carving out an Islamic state. Sadr was brilliant at branding himself as he rose to prominence. He named his newspaper, the means by which he disseminated his information, *al-Hawza al-Natiqa* (*The Speaking Jurisprudent*), underlining the distinction between him and the ayatollahs in Najaf. The same branding was evident in the name Mahdi Army, named after the imam who disappeared in the ninth century and is to return and lead the Shiite community. The ayatollahs are the Mahdi's temporary human representatives. It was clear that Muqtada wanted to challenge the ayatollahs to win the streets of Iraq. He was the new face of lay Shiism.

By 2004, the young Sadr had managed to enrage US proconsul L. Paul Bremer, who shut down Sadr's newspaper and targeted the Mahdi Army for dissolution. But these moves only enhanced Sadr's street credentials, making it easier for him to regroup. The Mahdi Army led two anti-occupation uprisings in 2004, taking the city of Najaf hostage, while Ayatollah Sistani and his cohort watched from their homes. Around this time, Sistani and Sadr were dubbed the most important religious and political figures in Iraq, in that order.

Despite Sadr's provocations, Sistani and the other ayatollahs largely ignored his rise for a time. Without mentioning names, the clerics wrote extensively on the need to respect the hierarchical structure and warned of the dangers of interpretation by unqualified persons. At a meeting in October 2003, Sistani did urge Sadr to dismantle his militia and deliver the weapons to the competent authorities.[19] Sadr ignored his advice then. But, his popularity notwithstanding, several of Sadr's moves had clearly alienated mainstream Shiites, especially the property owners who did not like the fatwa permitting looting or the transformation of Najaf into a war zone. These overreaches warranted a strong response from the ayatollahs.

Sadr's actions also provoked a larger, existential question for them: Could religious structures withstand more popular encroachment? Sadr could draw thousands of followers to the street under the banner of Shiite Islam in a matter of seconds. Sadr could and did act unilaterally, often directly challenging the clerics, and they were then forced to defend their positions and the *hawza*. The ayatollahs realized they had to persuade the populace to follow them and not Sadr.

The ayatollahs' dilemma resembled the experience of Western Christianity at the time of the Reformation. Charles Taylor argues that "orthodoxy [was] becoming epistemologically irrelevant and the collective structures of authorities that ultimately found their justification in these constructions of religious knowledge [were] becoming redundant."[20] The ayatollahs of Iraq, faced with this question in 2003, understood the tension between their centuries-old, hierarchical, ostensibly "rigid" institution and the need to justify and perhaps reinvent their own authority alongside the new political order in Iraq. They did not want their orthodoxy to become "epistemologically irrelevant" and therefore worked to ensure its adaptability and continued accessibility to the people.

And as it happened, counterintuitive as it sounds, the *hawza* would survive and thrive precisely because of the structure of the institution, premised as it is on a reciprocal relationship between clerics and followers that is unique to Shiism. To elaborate: The main (Twelver) branch of Shiism follows the line of twelve imams, up to the Mahdi, who, as a messianic figure, is in occultation and is expected to return one day to lead the community. The imam, believed to be infallible, is the political and religious leader of the community. In theory, Shiites accept no authority on Earth except the Mahdi, but in his absence the members of the clerical class act as his representatives. Advanced clerics become *mujtahids,* yet few can gain a large enough number of followers to rise in the ranks. These *mujtahids,* given the title of *marja' al-taqlid* (source of emulation), give authoritative opinions on disputed questions and are ayatollahs. They issue fatwas, compete with other ayatollahs to gain more followers, and run their own madrasas. Their uniqueness is also a product of their historical independence from government, as described earlier. Unlike Sunni clerics, who are now appointed by the government, Shiites are free to choose their own ayatollah, sometimes across borders and boundaries. A Shiite in Iraq can follow an ayatollah in Iran, Lebanon, Kuwait, or elsewhere—paying him dues and abiding by his rulings. This reciprocal relationship creates contingencies. It allows followers to keep ayatollahs in the loop about their interests. It also helps ayatollahs to rise in status, compete with other ayatollahs, and build momentum to contest the state if necessary. The process has a constant and embedded "democratic" and participatory aspect.

That is not to say that these discussions cannot happen among Sunnis or that they cannot happen in secular terms for Muslims. Sami Zubaida wrote a response to the repeated calls for an "Islamic Reformation." The assumption was that because there had been a Protestant Reformation, a purportedly liberal one, we should await the remedy for the fundamentalism that is currently plaguing Islamism. He addresses the underlying assumption that Islam is "petrified" and therefore has not undergone a "reformation." Beyond the problematic assumed Christian blueprint that he points out, he goes on to make several points. He makes clear that Islam has undergone many "reformations," one of which is Wahhabism. He also points out that the Protestant Reformation was not a liberal enterprise. The movement reformed the Christianity of the Catholic Church, which was based on church authority and hierarchy. He defined "reform" as relative, according to historical context. There is no such thing as one reform, but rather repeated cycles of reform. Therefore, Wahhabism was claimed as a "reformation," or *islah,* and was recognized by some as such, for its call to a return to scriptures and a rejection of the practices of saint worship.[21]

The US occupation of Iraq gave the *hawza* the opportunity to prove its mettle as an institution. The US government, upon invading Iraq in 2003, was looking at Iraq through the lens of Iran's 1979 revolution. The United States distrusted the clerics, probably remembering Khomeini's words upon his return to Iran in 1979: "Death to America." The US approach to rebuilding Iraq, under Bremer's lead, with a secular, pro-US government dominated by former exiles, was disconnected from the local population. The crucial grassroots voices, connected to Sadr and Sistani, were not taken seriously by Bremer or his bosses in Washington. Instead, Sistani and Sadr would compete in the informal public sphere to contest the US occupation and to call for an independent Iraq with a government system that reflected their own culture and traditions.

In response to Sadr's actions, Sistani set the stage for a discourse that made room for himself and the *hawza,* not only as important actors in this new political milieu but also as *the* most important political actors on the scene. The other ayatollahs would follow suit.

Sistani issued a series of fatwas and decrees about the rule of law, the illegality of militias and looting, and respect for government. Dozens and dozens of questions about lawbreaking and squatting were always answered with the same response: Sistani preferred order to chaos, legitimate to illegitimate means, and working within the system to action outside it. During this stream of opinions, Sistani managed to diminish the importance of Sadr, rarely speaking to him and sidestepping reporters' questions about him. Sadr would have some successes, but at the end of the day the *hawza* would triumph. Sadr discovered that in the world of Shiism, respect for the ayatollah and the traditional hierarchy meant success. Moreover, the *hawza* could modernize. Sadr decided that his political path required that he improve his religious credentials. He went to Iran in 2008 to study to become an ayatollah.

Much had happened on the ground before Sadr made this decision. For two years the Sadrists had refused to engage with the US-sponsored political transition except to denounce it. But in 2005, as elections approached for a transitional national assembly, Sadr opted to send his supporters into parliamentary politics. Sadr himself stayed out of formal politics, but his movement had representatives in the Shiite Islamist bloc that dominated the assembly chosen in 2005, the United Iraqi Alliance.

Sadr had the advantage of bouncing back and forth between the formal and informal political system. In the informal realm, he retained command of the Mahdi Army, and his militia forces would continue to engage in violence to resist the occupation until 2008. He also had a commitment to social welfare programs. The Sadrist movement broadened its provision of social benefits through "brick-and-mortar" offices.[22] Simultaneously, he fielded his candidates for government posts. This strategy allowed Sadr to engage in the state-building process at the same time that he resisted the occupation and challenged Sistani. At one crucial juncture, Iraq's governing coalition was in danger of collapse only a few months after the formation of the first permanent government under Prime Minister Nouri al-Maliki. It was December 2006, and Sadr had made the decision to field candidates in the United Iraqi Alliance, the Shiite bloc that went on to win the majority of seats and form the government. Sadr, outraged at Maliki's decision to meet President George W. Bush in Jordan, pulled his thirty lawmakers and six cabinet ministers out of the government. This move, which threatened the disintegration of the coalition, prompted government officials to send a delegation to Najaf.[23]

The delegation hoped to get reassurances from Sistani that the coalition should stand. He remained silent. The delegates met with Sadr but were afraid to ask him to dissolve his militia, as per their public demand, because their priority at the time was to reintegrate his followers back into the cabinet and Parliament. For a brief period, Sadr was powerful.

Yet Sadr would evolve politically. By 2007, he was preaching about Sunni-Shiite unity in his sermons and interviews. He pledged to stand "shoulder to shoulder with Sunnis" and to extend a hand to Christians as well.[24] By 2008, he would make an official turn toward political and social work, with less emphasis on militia activities. He realized that civil disobedience was a better method of communication within the existing state structure. Sadr launched a nationwide civil disobedience campaign to protest the Mahdi Army's raids and detentions.[25] Civil disobedience, while sometimes associated with acts that violate the law, is considered a legitimate form of political behavior and a normal form of resistance in democracies. It has historically been used to protest unjust policies that violate the higher standards and ideals to which democracies aspire.[26] Sadr thus understood that Iraqis had chosen the path of the rule of law, and he was now willing to follow the will of the majority.

He was becoming politically mature, much as Yitzhak Nakash had predicted that Shiite activism would evolve and become accommodationist. His decision to dissolve the majority of the Mahdi Army in August 2008 was a reflection of that maturity. Sadr ordered his militiamen to disarm, with the exception of the elite fighting units that would be called to resist if the United States did not set a date for withdrawal of troops from Iraq. The decision to disarm must have been driven in part by the realities Sadr faced. One reality was the powerful discourse of Sistani that painted militias as a violation of both religion and the law. Sadr knew he had to conform to Sistani's will, especially when it was clear that the Mahdi Army was involved in acts of sabotage and massive violations of human rights.

In 2003 Sadr wanted to declare himself a *marja'*. Because of his protection by Ayatollah Kazem al-Haeri in Iran and his father's prestige, Sadr thought he could make this declaration. True, Ali Khamenei of Iran was elevated to ayatollah status without having risen through the ranks. Yet it was not a self-declaration—Ayatollah Khomeini had designated Khamenei as his successor prior to his death in 1989.[27] Sadr's plan would fail. The *hawza* and the old hierarchical structure would endure.

The shifts in the street and in Sadr's aspirations for himself happened alongside state consolidation in Iraq. Sadr, unlike other Shiite Islamists, aligned himself with centralists and eventually with the position of Sistani and the *hawza*. Sadr, who had followed Haeri in Iran without question, began moving away from him. In one example, Ayatollah Haeri issued a fatwa on June 3, 2012, that forbade voting for secular candidates in elections. Sadr rejected the fatwa on the grounds that it was "impossible to distinguish between secularists and Islamists." Haeri was banking on the fact that not only Sadr, but also his broader movement, would follow this decree, based on the tradition that after the death of Sadr's father, Muhammad Sadiq, all of his followers would be inherited by Haeri.[28] Instead, Sadr announced that he would "not adhere to any fatwa issued by Haeri, and that he would not back down from his decision to withdraw confidence from Maliki unless Grand Ayatollah Ali Al-Sistani or Sheikh Ishaq al-Fayyad issued a fatwa," on the premise that these two authorities "issue fatwas for the benefit of Iraq, not other countries." Sadr's supporters agreed with him on the premise that a fatwa should not be issued to exert political pressure or favor one political party over another one. In this case, the fatwa would lose its legitimacy. They made the decision not to follow Haeri, while at the same time granting "respect" to Haeri.[29] As this example shows, Sadr had come to understand that Sistani had framed the nationalist vision for Iraq. In essence, Sadr had committed to following Sistani's narrative—an Iraq-centric one, resistant to pressure from Iran-based ayatollahs. Their narratives had merged.

On February 15, 2014, that seed would come to fruition. Sadr officially announced his "non-intervention on all political matters" in the interest of protecting his family's reputation. He also announced that all of his offices, centers, and associations inside and outside of Iraq would be closed, with the exception of nineteen cultural and charity institutions. No bloc would represent his movement inside or outside the government. His only reentry into politics, by use of his militia, renamed the Peace Companies in 2014, was to counter ISIS. He first called on it to protect Shiite shrines, and later in 2015 he offered help in battles against ISIS, all in the interest of maintaining the integrity of Iraq. Some commentators believed that Sadr's "peace companies" were a new label for his deadly Mahdi Army. When his militia returned to Sadr City in June 2014, for example, thousands of fighters marched through the streets with machine guns, grenades, and suicide belts strapped to their chests. They chanted, "I will purify Mosul, I am a Sadrist."[30]

Sadr's move was unexpected. His supporters heard the news through the media. As observers questioned his sudden retreat from politics, one thing to consider was that Sadr had come to terms with the special place of the *hawza* in the religio-political dynamics of Iraq. In an interview with *al-Hayat* in 2013, Sadr noted the lack of Arab or Western enthusiasm for him as an Iraqi leader with popular support. On the domestic front, Sadr expressed his unwillingness to turn his "popular current" into a political party, partially because of the divisions within the state and his sense that Iraq was headed for partition, with no hope for political change. These sentiments were all indications that Sadr did not want to be absorbed into the political system proper.[31] As a cleric on the rise, he would be able to carry the aura of his family, balance multiple centers of power, and operate parallel to the state should he rise to the rank of ayatollah in the future. He had watched Sistani do it and maintain his legitimacy and clout.

Sadr's evolution vividly illustrates the thesis of Robert Gleave that the *hawza* would modernize and eventually prevail, leaving little room for lay challenges, even if they might dominate for some time. Gleave sees post-2003 Iraq as enmeshed in a process of globalization, in line with the thinking of Nakash and Volpi and Turner. He explains that the process of globalization is normally conceived as a challenge to traditional authority structures—in this case, the structure of the *hawza* and the ayatollahs' position within it. This traditional argument holds that the maintenance of these structures depends on participants' continued isolation from outside influences that might disturb the structure's integrity. Zygmunt Bauman characterizes globalization as a time period of "epistemological anarchy," in which no one seems to be in control or even knows what "in control" would be like.[32] The scholarly consensus is that traditional authority structures ultimately do not stand a chance in the face of the rapid technological, economic, and political changes that constitute this "anarchy." Gleave objects that this scholarship takes the forces of globalization as inevitable. More importantly, he revises the notion that there is an "inability" of traditional authority structures to resist the forces of globalization because they are based on "ingrained and irrational deference."[33] Instead, he helps us make sense of exactly how and why, contrary to social science, the clerics, rather than resisting the forces of modernization, update their institution to make it relevant.

Gleave argues that not only has the *hawza* survived; it has also adapted and gained increased structural stability after the fall of Saddam Hussein.[34] In contrast to the dominant lay Sunni developments, he argues that the influence of lay Shiite thinkers has been minimal in Iraq. The very survival of the *hawza,* which diminished the influence of these lay thinkers, can be attributed to its members' ability to adjust their thinking to modern times; their discussions are in and of themselves modern. They have no choice but to keep one foot in the *hawza* and one foot on the street. That is, by definition, the way the institution survives. It needs the endorsement and the reciprocity of the people. Accordingly, the dominant writings and thoughts—the modern ones—on religious and political matters have originated from the *hawza.* There is a connection here to the argument that Nakash makes about the nature of the *hawza* as an institution and why it is inherently democratic. That embedded structural connection between state and society, through the *hawza,* obliges the ayatollahs to be accommodationists.

Yet the influence of Sadr and his brand of lay Shiism grew beyond the parameters of what Gleave theorized. He predicted that the influence of lay Shiite thinkers would be minimal and that the ayatollahs, because of their ties within society, would regroup and triumph. This would happen, he argued, because the lay thinkers failed to compete persuasively with the traditional clerical class, propose a coherent ideology, or gain extensive support among the international Shiite community.[35] It is true that, overall, the ayatollahs maintained their status. But it is also the case that while

Sistani is known as the most popular politician in Iraq, Sadr is a close second. Although Sistani and his cohort survived in the end, the political landscape in Iraq now has a new dimension.

Sadr did not quite hold true to his promise of nonintervention in politics. In 2014 Prime Minister Maliki was replaced by Haider al-Abadi, a change prompted by the influence of Sistani. Sistani welcomed Abadi to office in the hope of reform but then receded from view. Abadi did not deliver, and in July 2015 widespread protests in Iraq called for accountability and improved services. Soon, Sadr co-opted these protests and positioned himself as a rival to Abadi. He called for massive sit-ins to pressure Abadi to enact reforms. However, he did not call for violence, and he never challenged Sistani. Sadr used his power as a newly regularized feature of Iraqi politics to hold the government accountable.

In this sense, Gleave is correct that, for the moment, the lay trend does not threaten the clerical hierarchy or the institution itself. Yet, with resurgent violence and the new political atmosphere, it is hard to predict the future. Sistani's critics are increasingly asking for more intervention on his part. On May 1, 2016, after months of protests over stalled political reforms, thousands of Sadr supporters stormed Parliament in the Green Zone. They threatened more mass protests to follow. This movement was bolstered by earlier statements from Sistani, who had called the reform process "slow." But then three months prior to the storming of Parliament, Sistani declared "silence" on the matter. Was this a position of neutrality or a boycott of Abadi? Was it coordination with Sadr? In any case, Sistani's "silence" again allowed Sadr to fill the vacuum and threaten to "remove and uproot the political system." Sadr's power rests in his ability to bridge the formal and informal political spheres.

Lay interpreters of Sunni Islam presented another challenge to the ayatollahs. One such group, the Association of Muslim Scholars (AMS), was formed in 2003 by Muhammad Ayyash al-Kubaysi (d. 2007), with the hope of uniting Sunnis behind a program of political activism.[36] In a series of writings, Kubaysi called for a boycott of the political transition as long as Iraq remained under occupation, labeling resistance to occupation a form of jihad.

The AMS claimed to hold power similar to that of the Shiite religious authorities. Acting as an association rather than a political party, the group developed a platform similar to the Shiite establishment. They claimed the right to issue fatwas, like Ayatollah Sistani, that applied to all Muslims, Sunni and Shiite.[37] Highly organized, the group disseminated its ideas and rulings through its website.[38]

The AMS's main discursive innovation was its emphasis on the "jurisprudence of resistance," or *fiqh al-muqawama.* Following Kubaysi, the Sunni clerics wrote that resistance was *jihad al-fard*—an obligation for all Muslims, regardless of sect.[39] The AMS called for armed insurgency only against occupying forces, warning that attacks against civilians were illegitimate under international law.[40] It also declared that sectarian killings were not allowed under Islamic law and that such attacks would reduce the credibility of the Iraqi resistance in the Islamic and Arab world.[41]

This challenge to the authority of the ayatollahs coincided with discursive battles within the Sunni community. The Sunnis were also struggling to make sense of what was going on in post-Saddam Iraq. In one sense, a new sectarian narrative had already been written for them, as they were all lumped together as "the Sunnis," who had to be removed from power. On the other hand, for the first time in decades they were not co-opted by the state.

Ariel Ahram explores the new discourse that emerged from Sunni Islamists after 2003 in their efforts to find alternative visions for legitimate rule. To do so, he analyzes letters written by new Sunni Islamist groups to the UN envoy Lakhdar Brahimi in early 2004. The US-sponsored state-building process was under way, with the main Iraqi participants being the Shiite Islamist and Kurdish parties. Sunni Arab groups were either excluded from the process or chose to boycott it.[42] Brahimi had gone to Iraq that January to investigate the possibility of conducting early general elections as part of Iraq's transition to sovereignty. Ahram finds that "democracy" was an inescapable framework for the Sunni Islamists, as it was for everyone else. But unlike the ayatollahs, for instance, the Sunni Islamists were conducting a "monologue" rather than a discussion or a debate. Because the Sunnis did not have a *hawza* to help them navigate the new political scene[43] and Saddam's regime had opportunistically used Sunni Islam for its own ends, the Sunnis faced a certain "crisis of identity."

Interestingly, the Sunni Islamists sent their appeals to the United Nations. It was an attempt to "normalize" themselves after they had been labeled the enemy by the United States. Sistani took a similar approach as he sought multiple interventions from UN representatives over the years.

Religious actors looked past the United States. Sunni groups such as the Council of Muslim Clerics (CMC) and the United Patriotic Movement (UPM) wrote to Brahimi in an attempt to distance themselves from extremism and to make clear that they were resisting the Coalition Provisional Authority (CPA) and the "riffraff" (*habb wa dabb*)—the Shiite parties that had returned from exile.[44] They pointedly framed their resistance as a democratic struggle. However, the CMC wrote that democracy and institution building were of secondary concern and could begin only once the occupation had ended. They were sarcastic about the possibility of building democracy under occupation. Yet the Sunni groups studied by Ahram also realized that they needed to balance criticism of the occupation with the language of inclusion, making room for Iraqis in their vision for the future.

However, the Sunni Islamist circles did not have an interpretive monopoly. Alongside the AMS and similar groups were the hard-line *salafi* (puritanical Sunni Muslim) trends that gave rise to extremist armed groups such as al-Qaeda in Mesopotamia and, later, ISIS.

Seeking explanations for the brutal sectarian violence of these groups, some observers have focused heavily on the teachings of Muhammad ibn Abd al-Wahhab (d. 1792), who called upon Muslims to embrace a puritanical, literal reading of Islam. Wahhabism is outside the four main Sunni schools of jurisprudence, and historically many of its adherents have preached that Shiites are infidels. In Saudi Arabia, where the state is backed by a Wahhabi clerical establishment, the Shiite minority has faced severe and recurrent repression. Their seminaries were closed and their libraries burned, mosques and religious institutions were destroyed, and Shiites were forbidden from performing rituals in public.[45] It is well documented that the Saudi state has bankrolled extensive proselytizing by Wahhabi clerics across the Islamic world, so there may seem to be a straight line between Wahhabi teachings and the rise of, say, Abu Musab al-Zarqawi in Iraq. This Sunni extremist's writings called Shiites "serpents and snakes" and "the enemy within that needed to be exterminated." Once that mission was completed, Zarqawi's group, al-Qaeda in Mesopotamia, could concentrate on targeting the "far enemy, the West."

Wahhabi doctrine is undoubtedly a contributing factor to the sectarian violence in Iraq, but the weight that scholars, even Nakash, give it tends to yield a reductionist picture. Juan Cole offers an important corrective.

He argues that the eighteenth-century Wahhabis were primarily a puritanical movement aimed at ridding Arabia of pagan practices. By the twentieth century, the radical elements in the movement had been tamed under the Saudi government. Cole makes the case that Saudi proselytizing abroad is not the sole source of sectarianism, terrorism, or anti-Western sentiment. He shifts attention to the important explanatory variable of foreign invasion and occupation: Wahhabism became associated with violent extremism in the 1980s, when the United States, Saudi Arabia, and Pakistan recruited the mujahideen to fight against the Soviet occupation of Afghanistan. Ideology alone cannot explain terrorism, Cole continues. He offers the example of Qatar, where Wahhabism is also the official religion but there is no history of proselytizing associated with armed conflict.[46] In essence, cultures and religions do not commit acts of violence; people do.

The strain of *salafism* behind the sectarian violence in Iraq was introduced not by Wahhabi preachers but by Zarqawi, a Jordanian-born militant responsible for a series of attacks, bombings, and beheadings. In 2003 he formed al-Qaeda in Mesopotamia, also called al-Qaeda in Iraq, to oppose Western military forces "on Islamic land." However, Zarqawi perceived his movement as transcending Iraq's borders and soon pledged allegiance to Osama bin Laden, joining the broader al-Qaeda organization in 2004. His goal in Iraq was to attack the Shiites indiscriminately, hoping that the reprisals and chaos that ensued would speed the withdrawal of US forces. Zarqawi was killed by coalition forces in 2006, but not before his ideas would stimulate a new discourse against Shiites—a discourse the ayatollahs would work hard, though often unsuccessfully, to counter. The violence would spiral out of control.

In a 2005 letter to Osama bin Laden, Zarqawi summarized the situation as he saw it. The Americans came to Iraq with "haughtiness and pride toward God and His Prophet," thinking the occupation would be easy, but then they collided with a very different reality. The operations of the "brother mujahidin" began immediately, forcing the Americans to conclude a deal with the Shiites, "the most evil of mankind." The Shiites would get "two thirds of the booty for having stood in the ranks of the Crusaders against the mujahidin." Hence Zarqawi's two priorities: ending the occupation by violent means and destroying the Shiites.

Zarqawi's call to violent action against Shiites was based on his belief that they were the "insurmountable obstacle, the lurking snake, the crafty

and malicious scorpion, the spying enemy, and the penetrating venom."
The battle against the Shiites, he argued, was fierce because they wear the
garb "of a friend," but any true observer would realize that Shiism is the
"looming danger and the true challenge . . . the enemy." Zarqawi went on
to say that Shiism "has nothing to do with Islam," owing to its "patent
polytheism, worshipping at graves," and "circumambulating shrines." He
said that Shiites have "hidden rancor" toward the Sunnis and that they lie.
He declared that the ayatollahs' political shrewdness had allowed them to
mask their true intention to wage sectarian war against the Sunnis.

This trick, Zarqawi claimed, was in keeping with the Shiite practice of
dissimulation, "maliciously and cunningly" hiding their real motivations.
He argued that the ayatollahs knew full well that Sunnis from the "Islamic
nation" abroad would rise to defend the Sunnis in Iraq if the ayatollahs'
game were exposed. Sheer numbers meant that the Shiites would lose.
Zarqawi therefore believed that he had to amplify his message beyond
Iraq's borders. His attacks would provoke the Shiites into showing the
Sunnis their "rabies." He urged the insurgents to "pull out their teeth
before the inevitable battle."[47]

Zarqawi's rhetoric that Sunnis and Shiites were destined to fight each
other intersected to some degree with the dominant narrative informing US
policy. But rather than continuing a "timeless" tradition of sectarianism in
Iraq, as the United States imagined, in fact Zarqawi's language departed
significantly from historical precedent. In the past, the secular-minded
state elites had used the discourse of Arabism, not religious difference, to
exclude Shiites. But Zarqawi was operating in the dangerous "free-for-
all" that Volpi and Turner warned about, an environment where extreme
interpretations of "Muslim idiom," in Charles Taylor's terms, could take
root. His ideas were sanctioned not by a strong central state but by substate actors flourishing in wake of such a state's destruction.

Al-Qaeda in Mesopotamia nevertheless lost its currency by 2007, as
many recruits were rerouted to the "awakenings," Sunni tribal groups
that fought against the radical Islamists. Also called the "Sons of Iraq,"
these former insurgents gave up their struggle and began working to reintegrate into the state. The idea of using tribes as a force against the
insurgents was formalized in late 2006, beginning with tribal leaders in
Ramadi, in an effort to drive out al-Qaeda. Within a year, close to 100,000
former insurgents switched from fighting for al-Qaeda to fighting against

it. By mid-2007, major zones of insurgency such as Ramadi and Falluja were deemed largely peaceful. The killing of Shiites had lost its appeal to the majority of earlier recruits. The sectarian ideology of Zarqawi was not rooted in the culture. Myriam Benraad demonstrated that although the tribal awakenings were successful early on, this situation would not last. By 2009, al-Qaeda had new ground in which to operate, especially in Anbar province, in part because of the deteriorating security situation in the country. The tribal movement was exposed to massive retaliatory attacks. Over the next few years, some fighters had rejoined ranks with al-Qaeda, although exact figures were hard to determine. Benraad cautioned that this outcome was a by-product of tribal engagement rather than a matter of genuine state and nation building. Tribal alliances, she argued, would yield a short-term security benefit, not long-term institutional change.[48] As early as 2004, in correspondence with Zarqawi, al-Qaeda lieutenant Ayman al-Zawahiri had warned that the wanton sectarian violence would eventually alienate the population.

But the same type of terrorism would resurface, this time perpetrated by the self-proclaimed Islamic State, or ISIS, led by Abu Bakr al-Baghdadi. ISIS expanded rapidly after 2011, in part because of the presence in its top echelons of ex-Ba'athists who had held senior positions under Saddam Hussein. Its narrative focused on the corruption and impious leadership of the Maliki government, the malign influence of the West, and the need for immediate, violent revolution requiring purges of the population, mainly of Shiites. By October 2014, the self-declared ISIS "caliphate" was in control of territory that stretched along roads and rivers from north of Aleppo in Syria to Mosul in the North of Iraq to areas south of Baghdad. Estimates were that six to eight million people on either side of the Syria-Iraq border were living under ISIS rule.[49]

ISIS was a reconfigured variant of Zarqawi's group and took pride in claiming Zarqawi as its "founder and inspiration." But the doctrinal claims made by ISIS were even more extreme, so much so that, in essence, all who opposed them were apostates and infidels. Even Ayman al-Zawahiri, now successor to Osama bin Laden as head of transnational al-Qaeda, was compelled to disavow ISIS. Baghdadi called for literal interpretation of the Quran and Hadith, and justified any and all violence in the name of returning Islam to what he regarded as its purest form. All forms of practice, including Shiism, that did not conform to such interpretation were deemed blasphemies to be eradicated. ISIS leaders described Shiites as "filthy." In one statement, spokesman Abu Muhammad al-Adnani vowed to "spread terror" in the hearts of the Shiites until they were forced to flee the country. He said that the battle would not take place in Baghdad, but rather in the holy cities of "Najaf and Karbala."

The revival of Zarqawi-style anti-Shiism in the guise of ISIS was closely linked to the state-sanctioned sectarian tactics of former Prime Minister Maliki, which deeply alienated many Sunnis and pushed them to look for an outlet for their grievances. ISIS found an audience for its ridicule of Maliki as an "underwear merchant" and a "fool."[50] Yet, because the broader ISIS ideology was poorly rooted in Iraqi society, Baghdadi would struggle with local recruitment and had to rely heavily on foreign fighters. The Soufan Group, which tracks the flow of foreign fighters into and out of Iraq, had estimated that a total of 12,000 fighters from approximately eighty-one countries were active. By December 2015, that number more than doubled: The Soufan Group estimated that more than 31,000 people from eighty-six countries traveled to Syria and Iraq to join ISIS and other *salafi* groups. Newer recruits were coming mainly from western Europe, Russia, and central Asia. Some figures on foreign fighters include 5,000 from western Europe, 8,000 from northern Africa, and 8,240 from the Middle East. When broken down by largest group of fighters by country of origin, Tunisia sent more than any other country, 6,000. This was followed by Saudi Arabia, 2,500; Russia, 2,400; Turkey, 2,100; and Jordan, 2,000.[51] Most of the ISIS recruits from abroad were not well versed in Islam and could not challenge the distortions in Baghdadi's interpretations. Studies showed that recruits from outside Iraq and Syria came on the promise of a new life, for adventure, or because they were driven by depression, alienation, or even criminal purposes. However, the recruitment from abroad made the sectarian discourse harder to contain and harder for the ayatollahs to combat. Consequently, it would become common to see Sunni-Shiite conflict in Iraq as a reality that would be reproduced on a regional level.

Al-Qaeda in Mesopotamia and ISIS were hardly the only Sunni insurgent groups, of course. A 2006 International Crisis Group (ICG) study looked at the websites, pamphlets, recruitment methods, and tactics of nine organized Sunni insurgent groups.[52] ICG found no evidence that the insurgency was some master plan conceived by Saddam's regime before its demise. The insurgent groups, in fact, had no plan for assuming leadership in Iraq once they "succeeded" in driving US forces out of the country. They were heavily focused on the *salafi* brand of Islam and persistently unwilling to join the political process. Highly optimistic about victory but lacking a political vision, their early discourse was mainly about the US occupation and its intention to fragment Iraqis. By 2005, as the various insurgent groups became more consolidated, Zarqawi's call to target Shiites had some momentum. But by 2006, the study suggests, the insurgents had returned to an emphasis on the need to expel the occupiers, and nothing beyond that. Some groups were trying instead to roll back the sectarian discourse and called for national unity. They turned the blame for the violence on the United States and its "divide-and-rule" policies. Some insurgents even wanted to reach out to Western media outlets to clean up their reputations.

In the cacophony of post-2003 Iraq it would have been very easy for the centuries-old institution of the *hawza* to lose its voice or find it drowned out. The looting that followed the fall of Saddam's regime was an early indicator of not just the breakdown of law and order but also state collapse. US policies such as debaathification and the abolition of the Iraqi army officer corps exacerbated the disorder. The new political forces opposed to the US occupation were very assertive in building their constituencies and mobilizing them in the streets. Calls to expel the occupiers by any means necessary—including armed insurgency—resonated in wider and wider circles as time passed and incidents of violence multiplied. The same political forces harbored a deep antipathy for the US-sponsored state-building project meant to fill the vacuum. Attacks on recruiting stations for the new Iraqi security forces soon became as frequent as shots fired at US patrols.

The senior Shiite clerics of Iraq, by contrast, approached the invasion and subsequent state-building project with caution and pragmatism. The four grand ayatollahs of Najaf urged their followers—and, indeed, all Iraqis—not to confront the United States violently, and they avoided insulting their Iraqi opponents, opting instead for the moral high ground. The ayatollahs issued numerous calls for the dissolution of militias, respect for the rule of law, and basic cooperation with the US-sponsored state-building project. At the same time, they consistently exposed the undemocratic features of the various US plans for reconstruction. The rulings of Ayatollah Sistani, in particular, forced the United States to change those plans and engage with Iraqis about the essence and meaning of democracy. These interventions were an answer not just to the challenge of the US occupation but also to the unprecedented challenge to the clerical hierarchy coming from within the Shiite community. While surprising to many, the actions of the ayatollahs in post-2003 Iraq were actually in line with the nature of the *hawza* and the evolution of Shiism in contemporary times.

2

SISTANI, GUARDIAN OF THE DEMOCRATIC PROCESS

On January 20, 2003, two months before launching the invasion of Iraq, the Bush administration commissioned the Pentagon to establish the Office for Reconstruction and Humanitarian Assistance (ORHA) to oversee the country's political and economic reorganization. Jay Garner, head of ORHA, was told that his assignment would be short and easy. Douglas Feith, undersecretary of defense for policy and head of the Office of Special Plans, predicted that within 90 days or so, an interim government would be formed, permanent diplomatic relations with the United States established, and the withdrawal of US troops initiated. The Bush administration had been telling the American public for some time that a long-term occupation would not be necessary because Iraqis would greet the invaders as liberators. The assumption was that Saddam Hussein was the only obstacle to US reconstruction plans. His removal from power would leave the United States with a clean slate. At first, Garner wanted to keep the Ba'ath Party intact for the sake of stability and security, and rely on the existing state bureaucracy as his Iraqi partners, but this position was unpopular in the upper echelons of the Defense Department and with the vice president. The architects of the invasion in those offices wanted to work in the post-Saddam state-building enterprise with Iraqis who had been in exile under Saddam.

On April 21, 2003, exactly one month after the war began, ORHA was dissolved and Garner dismissed, to be replaced on May 11 by the Coalition Provisional Authority (CPA) led by L. Paul Bremer III, a former ambassador to the Netherlands and longtime State Department official. The CPA ruled Iraq until restoring limited sovereignty to an interim Iraqi government on June 28, 2004. As de facto viceroy, on the advice of the former exiles and the twin Kurdish parties, Bremer made several ideologically driven decisions that displayed little knowledge of and less regard for the political and social realities of Iraq. The list of decrees included the "debaathification" of the Iraqi state and the dissolution of the Iraqi Army officer corps through CPA Orders 1 and 2. Bremer pursued debaathification aggressively, depriving thousands of army officers and state employees of salaries, benefits, and access to state jobs in the future. He also wanted to privatize large segments of the economy, including the oil industry; reorganize higher education; and establish a liberal democratic system of government—all with no mechanism for consulting the majority of the Iraqi public. Those entrusted with carrying out these projects were junior CPA staffers and private contractors, many of whom had little or no experience in their areas of responsibility, and some of whom had secured their positions merely by having the right ideological leanings.[1]

What Bremer described as "the Iraqi face" of these projects was the Iraqi Governing Council, a body created by him with the idea that all of Iraq's ethno-religious communities should have proportional representation in government. Seats were allocated on the basis of communal affiliation rather than political beliefs or professional expertise. Although the council had little power, its composition set the precedent that the liberal democracy in post-Saddam Iraq would be arranged along confessional lines. According to this system, political and institutional power would be allocated among the country's religious and ethnic communities.

Along with the Bush administration and many mainstream media commentators, Bremer assumed that Iraqis who had known only dictatorship for so long would accept the US-designed reconstruction of their country without much question. This assumption was flawed, to say the least. Over the next fifteen months, as Bremer worked to reshape Iraq to his liking, he was met with stiff resistance from many quarters. Perhaps the biggest surprise to Bremer was the strong opposition to his plans by Ayatollah Ali al-Sistani, along with the other three grand ayatollahs of Iraq. The ayatollahs, as we will see in subsequent chapters, were thought to be adherents of the centuries-old quietist tradition who would abstain from politics. Instead, the ayatollahs monitored the political process with intense interest and intervened when they deemed it necessary. In contrast to received wisdom about ayatollahs, they have been and still are at the center of discussions about sovereignty, equality, transparency, and democracy in post-Saddam Iraq.[2]

Although this chapter focuses on Sistani, the three grand ayatollahs supported his fatwas and major positions on the democratic process. They also supported all of his major initiatives on elections and state legitimacy as well as his decision in 2014 to pressure Nouri al-Maliki not to seek a third term. My intention to focus this chapter on Sistani is to give the reader the full sense of Sistani's importance as a strategic actor in Iraqi politics. He was always the main, though not exclusive, actor who represented the spirit and practice of Najaf. The organization of this chapter, in its strict chronological format, is meant to convey to the reader the manner in which the politics of Iraq unfolded with Sistani at its center. This chapter, and the role of Sistani, give the reader a sense of the political culture of Najaf and Iraq more broadly. This overall picture helps to dispel some of the myths about Iraq and the assumptions about democracy, sectarianism, and religious actors more generally. Sistani's actions illustrate this remarkably.

In their political interventions, Sistani and his colleagues committed to follow the "will of the Iraqi people," a formula they used often, so that the political process would be deemed "legitimate." Their discourse on democracy was derived neither from the West nor from Iran, as outsiders might imagine, but was rich with references to universal concepts such as national unity, pluralism, legitimacy, the ballot box, and human rights. They were particularly keen to channel the offense that most Iraqis took to the notion of a confessional system of government. In the end, it was not the US "liberators" but the ayatollahs who were the guardians of democracy in Iraq after 2003.

This chapter therefore elaborates on the nuances of meaning in the discourse of Ayatollah Sistani as it engaged with the new state after 2003. During the transition phase, 2003–2006, he worked to ensure that the state was rooted in sound democratic principle and practice.

Democratic consolidation is a malleable concept in the "transitions to democracy" literature. There is no consensus on what the nebulous concept entails. By consolidation, I mean that the institutions in Iraq were put in place: A permanent constitution was drafted; new political parties emerged; parliamentary politics, however fractured, went on; elections were repeated; and there was turnover in leadership. I make no assumptions by using this term about the strength of democracy or possibility of regime collapse. My use of the term is meant to differentiate the era of transition (direct reconstruction) under the tutelage of the United States from the post-transition period, although the United States did not withdraw troops until December 2011. My study is bounded by time, 2003 to 2016, fully knowing that state consolidation takes decades. Moreover, I take seriously the statement by Ryan Crocker, former US ambassador to Iraq from 2007 to 2009, who, when asked about Iraq's potential to thrive, said, "[W]e are hard-wired into their political system. It won't really function without us."[3]

Although Sistani proved to be the most powerful political actor in Iraq, his commitment to democracy precluded him from disrupting the democratic process, even if it meant that the process would fail before his eyes.

The Transitional Phase Begins

Bremer initially thought he would be able to bypass the Iraqi majority in the reconstruction process. He relied for his understanding of the country on former exiles such as Ahmad Chalabi and Iyad Allawi, as well as the Kurds, who pushed for power sharing via an ethno-religious quota system. The new system was premised on identity politics, in which agreements and interests would be aligned with communal identity, rather than general notions of citizenship or commitment to national programs. This system, Bremer's Iraqi proxies thought, would safeguard against the resurgence of Sunni Arab rule. But, once institutionalized, this system would also normalize sectarian representation and shape the political culture that followed.

The transition phase, in which the mechanisms of the new state would be laid down, was crucial for the future of Iraq and was a test of the constitutional process in the decade to follow. The new political institutions were built alongside the reconstruction of the army and the police to fill the void left by the complete disappearance of all state institutions and services when Saddam fell. Yet before Iraqi institutions were established, Bremer thought he could rule by decree. He empowered the CPA itself to draft a new constitution for the country. This move was controversial because, among other things, the first draft suggested banning political parties opposed to the US occupation from participation in elections. So Bremer opted to create a council of Iraqis to draft a temporary national charter pending the restoration of Iraqi sovereignty.

As Bremer's plans for a constitution surfaced in the press, Sistani emerged on the political scene with his famous "democratic fatwa," issued on June 26, 2003. Sistani had been consulted by a group of believers about the CPA's intention to appoint members of a constitutional drafting council, whose work product would be put up for referendum, by "consulting with all social and political authorities in the country." Sistani replied:

> Those authorities do not have the power to appoint the members of the assembly charged with writing the constitution. Furthermore, there is no guarantee that this council will write a constitution which meets the higher interests of the Iraqi people and expresses its national identity, which is considered one of the primary pillars of Islam . . . the project mentioned is primarily unacceptable. Therefore a public election must be held to enable each eligible Iraqi to choose the person who represents him/her in the constituent council for writing the constitution. . . . All the believers must insist on this matter and they must contribute to it for it to perform well.[4]

In this fatwa, Sistani laid out the skeleton of the procedures he deemed appropriate for Iraq on its path to democracy. He insisted on direct elections, rather than appointments, to allow "every Iraqi" to vote for representatives to an elected constituent assembly. This insistence on the *procedure* of general elections, in the form of one person, one vote, would be repeated over the next year. In fact, the ayatollah's emphasis on voter inclusion predated the "democratic fatwa." On May 3, 2003, he was asked a similar question to which he replied, "The form of governance in Iraq is to be determined by the Iraqi people. The *marja'* does not play a role in either the authority or the governance [of the country]." And when asked if he wanted Shiites to cooperate with the CPA, Sistani answered, "We want to open the way to form the government emitted from the will of the Iraqi people, composed of all sects and ethnicities."[5] He did not single out specific groups or favor the Shiites because they were a numerical majority. He was careful and strategic, cognizant of the authoritarian legacy and the tactics employed by Saddam Hussein to empower one group at the expense of others. More importantly, he understood that Saddam's divide-and-rule tactics seemed to resurface with the proposed policies of the CPA, eerily reminiscent of Iraq's colonial past.

Sistani's impact was dramatic. He inserted important democratic discourse into the public sphere and often served as a foil to Bremer. Bremer's prerogative to sign off on every single document was likewise reminiscent of Saddam, who famously said, "It's the law if I write it down on paper."[6] As the viceroy, Bremer could impose a new law or abolish an old one with his signature.[7] Iraqis were accustomed to the whims of a dictator; Sistani was prepared for the implementation of the rule of law. Sistani understood that in order to break from authoritarian practice, he needed to emphasize contestation and participation, civic responsibilities, valid elections, and the legitimacy of the new state structure—accompanied by warnings about the dangers of delay.

Consistent with some thinking in the transitions literature, Bremer thought that elections would be a dangerous first step toward democracy. Bremer's plan was to instill a free-market capitalist democracy. Bremer's steps included a proposal to "corporatize and privatize state-owned enterprises." He said, "[I]f we don't get their economy right, no matter how fancy our political transformation, it won't work." He cared about setting up a free-trade zone hub that would benefit the international community. The proposed model assumed that the move toward capitalism, with the help of a new business class, would be the surest path to creating a viable middle class. This class would be essential to usher in political reform and democracy. The markets were of utmost importance, not elections.[8]

With what Samuel P. Huntington called the "third wave" of democratization, there were well more than one hundred new democracies in the world in the 1990s. They were "electoral democracies" insofar as free and fair elections had taken place, but they were not "liberal democracies" because they did not fully protect individual liberties and emphasize human rights. Critics such as Fareed Zakaria noted that promotion of elections in the developing world was responsible for what he called "the rise of illiberal democracy." Elections should therefore be delayed. This perspective favored "liberal autocracies" over "illiberal democracies." Zakaria went on to say that that the alternative to regimes such as the one in Saudi Arabia is not "Jeffersonian democracies" but rather "Taliban-style" theocracies. He described Arab rulers as autocratic, but as more "liberal, tolerant and pluralistic" than those who would likely replace them by way of elections. Specifically, he argued that Islamic parties, in their contempt for democracy, would use democracy for "one vote, one time." In cases of transition, Zakaria viewed the situation in Bosnia, where voters went to the polls within a year of the Dayton peace accords, as a hindrance to liberal democracy because it unleashed ethnic hatreds. He argued that the longer periods of state building in East Timor and Afghanistan were better models. He recommended a five-year period of transition, political reform, and institutional development before embarking on national multiparty elections.[9] He would recommend the delay for Iraq, which the local population and Iraq specialists would deem highly problematic. Zakaria's argument rested on the premise that a strong link between liberalism and democracy was ingrained in the West but lacking in other parts of the world.

This cautious discourse was prevalent in US circles and hindered the efforts to make the process an entirely Iraqi one, as Sistani had hoped. In one example, a former administration official was quoted off the record saying that the White House was relying on veto power by the Kurds and possibly Sunni Arabs to limit moves to form a "Shiite theocracy." As he said, "[T]his isn't going to be a Jeffersonian democracy," and "we are naive to think the Iraqis can draft a constitution and build a democracy without at least tipping a hat to the role of Islam."[10] So although there is excellent scholarship that refutes the Zakaria model, the point is that in policy circles, and in the events on the ground, this sentiment, which fears the "liberalism" deficit, carries weight. It assumes that left to their own devices, the Shiite majority, following a religious leader, would opt for some form of "illiberal democracy." It neglects to consider that power is diffuse and that although some Shiite groups did have political parties, we cannot assume we know what they "all want." The rhetoric that continued throughout the reconstruction process was obstructive. It treated "Shiism" as a monolith and assumed that all Shiite political activism is rooted in religious (Islamic) principles. The concept needs to be carefully unpacked. Most importantly, this repeated phrase, "illiberal democracy," which assumes that Shiite activism is the polar opposite of "Jeffersonian democracy," is highly problematic.

Would Iraqis opt for an anti-American Iranian theocracy? Would they respect the rights of minorities? Bremer might have had such questions on his mind, but Sistani was not willing to entertain them. Sistani's ideas about elections, which he tied to legitimacy, were consistent with those scholars who saw the other side of democracy. For instance, Marc Plattner argued that democracy and liberalism were not historically linked. The birthplace of liberalism, modern England, retained a highly restricted franchise throughout the nineteenth century. Instead, Plattner looked to John Locke's *Second Treatise of Government* as the source of liberalism because of its deeply egalitarian and majoritarian dimensions. Accordingly, political power was derived from the consent of individuals who were free and equal. In Locke's framework, the consent of all was essential to the political community and by extension the form of government they chose. Therefore, liberalism "unequivocally insisted upon the ultimate sovereignty of the people," a point that Sistani would make over and over.[11] Plattner argued for "founding elections" because, on the whole, countries that held elections were more liberal than those that did not, and countries that protected civil liberties were more likely to hold free elections than those that did not. He saw an "intrinsic link" and a "profound kinship" between liberalism and electoral democracy once the procedure was institutionalized.[12] Countries did not have to follow a Western path to democracy. Plattner took issue with the suggestion that in uncertain transition cases, Western policy should pursue gradual democratization. There is no principle that makes it acceptable to restrict suffrage and no legitimate mechanism other than elections for determining who will rule. In addition, it was unfounded to assume that Muslim communities would not vote to protect human rights—or would not be capable of protecting individual liberties—if left to found their institutions in the manner Sistani suggested. The whole conversation reeked of Orientalism, and of the language used by British imperial policy maker Gertrude Bell in letters to her father, wherein she said (without giving a reason) that power could never be handed over to "alien popes." Sistani resisted the resurrection of such notions.

Sistani then took the political scene by surprise again with a detailed statement about electoral procedure. In a follow-up to his June fatwa, he was asked to elaborate on the eligibility of voters and the selection of candidates. He replied that the constitutional drafting council members "must be elected by eligible Iraqi voters" and that the "terms and conditions for voting must be established, generalized, and transparent." He went on to say that a similar election had been arranged in East Timor under the supervision of the United Nations and wondered "why it [was] not possible to make such an arrangement in Iraq." He made clear that "there was no substitute for a direct election." It would not be possible to wait until the constitution was promulgated to vote because a constitution written by an assembly "which had not been elected by the people would not be acceptable." He said that his role was to "open the way for Iraqis to govern themselves without procrastination or prevarication."[13]

Sistani's fatwas stopped Bremer in his tracks, although it took several months for the viceroy to fully understand Sistani's informal power. On July 13, 2003, the CPA announced the formation of a twenty-five-member Iraqi Governing Council (IGC), to be entrusted with the task of rebuilding the state. It was composed of representatives from the country's main ethnic and sectarian groups (thirteen Shiites, five Sunni Arabs, and five Kurds, who were also Sunni, as well as an Assyrian Christian and a Turkmen). Three women were included. Although its purpose was to be broadly representative of Iraq's population, it was chosen to mirror the country's sectarian and ethnic makeup. Moreover, it assumed that political representation should be apportioned according to such quotas. In essence, the composition of the IGC reflected the CPA's view of Iraqi society, not how Iraqis identified themselves. Bremer may have assumed that such a "representative" drafting body would be deemed a legitimate compromise. He was mistaken. Twenty-four of the twenty-five members made their way to Najaf to meet with Sistani, and, to a person, they followed his recommendation that no temporary constitution be written prior to elections.

Through pressure from Sistani and others, Bremer was compelled to clarify that the IGC would be the provisional government only, serving as the transitional administration through a "cooperative" and "consultative" process with the CPA and the special representative of the UN secretary-general. The Iraqi Governing Council and the CPA were required to consult and coordinate on all matters, according to CPA Order 6. The IGC, ostensibly representative of the Iraqi population, would run the country until the constitution was written, elections held, and a permanent government formed. But it would soon become clear that legitimate civil institutions, grounded in Iraqi society, were hard to come by and that nation and state building under occupation would be riddled with problems, problems that Sistani would point out. Although Bremer retained most formal powers in the country, informal politics prevailed on this question.

Sistani was interested in the legitimacy of the new state structure. He wanted to distance himself from the "details of political work," as argued in chapter 4, and also from the United States, which he always referred to as the "occupying power." He was asked during this period if he had been invited to be on the IGC and if he was in negotiation with Washington. He rejoined that he would not participate in the council and that there was "no contact between His Eminence and the occupation authorities regarding the formation of this council or any other thing related to Iraq." He had "no information" about the council.[14]

In other proclamations, Sistani stated that he was "extremely worried about [US] purposes."[15] He replied "no" every single time about whether he communicated with the Bush administration. In fact, he never referred to the United States by name but called it either "the occupying power" or "the occupying authorities." He made clear on several occasions that these appellations were not a judgment on his part but rather the official terms used by the UN Security Council (and by Bremer himself).[16] He also often refused to comment on US actions or advise the Americans about how they could correct their mistakes. He talked little about the United States, in the same manner that he tried to diminish the importance of Muqtada al-Sadr or the insurgents by refusing to acknowledge them.

The United Nations figured prominently in Sistani's discourse. In all of his pronouncements, the ayatollah made clear that the UN was "central to establishing security and stability in Iraq during the transitional stage" and that its efforts were crucial to "supervise" and "monitor" the steps required to enable the Iraqis to "take sovereignty" of their country.[17] He also always stipulated that all military forces in Iraq must be there "under the umbrella of the United Nations."[18] Because the Security Council did not authorize the invasion and occupation, it was irrelevant to Sistani that the UN sent personnel to Iraq afterward. Whenever he was asked if he approved of the US presence, he queried, "How can we agree with the occupation?"[19] And he "did not see a difference" between US forces and other members of the US-led coalition, such as the Polish forces.[20] All were outsiders in Iraq by virtue of the fact that they were part of a military invasion that he and the international community deemed illegal. As for a possible Japanese presence in Iraq, Sistani replied that "the Iraqi people can look positively to its coming if it is conducted under the umbrella of the United Nations" and if it "provid[es] the conditions suitable to hold public elections."[21] (As it happened, Japan also sent troops to Iraq without a UN mandate.) The ayatollah always used the UN as the marker of legitimacy.

Sistani was repeatedly asked about the time line for US withdrawal and the subsequent role of the UN. He usually started by saying that there was no reasonable ground for the US presence to begin with, which left no room for the legitimacy of an occupation of any length. If foreign forces were needed to protect the country, then it must happen "under the umbrella" of the UN, according to Sistani.[22] No other options were legitimate. He was positive about the role of the French in Iraq because they had worked through UN channels, which was in accordance with the "interests of the people of Iraq."[23] Jolyon Howorth had called France the "defender of international legitimacy" for its ability to secure international agreements, to assert the centrality of the United Nations, and to gather international momentum behind the inspections process before the start of the war.[24]

Sistani focused heavily on the responsibilities of the United Nations to Iraq as well. He argued that because the UN had recognized the new state of Iraq, it should supervise the political process until it was stable and legitimate.[25] He was vague in his language here and elsewhere, but a logic ran through his statements: Legitimacy would be achieved when the political formation happened at the "will of all ethnicities and sects of the Iraqi people."[26]

Toward Iraqi Sovereignty

In November 2003 the CPA presented its plan for the transition to Iraqi sovereignty. The agreement signed on November 15 included the draft of a Transitional Administrative Law (TAL)—a provisional constitution—and a proposal for caucuses in each of Iraq's provinces to select a transitional national assembly. That assembly, in turn, would choose executive leadership by June 2004. Sistani expressed reservations. First and foremost, the agreement was predicated upon the continuation of the occupation, which automatically compromised its legitimacy. Second was the fact that the transitional national assembly would be selected by caucuses, not direct elections. Sistani had won his appeal for electoral democracy with his June fatwa, but Bremer seemed to miss Sistani's point about procedure.[27] Sistani had issued a string of statements that repeated the same message on the need for direct elections, but Bremer was not listening (or had gambled that he would be able to do what he wanted anyway). Now the ayatollah worried that caucuses might wind up choosing people who were not the "elected children of the people." He invoked that term, along with "ballot box," to highlight the disproportionate influence of former exiles in the state-building process and the presence of a foreign occupying power. Sistani argued that the "mechanism was not legitimate."[28] Homegrown democratic discourse was his best weapon.[29]

Sistani demanded a one-person, one-vote system that would consult a wider range of voices in this important interim phase. Sistani gave his fatwa on popular sovereignty to the reporter Anthony Shadid on November 27, 2003: "The mechanism for electing the members of the transitional legislature does not guarantee the formation of a parliament that truly represents the Iraqi people." He insisted that the mechanism be "changed to another method that would guarantee it, which is an election." That was the only guarantee of the formation of a parliament that "would derive from the will of the Iraqis and represent them in a just manner, and safeguard against challenges to its legitimacy."[30] In this same fatwa, Sistani offered the alternative of elections with ration cards serving as voter identification documents.

Tied to the November 15 agreement, the United States said that not enough time remained to prepare for free and fair elections that would transfer sovereignty to an interim Iraqi government by the established date of June 30, 2004.[31] Sistani then turned to the secretary-general of the United Nations, Kofi Annan, for advice. Seeking intervention from the UN, the only outside body Sistani deemed legitimate and neutral, was an important strategic move that would give Sistani leverage over Washington as he reasoned his way forward. Bremer also understood that he needed to seek out the help of Annan in the nation-building enterprise in Iraq. Indeed, after bypassing the UN in going to war, the United States was forced to return to the world body, in part because many countries wanted a UN resolution before they would join in the reconstruction efforts. But Sistani wanted to press the CPA to explain its unwillingness to hold elections right away. He continued to stress the issue of legitimacy and the fact that the interim government would have no domestic support. Annan had already sent a letter to Sistani, hand-delivered by the president of the IGC, Adnan Pachachi, in which the secretary-general recommended against early elections. A mere recommendation, even one furnished by the UN, without a fact-finding mission or investigation was not enough for the ayatollah. He pressed for more and received it. The CPA was forced to ask the UN team, headed by envoy Lakhdar Brahimi, about the feasibility of early elections for the interim government. Sistani not only requested an investigation of the possibility; he also wanted the team to "examine all aspects" and to "establish another mechanism" that would represent Iraqis in the temporary national council.[32] For his part, Bremer needed the UN stamp of approval for his plan to delay elections until after June 30.

After a lengthy investigation, Brahimi concluded that elections could be held no earlier than late 2004 or early 2005. Sistani accepted the decision. He issued a statement to the effect "that the report ensured the establishment of an integrated civil government that was based on direct national elections." He went on to say that the report revealed "serious flaws" in the November 15 agreement, which he listed one by one. He concluded that the only task left for the interim government was to establish the temporary constitution and that this "unelected body would cease" to exist by 2005.[33] He received guarantees from the UN to see the process through. This statement ensured that the UN's assessment of US actions would be broadcast.

At the same time, Sistani was careful not to overreach. In some ways, in fact, the ayatollah helped the US state-building project with his decision not to derail it. At the time that Sistani agreed to the UN recommendation, tens of thousands of protesters had taken to the streets in Basra to reiterate his demands for general elections. Many held signs that read "No to America." An aide to Sistani had also warned US officials in the days leading up to his UN announcement that the ayatollah had been contemplating the issuance of a fatwa against the proposed interim government. The United States was nonetheless reluctant to change its plans, perhaps without realizing that Sistani's fatwas in the early days of the war had made the occupation much easier for the United States. The ayatollah could have made things much worse, but he acknowledged that a weak Iraqi government would not be able to manage independent of the United States. Regardless of his disdain for the invasion, he repeatedly urged his followers to observe the rule of law, renounce violence, turn away from looting, and reject allegiance to militias. He always worked through the system.

The TAL was adopted on March 8, 2004. It remained in effect until the new government was formed, and it was replaced by the permanent constitution in May 2006. It was hailed by Iraqi and US leaders as a major achievement on the eve of the one-year anniversary of Saddam Hussein's removal from power. It was an aspirational document, as it laid out general principles that the authors hoped would guide the drafting of the permanent constitution. It had many elements of a modern state: a bill of rights, provisions for civilian control over the military, and a system of checks and balances. Its articles enshrined human rights and democratic rule. It allocated power among the branches of government and defined the role of the law. It contained compromise—Kurdish was recognized as an official language alongside Arabic, as was Kurdish identity. Massoud Barzani, the leader of the Kurdish Democratic Party, said that the constitution made the Kurds feel "equal to others," "not second-class citizens," as he switched from Kurdish to Arabic during his remarks about the achievement for his people.[34]

Although Sistani remained adamant that the unelected interim government lacked legitimacy, he turned his attention to the details of the TAL. He became increasingly specific about his reservations. One was that "sectarian interests would intervene" to delegitimize the constitutional process.[35] For instance, the TAL created a collective presidency, a three-person council consisting of a Kurd, a Sunni Arab, and a Shiite Arab—a predetermined ethno-sectarian structure. This system would lock

Iraq into a sectarian model of governance. Sistani warned that devotion to the ethno-sectarian model would block decision making by the council and damage the "unity of the country."[36]

Sistani returned to the United Nations to express his outrage with this sectarian framework, which he framed as offensive to the sensibilities of all Iraqis. He wrote a letter to Lakhdar Brahimi enumerating his complaints, this time taking a more forceful approach than in the last exchange. He wrote that the TAL had many "constraints" and that terms had been "dictated," which was the "most dangerous matter" that needed to be addressed. The collective presidency was clearly not supported by the people, "as ensured by public opinion polls as well as millions of signatures collected" calling for either rejection or amendment of the law. "Unless all three members agreed unanimously," which was unlikely given the different viewpoints, the presidential council would be unable to make decisions. Stalemate would require the intervention of an external actor, such as the United States. Sistani accordingly warned that the ethno-sectarian framework posed the dangers of "instability, segmentation and fragmentation" for the long-term future of Iraq.[37] Yet he did not issue a fatwa denouncing the TAL. It seemed, for the moment, that he wanted to exhaust diplomatic channels.

Significantly, Sistani took issue with Bremer's point that conditions in Iraq were not ripe for free and fair elections by the June 30, 2004, deadline. The ayatollah furnished evidence to the contrary. For instance, opinion polls and petitions in circulation demonstrated a politically mature Iraqi population in opposition to the proposed plan for the presidency. Thus, the ayatollah showed that he was in touch with the political trends in the country. He stressed that the TAL should never "acquire international legitimacy" and asked that this point be communicated to the Security Council.[38] In a follow-up letter to the UN in June before the adoption of Resolution 1546, which endorsed the impending handover of sovereignty and a timetable for national elections by January 2005, he sent an explicit message not to mention the TAL in the resolution because it was an interim document that was written "under the effect of occupation," that "did not comply with the law," and that was "rejected by the majority of the people."[39] Indeed, Resolution 1546 made no mention of the TAL. Sistani's hope was that, if not internationally recognized, the TAL would be ephemeral and would not lay the groundwork for the permanent constitution.

Essentially, Sistani had allowed the TAL to stand for the time being in order to preserve the unity of the country and to keep the momentum going toward the concrete goals of a date certain for general elections and the writing of a permanent constitution. There were a few problems, however. This interim constitution provided a federal structure: In fact, it defined Iraq as a federal state, which granted considerable authority to individual regions. The Kurds, despite opposition from others, succeeded in inserting a provision in the TAL that allowed any three provinces to vote down, by a two-thirds majority, the permanent constitution. Because the Kurds constituted a majority of the population in Suleimaniya, Erbil, and Dohuk provinces, this provision effectively granted them veto power over the permanent constitution, which was to be written *after* national elections were held. They were also allowed to maintain their *peshmerga* (literally, "those who face death") militia until its status was determined later. The status of other militias, such as ones associated with Shiite political parties, was not addressed in the TAL. Sistani had a policy of treating all militias the same—they were all prohibited, and the only legal forces were those associated with the government. Moreover, changes to the document would not be allowed without the approval of the government and the new national assembly, to be elected at the beginning of 2005.[40]

Sistani addressed this issue from a nationalist perspective, consistent with his discourse on all other issues. He was concerned with the distribution of power and the extent to which it threatened the unity of the country. For Sistani, the problem was the prospect of fragmentation and partition, not an attempt to single out "Kurd" or "Sunni." That approach was consistent with his Iraq-centric narrative since 2003. He exercised great restraint despite the fact that the Kurds were able to enter the new political pact with a disproportionate amount of power. He was neutral, or nonintrusive, on the question of federalism. When asked, Sistani said, "The origins of federalism and its suitable type shall be determined by the Iraqi people through elections" and "nothing shall be broadcast until that time." He did not want to influence the process. He assured his followers that those entrusted with the task would find "the perfect formula to save the Iraqi unit and the rights of all its ethnicities and nationalities."[41] Instead, he highlighted national unity and anti-sectarianism in the broadest terms possible. Likewise, his discussions of democracy were always inclusive, and he never referred to a group directly. When he was pressed to comment on the majority Shiites, perhaps *favored* to rule because of their sheer numbers, Sistani resisted the categorization. He made no distinction, insisting on the equality of Shiites with other Iraqis. Sistani clarified that Shiite needs were the "same as those of all Iraqis," which included the "fulfillment of their rights without sectarian discrimination."[42] He did not support the formation of any militia, not even for the protection of holy sites. He issued dozens of fatwas and statements that declared all militias illegal.[43] With regard to the form of government, he reiterated that it should be determined by all, regardless of the political clout of any particular faction and with a commitment to sovereignty, in the spirit that Plattner described.

Sistani was not a seasoned politician, but he had the political instincts to understand the deep implications of the foundational documents and institutions. The structural sectarianism of the IGC and the TAL would have repercussions, both locally and regionally. It was early 2004 when the TAL took effect, and at the time, there was little talk of civil war or violence that could threaten the integrity of the state. But Sistani could foresee the dangers of constructing a state along sectarian lines. He was hardly alone: Area specialists had long talked about the problems of the Lebanese model and how it would be a bad one for Iraq. Overall, his warnings about fragmentation referred not to the Kurds but to the legitimacy of the process and the integrity of the state. Indeed, the bulk of his discourse here was about the sectarian fighting that would engulf Iraq. His narrative about the Sunni-Shiite divide was partially driven by his larger point that "if foreign hands did not interfere in Iraqi affairs, the people would be more harmonized and converged."[44] Sistani issued early warnings about fragmentation because he saw a direct link between the state structure and the violence on the ground, not because he wanted to target a particular ethnic group. In fact, his message was the opposite: Disenfranchised groups that found no outlet through the political system opted for violence. It was a recipe for disaster.

Elections and a New Constitution

With elections for an interim national assembly scheduled for January 30, 2005, Sistani refocused his attention again. The stakes were high. The 275-member parliament was charged with writing the permanent constitution and exercising all legislative functions under the Iraqi Transitional

Government until the new constitution was adopted by referendum on October 15, 2005. Elections were to follow in December 2005 for the formation of the first assembly under the permanent constitution. On October 10, 2004, Sistani was asked by a group of his followers about how they should interact with the voting process. He responded with a fatwa on how they should proceed. He urged male and female citizens to confirm that they were properly registered. He insisted on the formation of "popular committees" to assist in the process and deemed it most important that "all Iraqis shall participate."[45] According to one Iraq specialist, it was a "top-level clerical commitment to participatory democracy unparalleled in earlier Iraqi history."[46] The go-vote fatwa was for all Iraqis, not only his followers.

Sistani framed the act of voting as a religious duty. He must have reasoned that Iraqis would be able to work as a collective, as he reiterated tirelessly for over a year, to find a model that would be inclusive of all Iraqis. He did not issue multiple fatwas, as he did in the past. Consistent with his commitment to refrain from meddling in the details of political work, he made clear that he would "pave the way" but not lay the tiles. To that end, his October fatwa was a general call to *all* Iraqis to vote. When it came to the January 2005 elections, everyone expected Sistani to issue another fatwa or to endorse the Shiite Islamist coalition, the United Iraqi Alliance (UIA).[47] He could have thrown his support behind the Shiite bloc in an effort to determine who would control the country. But had he outwardly endorsed the UIA or issued a fatwa (or multiple fatwas) regarding the January elections, commentators and local politicians would have perceived him with suspicion—as sectarian. Media outlets did circulate stories claiming that Sistani endorsed the UIA. However, little evidence suggests that Sistani supported the coalition.[48]

The question of whether Sistani endorsed the United Iraqi Alliance was an important discussion topic for journalists and analysts. The majority of scholars agreed that Sistani endorsed the UIA, but another way to interpret the fatwa is that he gave the UIA his "blessing." In the next sentence, however, he went on to say that he "endorsed" all political parties in the elections. When asked to elaborate, he made clear that parties should not use his name or influence opportunistically. However, his representatives and wider web of associates may have given endorsements to the UIA, which resulted in the scholarly consensus that "Sistani" supported the

UIA in 2005. The ayatollah replied to a question about this matter on December 16, 2004. He said that although he gave his "blessing" to the UIA, he also "supported" all political parties in the elections. He made clear that he had not issued a fatwa in support of one political party over others and expressed dismay at the opportunism displayed by those using his name to pursue votes.[49] Shortly after the elections, Sistani made a statement through one of his representatives, Hamid Al-Khafaf, to address any remarks made by Sistani regarding the constitution and the process to date, making it clear that Sistani had not issued any new statements and had not changed any of his "previous attitudes in recent days." He confirmed his previous position with regard to the permanent constitution and its need to respect the identity of the Iraqi people. He remained committed to the original details formulated by the people's representatives elected in the national association. During the campaign, UIA posters featuring his portrait were plastered all over cities, including polling places. He called on "those persons who loved him to stop those acts."[50] His response meant that he wanted to distance himself from the process. It was also usually the case that authoritarian leaders in the region had their posters splattered all over cities as mythical and godlike figures. That was not an image that appealed to Sistani. He had tried not to cross the line between influencing politics and participating in it. This was not the time to begin.

Eerily, during the run-up to the January elections, when Iraqis should have been jubilant, violence was on the rise, and the attacks took on increasingly sectarian overtones. Iraq was headed toward civil war. The UIA and the Kurdish parties triumphed in the elections, but Sunni Arabs had largely abstained. They composed nearly 20 percent of the population but less than 2 percent of the voters. The level of violence in Sunni Arab areas was high. In turn, many Sunni groups, such as the Association of Muslim Scholars, boycotted the elections. The low turnout threatened the legitimacy of the whole process, which pushed the election winners to guarantee future Sunni Arab participation in the constitution-writing process. Sunnis secured only 17 out of the 275 seats in the assembly. Six months later, in June 2005, Sistani pushed for changes to the voting system that would increase the chances that Sunnis could gain representation in future parliaments. Sistani outlined a proposal that eliminated the system used in the January election. Accordingly, voters in national elections would select leaders from the 19 provinces rather than from a single countrywide list. The new province-based proposal would set aside a number of seats in proportion to population. It was not based on voter turnout. Sistani made clear that the importance of this new voting system reflected the delicate political situation in the country. He was acting because "a lot of mistakes" were made in the past. As usual, Sistani wanted "all the people" to partake in the democratic experience.[51]

After the new government assumed power in May, the drafters of the permanent constitution debated the remaining contentious issues. It was federalism, and the perceived potential for Iraq to break up into several regions, that caused more tension than any other issue. Drafts about the concept of federalism were put forth by the Kurds and embraced by the party of slain Ayatollah Baqir al-Hakim, the Supreme Council for the Islamic Revolution in Iraq (SCIRI). Sistani did not interfere with these debates but allowed the factions to negotiate. He kept quiet not because the points were trivial but rather because the groups needed to work out their differences. In the same way that he did not want the United States or the IGC to "dictate" policy, he understood that he should not meddle either. Rather, political parties that were democratically elected (albeit in flawed circumstances) had a better chance of evolving through multiple interactions with the political system. As it turned out, however, the bargaining over points in the permanent constitution was carried out in ethnic and regional terms, as Sistani had predicted. Group interests were already enshrined in the TAL, the document which constitutional specialist Andrew Arato referred to as the "straightjacket" that was in part responsible for some of the political consequences that would follow.[52]

The permanent constitution met many of the Kurdish demands for substantial autonomy by way of federalism as defined by "regions." Kurds maintained all of their power from the TAL and gained even more jurisdiction over the central government. Article 117 of the constitution recognized the three Kurdish provinces of Dohuk, Erbil, and Suleimaniya as legal regions, which formed the Kurdistan Regional Government (KRG). The KRG had the power to amend the application of national laws not specifically under national government purview and also to maintain its own security forces. In addition to this, the KRG had the right to establish embassies abroad (Article 117). Kurdish was recognized as an official language (alongside Arabic), according to Article 4 of the Iraqi Constitution. At the time that provincial council elections were held nationwide in Iraq in January 2005, they were also conducted for the Kurdistan National Assembly, the separate parliament for the KRG. The Kurdistan National Assembly selected Massoud Barzani as president of Kurdistan on June 12, 2005.[53] Abd al-Aziz al-Hakim, who favored a great deal of autonomy in the South, delivered a "bombshell announcement" in which he demanded a region of nine southern Shiite provinces. He envisioned a regional confederation that mirrored the one formed by the Kurds. The proposal was a break from the more "centralist" position taken by Prime Minister Ibrahim Jaafari, who, at the time, wanted to deal with the nine provinces separately.[54] This powerful region would contain up to 80 percent of Iraq's oil and half the population.[55] It would amount to a de facto Shiite supra-region or, worse, a Shiite entity that had overwhelming control over the central government. The Kurds would reject such a preponderance of power. And the Sunni Arabs would see themselves left in the center, resource-poor and powerless. Federalism held no appeal for them. The Hakim proposal went against Sistani's desire to treat all Iraqis as equals. It also bumped up against his Iraqi unity narrative and led policy makers to embark on proposals for a "soft partition" of Iraq.[56] Most importantly, Hakim's proposal did not represent a "Shiite" point of view. Shiites overwhelmingly preferred the centralist position with "asymmetric federalism" that was limited to the Kurds only.[57] In the year to follow, there was a fledgling call among some Shiites in Basra for a small federal region made up of the southern port city and its adjacent governorates. But even such limited schemes were not very popular. The Sadrist and Da'wa factions within the Shiite bloc favored a centralist position. Even SCIRI softened its tone on federalism by 2007, moving away from dreams of a large-scale federal entity. Instead, SCIRI officials stressed constitutionality and the "popular will" of the Iraqis.[58] It was clear that the skepticism of the average voter about federalism had shaped their thinking.

But it was the language of the constitution on federalism that paved the way for the "fragmentation" that Sistani had warned about all along. Article 118 of the constitution declared that provinces had the right to form regions if a simple majority of voters approved. In fact, future regionalization was guaranteed through interpretation and implementation of Articles 112–117. Over the next few years, Iraqis would have to discuss the process of region formation and determine the powers these regions would have, especially as they related to oil and broader fiscal policies.

Sistani did not engage this federalism debate at the grassroots level with fatwas as he did regarding elections. In fact, after the constitution was finalized, Sistani did not oppose it, despite all of the problems it presented. He urged all citizens of Iraq to vote "yes" for the constitution, "despite the failure to address some of its shortcomings."[59]

The constitution was ratified on October 15, 2005. At this time, Sistani was drained, as he came to the realization that the factions, particularly the Kurds and SCIRI, were clinging to maximalist positions to bargain for greatest gain from the political system. A believer approached him regarding the upcoming December 15 general elections to choose the 275-member Iraqi Council of Representatives. In this election, seats were allocated through proportional representation in order to guarantee Sunni representation in Parliament. Sunni voters had largely boycotted the January 2005 elections but participated in December even though many were unhappy with the federalism articles in the constitution. They did not boycott the elections because of the agreement that the Constitutional Review Committee would be formed under the first Parliament, which would prepare proposals for amendments that could be adopted in a clear and simplified procedure. In December, Sunnis managed to win 60 of the 275 seats in Parliament.

Sistani offered a short decree, insisted that all men and women should vote, and hoped for a "strong presence." He also asked voters not to "split votes or waste them."[60] Given the political wrangling at the time, some analysts suggested that this request was a "veiled endorsement of the UIA," which managed to win more seats in December than in January.[61] The UIA did represent the majority, so a win was not a surprise. However, some centralist voices within the group were loud yet still ignored. The UIA's policies did not reflect the full array of Iraqi voices, but rather the voices of those who were in power, those individuals who had been in close communication with the United States before and after the invasion. This line of communication distorted the "Shiite view" and led the United States to assume that the majority of Shiites overwhelmingly supported federalism. Senator Joe Biden's proposal for a "soft partition" of Iraq in May 2006 may have been influenced by these voices. The problem with Biden's plan to create "one Iraq with three regions" was that the constitution of Iraq does not recognize federalism as a general principle of government for Iraq. The creation of any new federal units outside of

Kurdistan was left to the Iraqi people, through referendums. Biden's statement therefore violated Iraq's constitution, which doesn't allow outsiders to dictate the structure of the state. New federal units have to be chosen by Iraqis, "from below."[62]

Federalism, if viewed through the lens of Sistani, was not about whether the constitution would set a precedent for the dismemberment of Iraq. Dismemberment would be consistent with a long history of a people who were in fact "lumped together" and lacked a national identity. Such is the argument of the "artificiality of Iraq" thesis that Sistani worked to debunk, as seen in chapter 5. If, on the other hand, and consistent with the Sistani narrative, Iraqis were unified in their nationalism, the constitution was less likely to give form to widespread movements that would break Iraq into separate regions. Even if the central government were deemed corrupt and illegitimate, an issue Sistani addressed repeatedly under the Maliki government, there would be no resurgence of the federalism model. In fact, there was no general decline in Iraqi nationalism, but there was a decline in support for the policies that were inconsistent with the historical narrative that Sistani preferred.

However, Sistani understood that key players could mold political outcomes to their benefit regardless of the popular will in Iraq. Thus, he was insistent on a state structure that would allow all Iraqis to participate in the process as fully as possible. Sistani saw imperfections in the permanent constitution, but at the same time he was pleased that the explicit allocation of government positions based on ethno-religious affiliation (as stipulated in the TAL) was removed.

Religion, and specifically the place of Islam in the constitution and the state, was a second contentious issue in the negotiations over the text of the constitution. However, it was not central to Sistani's discourse or high on his list of priorities. His fatwas, speeches, and pronouncements rarely centered on Islam. It was the more-conservative lay Shiite groups, such as SCIRI, that wanted particular language regarding the place of Islam in the state and its prominence with regard to personal status law. These groups did not represent the *hawza* or offer interpretations based on jurisprudence. In many ways, Sistani's low-key engagement with this issue illustrates Charles Taylor's proposition advanced in chapter 1 that modernity leads to the increase of individuated responses to questions in Islam. Sistani could not give voice to all the possible Shiite ideas about the constitution, nor can he be held responsible for all of them because he heads the *hawza*. Yet his response could not disregard Islam in favor of a completely secular state. That would go against his commitment to preserve Islam as a moral basis of society. Sistani's goal in the constitutional debate was to ensure that the national identity of the majority would be safeguarded and balanced with democratic goals.

The Islamic content of the constitution sowed a great deal of confusion among US and other Western journalists and policy makers. Speculation about Shiite ayatollahs and their intentions to create a constitution "based solely on Islamic law" began circulating in 2003. After the January 2005 elections, the questions about what shape the discussions surrounding Islam would take continued, sometimes without context.[63] Some scholars surmised that "Sistani and the other grand ayatollahs will press for as much Shariah—or Islamic law—as possible in Iraqi law." The thinking was that "they can afford to be patient if they can't push through everything right now."[64] Yet these discussions began before the permanent constitution was even drafted.

The main concern regarded Article 2, which read as follows:

> *First:* Islam is the official religion of the State and is a fundamental source of legislation.
>
> A. No law may be enacted that contradicts the established provisions of Islam.
> B. No law may be enacted that contradicts the principles of democracy.
> C. No law may be enacted that contradicts the rights and basic freedoms stipulated in this Constitution.
>
> *Second:* This constitution guarantees the Islamic identity of the majority of the Iraqi people and guarantees the full religious rights to freedom of religious belief and practice of all individuals. . . .[65]

This language was not only vague, but it also seemed contradictory to some commentators in the sense that it did not provide a blueprint for everyday governance or a way in which courts could proceed in cases. It was not meant to provide such clarity, however. This article, like all other articles before it in Arab constitutions, including previous versions of Iraq's constitution, recognized Islam as the state's official religion in a ceremonial, symbolic nod to religion and culture. Constitutional debates in other Arab countries had centered on whether Islam was *a* source of legislation or *the* source of legislation. In Egypt, for example, Article 2 of the constitution was amended from the 1971 version that read "principles of Islamic sharia are a source of legislation" to the 1981 version that read that the "principles of Islamic sharia are the main source of legislation." Nathan Brown, an expert on constitutions in the Middle East, wondered whether this change was the regime's attempt to enhance its Islamic credentials. After all, this change followed the time when the Supreme Constitutional Court was able to secure its independence and potentially enforce its "conception" of the meaning of Islamic law. However, Brown reasoned that the court had not used this change to enforce its limits of Egypt's legal order. Legal rulings that followed demonstrated that sharia could not operate as a binding law in its own right.[66]

If this case and other similar ones in the region are illustrative, then there should be nothing innately threatening about the language contained in Articles 1 and 2 of the Iraqi Constitution.[67] We would have to consider the broader role of the courts and the conservative actors—in this case, "Shiite Islamists" such as members of SCIRI who had participated in drafting the constitution. Some critics of the constitution wanted the articles to be explicit and noncontradictory, and took issue with gendered language in the preamble stating that "we have honored the sons of Adam," rather than the sons and daughters of Adam. Shak Hanish wrote that the constitutional articles endorsing principles such as human rights are impossible if they are subject to the clause that they could not run contrary to the provisions of Islam. He argued that all Islamic religious rhetoric contradicts modern conceptions of rights and equality. The document, according to his analysis, was "conservative and even reactionary" in its high regard for Islam that welcomes conservative jurisprudence. The "ambiguity" paves the way for what Hanish perceived to be the inevitability that "Islamic states," given their histories, will be "hostile to the concept of freedom and democracy as we understand them today." Hanish's analysis included a line-by-line analysis in order to demonstrate that the articles of the constitution were contradictory and vague. He also made the case that the constitution was a step backward with regard to human rights and the role of women in society more generally. This was caused by the obstacles and restrictions placed on interpretation, according to Hanish, from the prominence given to Islam in the document. Yet Hanish, like some of the other analysts engaging in the discourse surrounding Islamist participation on the topic, makes assumptions about "Islamist" goals and how Islamists would behave once in a position of power.[68]

Rather than viewing the document as "ambiguous," it is more useful to view the document as "flexible," as Haider Hamoudi called it. He argued that the language was "wisely designed" to allow for the constitution to evolve and be updated over time. A constitution must be flexible so that it can outlive political trends and increase in legitimacy as the state consolidates.[69] Hamoudi argued that the flaw in some interpretations of the constitution is that they had implicitly adopted a "rigid and formalistic model of legal and constitutional change," whereby changes to the document are envisioned only by way of formal amendment. Hamoudi, who invoked the US constitution as an example, argued that constitutional theorists have provided a narrative of continual evolution of constitutional meaning: Social and political change will occur, and in all political systems, old and new, flexible language is required to address them. If we follow Hamoudi's logic, the constitution allows for inclusion of people from all political leanings but needs to take into account the political culture and "popular will" that Sistani conjured with his recruitment of people to the polls. A suggestion to ban the headscarf would be highly unpopular at present, for example. Hamoudi therefore suggested that the language offers a space for engagement that can keep discussions in line with the prevailing sentiments in Iraq. To support his idea, he wondered what would happen if the document were not flexible. First, there would need to be frequent amendments to take into account electoral results. Second, there would be an impasse with regard to the role of religion in the state.

Hamoudi's constitutional interpretation helps to situate Sistani's position of noninterference on the question of Islam and the constitution. Sistani did not offer explicit details of what should be included in the constitution as articles, but he made clear that that the charter should accommodate Islamic ideals. It was Hamoudi who, after his encounters with the ayatollahs in 2009, coined the phrase "Najaf mantra," a commitment on the clerics' part to guide citizens without taking on a direct role in government. Therefore, it made sense that Sistani would deliver his position through a series of fatwas on the broader political process rather than meddle in the "details of political work."

To understand Sistani's position on the topic, we can piece together his fatwas and rulings on the role of religion in the state, even before the constitutional process was under way. He responded to such a question in 2003 by saying that a government that emerged by the "will of the majority" must respect the religion of the majority and "shall not contradict the people's provisions." In a follow-up question about the biggest threat to Iraq, Sistani responded with "the obliteration of its cultural identity, one of the most important pillars of Islam."[70] In other fatwas, Sistani was asked if the government should be modeled on Iran or whether it should be an "Islamic government." He answered that the Iranian model was "out of the question," but he made clear that the government must "respect Islam" because it is the religion of the majority.[71] In this same statement, he said that the government should not contradict the teachings of Islam. But he also said that he was unable to dictate the type of government, which should follow the will of the people as revealed by elections. His job, as he saw it, was to "open the way for them."[72] Sistani wanted Islam to serve as a moral basis of society but was unwilling to delineate exactly what that entailed.

His fatwa regarding the proposed constitution-drafting council in 2003 was concerned that the occupation authorities had no power to appoint members without elections. But it was equally concerned that the constitution would not express Iraq's "national identity," which Sistani repeatedly referred to as a "primary pillar of Islam and the noble social values."[73] He was asked about the aspects of Islamic law he wanted to see enshrined in the constitution. To this he replied, "[R]eligious constants, ethical principles, and social values must be the primary pillars" of the constitution.[74] A direct question about the role of religion in the forthcoming constitution prompted Sistani to respond that the specifics would be determined by the members of the elected council.[75] He often added that that "Islam is the religion of the majority of Iraqis. If the constitution is written by the persons elected by the Iraqi people, it would then represent Islamic values and its tolerant teachings."[76]

While he gave his opinion on Islam, he always balanced it with an assurance that free and fair elections would reveal Iraqi public opinion on the question. Sistani added that the constitution should also enshrine principles such as consultation, pluralism, respect for the opinion of others, justice, and equality. Sistani expanded his notion of the type of state in a response to a question on February 12, 2004. He insisted that the form of government should be left to the will of the Iraqi people. He added that those involved in the process should safeguard the rights of minorities and agree upon principles of justice and equality, in addition to the principles of pluralism, a commitment to the ballot box, and a peaceful transfer of power.[77]

He assured his followers that in Iraq, the "primary political and social forces" were not in favor of establishing a religious government. He called instead for the formation of a government that "respected the religious constants" of the majority of the population.[78] It was an embrace of a secular government that was inspired by Islam and protected its cultural role in society.

What Sistani had not calculated in his early pronouncements was that the makeup of the IGC and the foundation of the TAL would determine the political maneuvering of the constitution-writing process. He had envisioned a process that was more representative of the population.

Sistani's fatwas revealed much about his commitment to laying the foundation for democracy on his terms. His fatwas suggested that he was not interested in empowering the Shiite majority at the expense of others. He was also not interested in the creation of an Islamic state, but instead wanted to ensure that the "cultural identity" of Iraqis was not "obliterated" in the transition. We can reach back to history to find precedents for Sistani's behavior in the advocacy of pro-democracy ayatollahs during the 1906 Constitutional Revolution in Iran. As Babak Rahimi argues, Sistani could be viewed as adhering to a tradition in which a cleric guides the Muslim community while securing a "social contract" between ruler and ruled by promoting the ideals of Islam.[79] Yet there was much more. Sistani's conceptions of rights and liberties were shaped in an era different from his predecessors'. Yes, his actions took into account previous clerical judgments. But his notions of sovereignty must have also been shaped by contemporary ideals, as illustrated by his strict adherence to the judgments of the United Nations and repeated reference to that institution and associated documents. After all, it was Article 21 of the Universal Declaration of Human Rights that made clear the right of all people to take part in their country's governance and to freely choose representatives.[80] The commitment to the UN eventually served Sistani well. Sistani would use the UN repeatedly. And the UN in turn recognized him as the "sole" actor needed in Iraq at important junctures.

Above all, Sistani's language about democracy centered on cultural authenticity. It revealed that some Islamic actors are in line with the philosophy of Mark Juergensmeyer, who argued that religion could serve as a basis for nationalism and be a legitimate political ideology for state building. He treated Islam as a modern and legitimate form of expression, one that could play a positive role in the political landscape of modern nations. Accordingly, it was the synthesis of traditional religion and secular nationalism, typified by Sistani, that Juergensmeyer argued could enhance democratic values and human rights in modern nation-states.[81] When Sistani talked about respect for Islam and exhorted the government not to "contradict the teachings of Islam,"[82] some scholars were alarmed. But attention to flexibility in the constitutional process could help make sense of Sistani's desire to reconcile a deep connection to Islam with democratic thought. The state-building process in the Middle East took place under the tutelage of the world powers after World War I, with further interventions through World War II. The British and French had had a hand in the leadership, constitution writing, and parliamentary process of these states once before. Sistani was trying not to repeat the patterns of colonialism; hence, he built his discourse about democracy on indigenous Iraqi foundations.

SISTANI, A GUIDE ONLY

In June 2016, after six months in the Persian Gulf, the aircraft carrier *USS Harry Truman* moved to the Mediterranean Sea, from where its bombers had a faster route to the sites in Syria and Iraq occupied by the Islamic State, or ISIS. The *Truman* had already been instrumental in Operation Inherent Resolve, dropping more bombs on ISIS than any other vessel in the US fleet. The operation's initial goal was to win back Falluja, the first Iraqi city to fall to ISIS fighters in 2014 and one of the two Iraqi strongholds for the group, along with Mosul, which it took later that year. As of this writing, ISIS had lost Falluja and Mosul, along with more than 40 percent of the territory it gained since the US-led international coalition began bombing. Anti-ISIS forces, including US, Iraqi, and Iranian forces, were also succeeding on the ground. But a resolution of the political situation that aided the rise of ISIS in Iraq was an entirely different matter.

The emergence of ISIS as a military power capable of occupying major cities and—at least for a time—building a quasi-state in Iraq was a function of the civil and proxy war in neighboring Syria. But it was also, in many ways, the culmination of the tumultuous decade in Iraq after the mid-2004 handover of formal sovereignty from the Coalition Provisional Authority (CPA) to an interim Iraqi government. The constitutional referendum and series of elections in the years following the handover empowered formerly exiled politicians who constructed, in both law and government practice, a de facto confessional state headquartered in Baghdad. This state's narrowly sectarian agenda alienated Sunni Arabs and others; meanwhile, its negligence and corruption angered millions of Iraqis of all religio-ethnic affiliations. ISIS was one of several groups that attempted to exploit the gap in governance.

For several years after the handover of sovereignty, Grand Ayatollah Ali al-Sistani remained a highly visible, though informal, actor on the Iraqi political stage. As he had done under the CPA, and during the ensuing year and a half of transition, he intervened with fatwas and statements to remind Iraqis and the broader international community of the importance of elections, popular sovereignty, and state legitimacy in the project to build democracy in Iraq. Yet although Sistani operated with vigor alongside the formal state structure, he was walking a fine line. At times he delivered opinions that compelled him to intervene in the political process. But his influence would have limits: He and the other grand ayatollahs were committed to serve as "guides only" to avoid the Iranian model of government entirely.

From the beginning of his entry onto the political scene in 2003, Sistani made the connection between the sectarian construction of the state and violence on the ground. He repeated over and over that rampant corruption and abuse of power by government officials would pave the way for terrorism and possibly worse. "Today," he told an Agence France Presse reporter in 2005, "if true reform is not realized by fighting corruption without mercy and realizing social justice on different levels, it is expected that circumstances will become worse than before. Iraq could be dragged to . . . partition and the like, God forbid."[1] The ayatollah found himself increasingly focused on government performance after February 22, 2006, when a massive bomb went off at the al-'Askari mosque in Samarra. The targeting of an important Shiite holy site unleashed large-scale sectarian violence throughout Iraq. Sunni mosques were attacked in reprisal, and imams were killed and kidnapped. Juan Cole recalled it as an "apocalyptic day in Iraq."[2]

Sistani had warned about this violence. The year 2005 had no precedent in Iraqi history, as citizens were engaging a new and reconfigured political landscape. Would this new state structure and the political culture it established be premised on ideas of inclusion, as Sistani had hoped, or would the electoral process instead be shaped by sectarian identities? Sistani would highlight the ways in which the government's inability to overcome Iraq's authoritarian legacy and weed out corruption under Prime Minister Nouri al-Maliki's two terms, from 2006 to 2014, threatened Iraq's road to democracy and the physical safety of Iraqi citizens.

Yet at the same time Sistani walked a fine line in when and how he was willing to address the "apocalyptic" conditions in Iraq. Sistani's logic was to be flexible, to react to new circumstances in order to offer the proper directives in the best interests of the country. His goal, as always, was to "pave the way." He was wise enough to understand that he had to step back and allow the political process to unfold. He needed to retreat at particular junctures and allow political factions to rise and fall, especially to allow the electorate to reflect which groups represented their "will," as he stated. Nonetheless, he "kept an eye" on the government from 2009 onward. He was at times perplexed and angry. In June 2011 he began boycotting politicians because of his perception that they were not following his directives. Yet his commitment to intervene when the stakes were high continued to be a game changer as violence perpetrated by ISIS ripped through the country. He maintained a delicate balance throughout because, given his long-term view of Iraq, even though sometimes it would be easier to issue a quick fatwa, his years of activism in Iraq had demonstrated that the way to reconciliation was through negotiation, the formation of coalitions, and the civic participation of the majority.

In April 2006, newly elected Prime Minister Maliki visited Sistani at his home in Najaf. It was an important visit, and Sistani issued a statement afterward to demonstrate that the clerical seal of approval gave added legitimacy to politicians. Sistani wanted Maliki to know that he would be "watching him closely." This visit was an attempt to establish the rules of the game so that Maliki understood Sistani's informal veto power in the system. The subsequent statement was a detailed account of Sistani's vision for the road ahead. Sistani insisted that the new government be "efficient" and be composed of members with "integrity and a good reputation." He warned that the government must safeguard "the higher national interest and ignore personal, sectarian and ethnic interests." He also stressed that the government's first mission should be security: to end "criminal operations" of all kinds in order to ensure "loyalty to the motherland." The government needed to undertake "significant measures" to fight the corruption that was spreading in government institutions and "provide public services, electricity, and water" to reduce the suffering of the people.[3]

The statistics were clear. According to the UNDP *Human Development Report of 2014,* households in Iraq were able to get up to fourteen hours of electricity per day when they combined public resources and a difficult-to-find private generator. Twenty percent of Iraqis consumed unsafe drinking water on a regular basis. Only 30 percent of households were able to access public sanitation networks.[4] Sistani also wanted to see the new government do its best to "remove the effects of the occupation." Although he wished Maliki well, he warned of great dangers ahead if the new prime minister did not take his advice. As *marja'*, his job was not to "flare up tensions" or "damage the public interest," but he would "monitor the governmental performance" and "determine the faults when necessary." Sistani ended his statement with strong support for "oppressed and disadvantaged people," wherever they were, "regardless of sect or ethnicity."[5]

In a follow-up meeting a few months later, Sistani addressed the problem of militias. For a country to be properly secure, as Max Weber classically noted, the national military must have a "monopoly over violence" and its security forces should be based on "proper national principles." Sistani warned that if Maliki could not collect unlicensed weapons and protect citizens, "other forces would do it." He saw in Maliki at the time the will to pursue national reconciliation and praised him for it. He urged him to keep the principles of "justice and equality" at the forefront of his reconciliation program, highlighting the need for a judiciary that would prosecute efficiently and justly. He warned that tactics furthering personal agendas would severely curtail political progress. Instead, the government should focus on respecting the will of the Iraqi people, as reflected through the creation of the permanent constitution.[6]

Sistani gave Maliki a lot to consider and a tall order to follow. Iraq's political landscape was complex. Even though the permanent constitution did not enshrine the terms of the TAL, state institutions had an unofficial sectarian quota system. In order to avoid sectarian infighting, US administrators split the most important positions in Iraq's parliament among the three main groups—Shiite Arabs, Sunni Arabs, and Kurds—which led people to vote for candidates based on sect or ethnicity, rather than merit. Based on this quota system, politicians found it beneficial to shoehorn themselves into such formations as the grand "Shiite alliance" that could win a majority and capture the post of prime minister. It also determined the logic behind the decisions that leaders such as Maliki would make to consolidate power and purge enemies.

Maliki had been a US favorite and came to power in part as a result of that support, despite his animosity toward the United States at the time. Yet he also had a long history as a self-styled soldier in the Shiite struggle as an oppressed majority. He joined Da'wa in 1967, when it was a secret organization dedicated to the formation of an Islamic party in Iraq. With the rise of Saddam to power, Maliki was left behind, despite his education, because he refused to join the Ba'ath Party. He witnessed crackdowns and executions of dissidents, was able to flee Iraq in 1980, and remained in exile until the 2003 invasion. From abroad, Maliki made it his mission to fight Saddam and for the rights of Shiites, especially the 150,000 who died during the 1991 uprising. Maliki was responsible for Da'wa military activities in Syria, Lebanon, and, to a lesser extent, Iran. That formative period did not lead him to see all Iraqis as oppressed. Instead, he saw his return as a way to redress the wrongs done to his sect. When he entered office in 2006, the police and army were overwhelmingly Shiite, many of them former militiamen who were in the business of ethnic cleansing. Early reports from civilian advisers to the US Army indicated that Maliki was not interested in hearing about massacres carried out by his army or seeking justice when death squads were unleashed.[7] That was not all. Without allowing the legal process to unfold, he ordered the execution of former President Saddam Hussein in a basement, bringing criticism from human rights organizations and deepening sectarian discord. Maliki's goal was authoritarian consolidation.

By the time Maliki had completed his first term in office, he had broken away from the United Iraqi Alliance. At the time that this large Shiite bloc won elections in 2005, it was composed of Maliki's Da'wa Party, the Sadrists, and SCIRI, which in 2007 renamed itself the Supreme Islamic Iraqi Council (ISCI). SCIRI announced its name change on May 11 to reflect the changing situation in Iraq. The "Revolution" portion of the name was a reference to the overthrow of the Baʿath regime, a time that had come to pass in Iraq.[8] Maliki left the bloc following the 2009 provincial elections and formed the State of Law Coalition for the 2010 general elections. He campaigned on a platform of establishing strong state institutions, reducing corruption, and providing services to the people. Yet future negotiations forced the Shiite parties together again, this time, because of the logic of the political structure, under a revised name: the Iraqi National Alliance (INA). Maliki had been able to consolidate his power to the extent that the political blocs were merely ceremonial. Still, he was in a tough position. In the March 2010 elections, he had garnered only eighty-nine seats to the ninety-one of his opponent, Iyad Allawi. Allawi managed to win votes for a secular, pro-Western bloc that was composed of Sunnis and Shiites. Had be been able to win a majority, perhaps Iraq would have been able to overcome its sectarian obstacles. Neither secured a majority, but Maliki was nonetheless able to form a government because of extra-constitutional measures.

Maliki had taken on an authoritarian persona as well. Despite these factors, Sistani maintained his commitment to remain neutral at this point in the political process. He issued a fatwa in advance of the January 2009 provincial elections in which he urged his followers to vote "despite dissatisfaction." He stressed his neutrality in the process but emphasized that voters should "screen and check who is qualified" before they cast their ballots.[9] It was a directive to scrutinize the increasing corruption and increasingly sectarian policies of the Maliki government. Sistani was aware of Maliki's increasingly authoritarian ways, including his version of debaathification, which he used selectively, to keep his opponents out of government. If former Baʿathists were his allies, they were protected from debaathification measures.

When it came to the impasse after the March election, Sistani reiterated his commitment to "guidance"; he would not manage the negotiations. His fatwa on the topic was also clear that he was "not affiliated with any organization involved in the elections." He again urged voters to choose wisely and to select candidates who were "committed to the stability of Iraq."[10] There was no room for misunderstanding him this time. He would offer no "blessing," as he did in the 2005 elections, but would leave open the possibility later if the system itself was threatened. It was clear to Sistani that the problems that plagued Iraq were not about who people chose at the polls. Deeper structural problems were at the core.

One problem was ISCI. Sadr al-Din al-Qabbanji, an ISCI leader, had issued statements that, given their majority status, the Shiites had the right to rule the country and indeed a duty to defend that right. In response, Sistani's office issued a statement that Iraq should not be ruled by a sectarian or ethnic majority, but instead a "political majority" that should emerge only after election outcomes.[11] Sistani's commitment not to meddle in administrative affairs prevented him from crossing the line into formal politics. He wanted to distance himself from ISCI, which was headed toward religious interpretations that he did not endorse. In addition to its position on federalism, that party had also proposed to enshrine Islamic law in the constitution against the wishes of Sistani. It was responsible for introducing a controversial amendment to Article 41 of the Iraqi constitution, the Jaafari personal status law, which rendered personal status a choice. Article 41 stated that Iraqis are free in their commitment to their personal status according to their religions, beliefs, or choices, and this shall be regulated by law. Article 42 stated that each individual shall have the freedom of thought, conscience, and belief. Taken together, these articles guaranteed religious freedom, but some critics saw the articles as a step backward from Iraq's 1959 Civil Code if there was room to enforce personal status law based on sharia. If the amendment passed, Iraqi Shiites could refer to sharia law, based on the principles of Jaafari jurisprudence (named after its founder, the sixth Shiite Imam Jaafar al-Sadiq), for personal status issues such as marriage, divorce, inheritance, and adoption. The proposed legislation encouraged sects to develop similar laws to set up separate courts that regulated affairs for the different religious communities. This would divide Iraqis and encourage the application of law by sect rather than by universal civil codes. The proposed law included 254 items based on a variety of interpretations of religious leaders. One item would reduce the legal marriage age for females to nine and males to fifteen. Human rights advocates worried that this would violate the rights of women and children and lead to an increase in child abuse and child marriage. Iraq's 1959 personal status law had set the legal marriage age for both males and females at eighteen.[12]

Sistani had wanted a civil state built on constitutional institutions. The issue would resurface, but like many other ISCI ideas, it gained little traction. Iraq's justice minister, Hassan al-Shammari, a member of the Virtue Party, tried to pass the Jaafari personal status law in December 2013 amid widespread resistance among voters and civil society organizations.[13] The bill was justified according to Article 41; however, it contradicted Article 2 regarding the prohibition of laws that contradict the rights and basic freedoms outlined in the constitution. The bill had passed through the council of ministers, although no official political or religious party offered to endorse it.

Indeed, just as with the issue of federalism, ISCI managed to lose ground on its own, without Sistani's interference. ISCI members had been in Iran in exile for years, and many observers wondered if they were, effectively, Iranian agents. The majority of them were out of touch with Iraqi society. The Sadrists, known as the centralists, were far more popular and in tune with the needs of Iraqis. By the time of the 2009 provincial elections, some called ISCI a 10 percent party. It was decimated in the electoral process across the country. After previously dominating most governorates south of Baghdad, it was not able to get 10 percent of the votes in most places and was hit especially hard in Najaf.[14] Sistani therefore did not need to meddle and direct the political process on issues such as federalism or the role of religion in the constitution. He had hoped that with time and through the electoral process, unpopular issues would fall by the wayside.

But another problem was Maliki. When he took office in 2010, it was a turning point in what Nicola Pratt called "renewed authoritarianism," whereby authoritarian leaders diversify their tactics to ensure that their power is not contested in the future.[15] Maliki refused to appoint a defense minister or an interior minister. He appointed senior military commanders rather than following the constitutional procedure, which mandated parliamentary approval of his nominees. He unleashed his Special Forces, known as the "Baghdad Operations Command," to kidnap and kill opponents. After US forces withdrew from Iraq in December 2011, Maliki ordered the arrest of Vice President Tariq al-Hashimi, the highest-ranking Sunni Arab in the government at the time. Maliki unleashed a sectarian machine to decimate his rivals. He forced out senior officials such as the governor of the Central Bank, who had tried to stop him from funneling money from Iraq's foreign reserves into the government budget. He purged Sunni Arabs from the bureaucracy, in a systematic and sustained manner, beginning with the creation of the Iraqi National Intelligence

Service. He resurrected Saddam-era laws that criminalized criticism of the head of state. The list was long. Maliki created the office of the commander in chief. He was able to gain control over the country's army and police, with local commanders reporting directly to him. He gained exclusive rights to draft legislation. Counterterrorism laws allowed for the indefinite detention of Iraqis without due process. This system resulted in tens of thousands of Sunni men in detention, subjected to torture and other interrogation tactics. Women held in custody have reported cases of sexual assault.[16]

Social unrest increased in 2011 and 2012. Antigovernment demonstrations swept throughout several major cities, including Baghdad and Karbala, and persisted for months. Protesters were concerned with the lack of public services, the rampant corruption, and the declining security. These protests took place beginning February 12, 2011, around the time of the protests in Egypt and Tunisia. They were inspired by the symbols in those countries. A young man in Iraq reportedly self-immolated, as had also happened in Tunisia; protesters planned a "Day of Rage" on February 25 to correspond to Egypt's Day of Rage. However, there were no demands for regime change. The demands were mainly for reform. Yet, as in the other cases in the region, Maliki promised reforms. To prevent further unrest, he announced that he would not run for a third term in 2014, and he called for a constitutional term limit. Part of the "renewed authoritarian" tactics that Maliki tried to implement included deflecting attention away from his shortcomings and offering goods to the people, in the form of sugar and free electricity. Regimes across the Arab world engaged in similar tactics.

Maliki was defiant. He labeled the protesters "terrorists" and proceeded to shell Anbar's two largest provinces, Falluja and Ramadi.[17] Dozens of Sunni Arab members of Parliament resigned. Sunni police abandoned their posts. Sistani immediately corrected the image of the protesters. They were "peaceful and civilized," not "terrorists," he said, and it was clear to him who had the "hidden agenda." The protests were a sign of the urgency of "tangible steps" to improve public services and root out corruption. He demanded that unacceptable privilege be abolished.[18] He asked Maliki to initiate reforms that might lead to systemic change, but Maliki was bent on entrenching himself in power.

Sistani was left with no choice but to engage in a boycott of Iraqi government officials beginning in June 2011. It was a sign of no confidence in the government, an expression of support for the demands of the protesters, and an indication that he would not allow his "seal of approval" to be used to lend legitimacy to the government. He would deliver indirect messages, through his representatives, during Friday prayers. Maliki had gone down a dark path as he unleashed his militias to weed out his opponents, including the Sadrists, who had formerly formed a political alliance with Da'wa to gain seats in Parliament. Maliki had made use of the Iranian connection and its extension, the Quds Force, which exercised great influence over his regime. Maliki's security in power was buttressed by his good relationship with Iran, which was a decisive factor in his ability to secure a second term in the first place. Indeed, Maliki's years in exile in Iran had given him experience in militia activity. This history in part explains why Sistani issued a decree in 2010 that called for the armed forces and the security services to refrain from partisan politics. Sistani had received the Iraqi general, Abboud Qanbar, deputy chief of operations, who gave him assurances that the army was ready to handle the security situation in the country in a transparent and professional manner. The ayatollah offered a "speech of guidance" urging that the armed forces and security agencies be shielded from political interference.[19] Unfortunately, that gesture would not prove beneficial.

Sistani had limits to what he was willing to do to stop Maliki. As grand ayatollah, he was acting in the interests of the people and was accountable to them. All along, Sistani acted according to the logic of his institution. The new social conditions in the post-Saddam era would invigorate the traditional institution and its democratic structure, rather than render it obsolete. It was built on accountability between Sistani and his followers, which meant that he acted in their interests in the way that politicians would act in a transparent "democratic" structure. That logic was embedded in the structure of the *hawza,* as Nakash and others have argued. Yet despite his position, we can perceive Sistani's nonaction as action. Sistani held his ground in boycotting the government because of what he was willing and able to do. The future of democracy could not rest with him alone. He understood the meaning of popular sovereignty.

There would be criticism of his stance of noninterference and several requests for him to "distribute *bayans*" (decrees) and "fix the current crisis." Especially as protests grew in 2012 and 2013, many in Iraq framed these requests as appeals to the ayatollah's religious duty. Now a reversal in the discourse occurred. Members of Parliament and actors in civil society tried to insist that it was unacceptable for the ayatollah to refrain from political activity. In one example, an Iraqi parliamentarian demanded direction from Sistani and insisted that he resume the issuance of *bayans* to prevent the country from being torn apart. In response, Sistani issued an indirect response, through his representative and leader for Friday prayers in Karbala, Sheikh Abd al-Mahdi al-Karbalai. It was clear that Sistani was not disengaged and disconnected. He delivered "five commandments" that should guide "politicians during this time period." He was willing to talk about politicians only, not the government as an entity. He wanted to communicate to the individual that he or she was heard. His commandments included the need for political parties to share responsibilities rather than pass the buck; to hear one another's claims and to study those within the law; to refrain from steps that would escalate the crisis in the streets; to insist that the security forces exercise restraint with protesters; and to understand that the crisis in the street was the result of the politicization of differences, which should be instead solved through an independent judiciary.[20]

Everyone, including the United Nations, was seeking someone above the fray to resolve the political stalemate and ease the social unrest. Sistani would meet twice with the special representative of the secretary-general for Iraq, Martin Kobler, regarding the need for political parties to engage in direct dialogue. Maliki had managed to divide and rule politicians. Kobler stressed the need to find a resolution based on "national unity" and the spirit of the constitution. He met alone with Sistani for several hours. He reported that Sistani had a "road map" to the end of the crisis.[21]

These meetings came on the heels of failed dialogue initiatives that were previously launched by Sunni and Shiite *waqfs* (charitable endowments) in Iraq. These intergovernmental institutions normally tend to religious affairs and are sought out for mediation, but they were linked to the Maliki government, which rendered them suspect. Iraqis had therefore reached out to Sistani because of his neutrality and his long record of transparency and commitment to anti-sectarian democratic principles. Kobler had reacted to the reality of the widespread Sunni, Shiite, and Kurdish calls for Sistani to intervene. Sistani had carved out a special place for himself in domestic politics over the years, and international actors came to believe that Iraq could not solve its political crisis without this single individual. Yet Sistani's position had been clear for three years—he insisted that Maliki "give justice to the Sunnis."[22] Sistani had closed his doors to government officials, but he left the line of communication open to members of civil society and heard grievances from a range of Sunni clerics. Sistani continued to deliver messages through his representatives, stating that the protesters' demands were "legitimate," in clear contrast to the actions of the government. The protesters were talking about widespread legitimate grievances. The grievances were not limited to Sunnis or, worse, the "terrorists" that Maliki wanted to label. Sistani made clear that they were problems that affected all Iraqis.

By late 2013, widespread protests, larger than in previous years, had prompted the government to implement strict security measures to regain control over the streets. When Sistani closed communication with the government, Maliki looked to Ayatollahs Kazem al-Haeri and Muhammad al-Asefi, both based in Iran, for fatwas to urge protesters to refrain from action. But the unrest continued. Sunni Arab officers had left a power vacuum when they abandoned their posts in key cities such as Falluja and Ramadi. It was filled by the rise of ISIS. ISIS would take control of Fallujah and Ramadi in January 2014 and then Mosul, Iraq's second-largest city, in June.

Sistani kept communication with the government severed despite the deteriorating political situation, in hopes that the ballot box would be the solution. Parliamentary elections were slated for April 2014. In the months leading up to the contests, he issued a series of fatwas. On February 24 he asked voters to "choose wisely" so that they would not regret their choice later. He painted a stark choice between good and bad, and implored Iraqis to differentiate between the two. He insisted that everyone "actively and consciously" participate in the upcoming elections. Yet the political and social landscape was increasingly precarious. Violence was on the rise, and the attacks by ISIS complicated the already fractured and sectarian political process.

Some reports indicated that Sistani also ordered his agents to maintain a distance from all parliamentary blocs and called on people not to vote for anyone involved in corruption or anyone associated with the previously failed government. Sistani had hoped for a clean slate and a new opportunity at democracy building.[23] He made statements, through his representatives, about "comprehensive change." However, Sistani was clear that it was not his role to support specific candidates. He insisted that the road was paved for Iraqi voters to "decide the fate of their country through elections." It was a big responsibility, to be sure, requiring study of past errors. One way to meet one's responsibility was to vote for qualified individual candidates and not for a tribe or sect.[24] Despite Sistani's clear language on the matter, Maliki continued to campaign. He addressed Shiites using sectarian rhetoric to gain their votes. He even asked to meet with Sistani, which Sistani refused. Thus, he sent a strong message to Maliki about his informal power and his respect for the process.

Sistani did his job, from his perspective. He tried to set the wheels in motion for the democratic process, despite his misgivings about Maliki's corruption. He intervened again, and in a powerful way, only when it was clear that no other option was available. Even then, he did not "meddle in the details of political work." He acted as a "guide" and lent legitimacy to the actions of those who were seeking his seal of approval. It was mid-June of 2014, and ISIS had begun advertising its executions of Iraqi soldiers as parts of the country had fallen out of government control. Divided political factions were unable to select a prime minister. Maliki had lost the support of much of his Da'wa Party, but he would not withdraw his bid for a third term. When Da'wa Party leaders reached out to Sistani for advice on how they should proceed, he took action.

He wrote a handwritten letter to Maliki, signed and stamped, which insisted on the selection of a new prime minister who had "wide national acceptance." Sistani's July 9 letter invoked "critical circumstances" and the need for a "new vision." The letter empowered Da'wa members to vote almost unanimously against Maliki's nomination. The Da'wa Party's leadership committee was composed of eleven senior members. Maliki was the party's secretary-general at the time and opposed any change in the leadership. The vote to select a new prime minister was ten out of eleven, with Maliki casting the only opposing vote. In turn, the party issued a statement that it would heed the advice of the ayatollah. Neither the United States nor Iran nor the United Nations could exert such pressure on Maliki to step aside. That is not to say that Maliki went down easily. He attempted last-minute maneuvers. His supporters suggested that because Sistani had only urged those in power not to "cling to it" and had not mentioned Maliki directly, there was wiggle room in interpreting the letter. But the phrasing was in keeping with Sistani's style over the years—diplomatic and brief. Maliki's options were limited. Even Ayatollah Ali Khamenei of Iran refused to support Maliki or anyone who would "sow sedition" in Iraq. Maliki's own party turned on him, at the final hour, with special appreciation to Sistani for his "significant role in maintaining national cohesion."[25]

Sistani's intervention did not break with his commitment to democracy; it embraced the rule of law. He did not face off with Maliki or confront him in front of his peers. He merely gave Da'wa members the political space and leverage to vote Maliki out of power. It was clear, given Sistani's clout, that he could have intervened sooner. But that would have defeated his greater purpose. He wanted all groups in Iraq to continue to participate in the political system. And Sistani's method of removing Maliki was especially shrewd—as usual, he did not involve political parties, factions, or sectarian groups. He allowed the formal political actors to maintain their integrity. It was his natural inclination not to capitalize on religion, ethnicity, or sect. That was not how he saw Iraqis. That was not how he envisioned democracy.

Sistani wanted the democratic principles he worked hard to enshrine in the discourse to become regularized. He therefore reserved his interventions for times of existential threat. Over the course of a decade, he insisted that he would not "meddle in the details of political work." Because he took on the role of arbiter and counselor, as the informal political process warranted, he invariably walked a fine line that he sometimes crossed. At times, he issued decrees that told people to "try not to split votes," which could be perceived as meddling in the details of political work. He tried to keep the democratic process moving in the direction that would safeguard national unity, the country's development along secular lines, and his own neutrality and independence regarding the state. Sistani gave himself a lot of leeway and kept all possibilities open as he remained committed to "pave the way" for the political process. He did not always succeed, yet this was an experiment after years of authoritarian rule and years of silence from the *hawza*. Like all political actors, he engaged the political system and recalibrated his engagement when warranted by new circumstances. It was clear, nonetheless, that Ayatollah Sistani was at the center of the political process, or at least hovering over it in powerful ways that those in formal institutions could not imagine.

Sistani's long-term impact on the political process remains difficult to assess. The state-building process in post-Saddam Iraq has been far from ordinary, making the position of the ayatollahs that much more complex.

Iraqis were tasked with rebuilding the state under the continued auspices of the United States rather than as a fully independent nation. And rather than an Iraq-centric model, the politicians in power chose an authoritarian and sectarian leader who moved the country backward. As Sistani had warned, state-level sectarianism so dovetailed with sectarian violence on the ground that the two were indistinguishable to the outside observer. Such attempts at national reconciliation as took place occurred alongside the decline of the central state. Even with the grand ayatollah's moral guidance, his commitment to "pave the way" for democracy, and his powerful influence over the political system, Iraq's prospects looked bleak.

On the one hand, it is hard to imagine peace or democracy in Iraq. More than a decade after the invasion, the sectarian political structure has not changed much. On the other hand, Iraqis have adjusted to the new political realities, often at the prompts of the grand ayatollahs, and have strongly resisted the narratives that were written for them by outside powers and their Iraqi proxies. Despite the flaws of the 2005 constitution and the de facto quota system that predetermines political outcomes, ordinary Iraqis have demonstrated an ability to coexist, over and again, as they had done historically. The desire for communal coexistence was most evident in the rounds of protest against the failing political structure that preceded the rise of ISIS.

When the protests first broke out in 2011, Sunnis and Shiites protested side by side. The demonstrations had a strong secular component, with many leftists pledging allegiance to the Iraqi Communist Party, for example. Prime Minister Maliki, bent on crushing the movement, arrested numerous protesters and sowed division among the rest, forcing a sectarian character upon the demonstrations as they tailed off.

The same was true for the widespread protests of 2013. Even when demonstrations took place in predominantly Sunni areas, they were not avowedly sectarian. Sunnis demanded equal rights under the law and an end to the counterterrorism laws that had been in place since the days of the US-led occupation. Again, Maliki spurned the movement, branding the participants as "terrorists" and jailing and torturing many. These conditions helped to fuel the antigovernment insurgency and made political reconciliation and progress toward democracy all the more difficult.

Protests erupted again in 2016, addressing the same government deficiencies as in 2011—poor public services, uneven access to electricity, and rampant corruption. The protests represented a "flourishing of cross-sectarian politics," as Anand Gopal observed. Demonstrators called for the end of religio-ethnic quotas in government and the eradication of the patronage system.[26]

As the grand ayatollah argued tirelessly in the aftermath of the US-led invasion, the civil strife that followed was not caused by ancient sectarian hatreds, as posited by US commentators and, for his own purposes, by Abu Musab al-Zarqawi, leader of al-Qaeda in Mesopotamia. Nor was it a "Shiite problem" resulting from that group's inescapable "culture of victimhood." The problems in Iraq were a result of the post-2003 order, a consequence of the new state structure that stacked the deck against peaceful coexistence and democracy. The ayatollah's interventions throughout the process were warnings of the likely consequences of the sectarian state model.

Despite the structural constraints, nothing about Iraq's future is foreordained. Besides the rounds of protest, there have been other examples of nonsectarian politics at work in recent years. As mentioned earlier, for instance, Iyad Allawi's Iraqiyya list won the most seats in the 2010 parliamentary elections, although it fell short of a majority. Allawi, a secular Shiite, drew support from millions of Sunni Arabs.

The widespread protests, aimed at government ineptitude and supported by key religious actors, suggest two things. First, the nonsectarian character of the protests was a testament to the Iraq-centric discourses of the ayatollahs over the years. Second, a strong chain of informal networks had been forged between religious actors and their followers. After all, the most common forms of political participation amid authoritarian conditions in the Middle East were informal. When the state represses, excludes, or fails to respond to the needs of the people, the people resort to the informal realm.[27] Such was the vacuum that Sistani and, later, Sadr were able to fill.

Sistani had used his informal political power to prevent Maliki from seeking a third term in 2014. In so doing, he had preserved his independence from the state and maintained a position of respect for the democratic process. Sistani's intervention followed his pledge to stop meeting with politicians in 2011. When Prime Minister Abadi was sworn into office on August 10, 2014, Sistani welcomed him and encouraged him to undertake reforms in order to protect the country's democratic and civil framework. Sistani was acting as a mediator, as he had done for years.

Sistani was vocal in the early days of Abadi's tenure, as he had been in Maliki's, in the hopes that the government could start off on the right track. Sistani made clear that his support was not unconditional and that his previous boycott had been a result of the government's inability to keep its promises to the Iraqi people. It was likewise clear that Sistani wanted the state to create equal opportunities for all Iraqis—Sunni Arabs, Shiite Arabs, Kurds, and others—and to enact reforms that would help the whole of the country prosper. Sistani was a bridge to society, and it would soon be evident that the prime minister would need his support.

At the end of July 2015, one year after Abadi took office, unrest again spread throughout Baghdad, as in previous years, over the inadequacy of public services. The organizers were largely peaceful civil society activists. Within days, the League of the Righteous, a militia, appeared on television to offer its endorsement of the protest. This extremist armed Shiite group, committed to fighting ISIS, had the support of former Prime Minister Maliki. In a public statement, the league's leader, Qais al-Khazali, recommended that Iraq's political system be changed from a parliamentary to a presidential one. His intention was to undermine Abadi and empower Maliki, by way of co-opting the protest movement. At this time, supporters of the League of the Righteous as well as other militias, such as the Hezbollah Brigades, were planning to join the protests and undercut their broad-based appeal. The consequences looked to be dire: Maliki and, by extension, Iranian proxies would find their way back to power in Iraq.[28]

Sistani, who had been hopeful about change in 2014, was critical of the slow pace of progress under Abadi in the succeeding year. He blamed the new prime minister for the growing divisions within society. Sistani had warned Abadi not to follow Maliki's dark path. Sistani's logic was that he would intervene "only at crucial junctures," "only when absolutely necessary," and never in the "details of political work." The grand ayatollah's strategic thinking in 2014, as in 2006, was to be a "guide" and to "keep an eye on the government." Although he was displeased with Abadi, the elderly cleric was warier still of the greater Iranian influence that would come about if the prime minister was replaced.

Sistani decided to save Abadi. He issued a fatwa pledging his support for the prime minister on the condition that "partisan and sectarian quotas" were abolished. Thousands demonstrated in support of the fatwa. Abadi promised to abide by Sistani's demands and declared his "total commitment to the directions of the religious *marja'iyya,* which has voiced the concerns and aspirations of the Iraqi people."[29] Sistani's representative, Ahmad al-Safi, said that the premier should be "more daring and courageous" and "make political parties accountable" by identifying who exactly was hampering reform.[30] Abadi responded by unveiling reforms such as the reduction of expensive perks for government officials and the elimination of the posts of three deputy prime ministers and three vice presidents, including the one held by former Prime Minister Maliki. It was clear that Sistani was seeking to redress aspects of the political system that disheartened Sunnis as well as Shiites.

For the moment, the ayatollah was successful. Rather than turning to the militias, the protesters expressed support for Abadi and his backer in Najaf. Yet again, Sistani was able to pull the center of political gravity away from Iranian-backed elements and prevent an extremist group from co-opting a peaceful protest movement.

But Sistani cannot save the Iraqi political system singlehandedly. What will happen after his death or departure from the public sphere? The other three grand ayatollahs do not have his political clout and may not be able to exert the same influence. Moreover, Sistani has set limits for himself. The ayatollah operates in the informal political realm, after all, and he has no blueprint for when and how he should intervene. True, he has always respected the democratic process. Even when he opposed a third term for Maliki, he did not overstep his self-drawn boundary. He expressed his discontent through indirect messages and allowed Maliki's own party to vote him out. Sistani has continued to watch the political process, but he is also committed to allowing the political system to mature and evolve. To that end, he is not willing to take the lead or put himself in the spotlight. He does not want to become the political system.

In contrast to previous occasions, in mid-2015 the ayatollah's calls for reform collided with the interests of an entrenched and venal elite that had accrued many advantages. This elite had already managed to block attempts to reduce its prerogatives. Corruption was such a major problem that Transparency International ranked Iraq 161 on a list of 167 countries (with 1 being the cleanest) in its 2015 Corruption Perceptions Index. A pervasive culture of bribery and nepotism affected the award-ing of government contracts, and because the government was run by Shiite Islamist parties, these practices disproportionately favored Shiites.

Meanwhile, tax officials were creating fake companies to siphon off millions of dollars in tax rebates. The barrier to reform was high. People had lost confidence in the government but still had hope for the informal channel of the *marja'iyya,* with its moral authority. Many Iraqis wanted Sistani to intervene because they viewed corruption as an issue of moral conduct rather than politics as usual. Yet Sistani did not publicly denounce leaders. In his diplomatic style, he spoke out through his representatives and did not single out Abadi. He reasoned that "once the laws are not respected, corruption is spread on earth, and those who have violated the laws are cursed."[31] Yet this statement fell short of his previous interventions.

Given the fluidity of the informal realm, Sistani must have understood that although he wanted to allow the political process to unfold organically, there would be other actors who would fill the political void after he withdrew from politics. Sadr appears to be willing to assume that role. He has had an "outsized influence" on Iraqi politics ever since 2003. In the early days of the US-led occupation, he was able to mobilize thousands of Shiites in street protests, form a powerful militia, and play the role of "kingmaker" in the selection of prime ministers.[32] In 2007, at a peak of civil strife, he was able to order his armed loyalists to stand down. Even when Sadr withdrew from politics for a time in 2011, his supporters continued to run for office. He returned to the forefront of the political process in 2016, as Sistani, for the moment, had receded from view.

Perhaps the shift to Sadr was a moment of reckoning. People had called on Sistani to act, but he was unwilling. On April 30, 2016, after protests over stalled reforms, Sadr supporters stormed the Green Zone, the location of the government headquarters. Sadr threatened mass protests during the following month if his demands were not met. This time he could no longer be labeled the "firebrand cleric" trying to carve out a place for himself in the sectarian landscape as in earlier years. Over the years, he was able to claim the nationalist mantle and distinguish his movement from others who did not put Iraqi interests first. He had led mass protests in February that called for an end to political corruption and financial mismanagement. This platform drew tens of thousands into the streets. Sadr made demands on Abadi, much as Sistani had done, to form a new government that would implement political reforms. This time Sadr, not Sistani, would be "watching the government closely" because Abadi had fallen short on his promises. The premier had yet to eliminate the three vice presidential posts, cut government spending, or remove sectarian quotas in political appointments. Sistani described the situation as "alarming" but said that he saw no need to "reiterate his directives" that had not been taken seriously.[33]

Sadr, in his face-off with Abadi, did not call for the prime minister to step down. He called for reforms, on a nationalist platform, in the interest of preserving the government and ensuring the equal treatment of all Iraqis under the law. Like Sistani in the previous year, he wanted to extend support to the government and drown out the alternative narratives of ISIS and Iranian-backed militias. He carried out Sistani's former role, possibly overshadowing the grand ayatollah. After all, there was no indication that Sistani would have been willing to storm the Green Zone. Sadr had also never imposed limits on himself, despite the fact that he was on his way to becoming an ayatollah. Sadr has never laid out his political program in detail. In future decades, his position may change, and the *hawza,* should it see fit, may rein him in.

Sadr had challenged Sistani for dominance of the informal public sphere on previous occasions. Sadr's followers once tried to force Sistani to leave the country. But this time was different. The two men seemed to be speaking in the same terms. Rising above the fray, Sadr stepped in to guide a protest movement in order to ensure that the demands remained nonsectarian. He had the benefit of both formal and informal channels. On the formal level, in 2015 the Sadr movement had thirty-four lawmakers in Iraq's 328-seat parliament and held three key professional and service portfolios in the cabinet: the Ministries of Commerce, Municipalities, and Construction and Housing.[34] In the early days after the fall of Saddam Hussein, the "firebrand cleric" threw down the gauntlet to the ayatollah in Najaf; he seemed bent on being the bad boy on the block. Over the years, however, he matured politically.

Abadi understood Sadr's political power—under the pressure of the storming of the Green Zone, he formed a new cabinet of technocrats.[35] Sadr rejoined the Iraqi National Alliance in October 2016. The alliance was composed of Shiite Islamist parties—the Islamic Supreme Council, the National Reform Movement, and the State of Law. Sadr had previously accused the alliance of shielding corrupt leaders, but now he suspended his conditions for rejoining for the greater good of Iraq. He called for the abolition of the practice by which the alliance nominated government ministers and for an amendment to the electoral commission charter. With Mosul on the way to liberation from ISIS, Sadr was not the only one who was envisioning a new Iraq. Sistani had laid the groundwork with democratic principles and moral guidance. Others would have to work hard to fix the structural problems.

Sadr's resurgence must be understood in the context of the limits that the grand ayatollahs set for themselves from the beginning: to serve as "guides" only and "not to play a direct role in the government."[36] Yet the narratives of Najaf and Sadr City eventually merged. Sadr and Sistani had the same goals: to work toward an Iraq-centric polity and to block Iranian meddling in Iraqi affairs. Both had matured politically, and both were pulled to the center of the political system. Even as informal actors, free from the constraints of the formal political system, they found themselves subject to some of the same scrutiny. However, here is a larger question about Iraq's future: Can the political system survive if it is influenced by, and somewhat dependent on, the "good will" of informal political actors?

4

Quietists Turned Activists?

Prior to the US invasion of Iraq in 2003, Ayatollah Ali al-Sistani issued only one "political" fatwa—a criticism of the Israeli military operations in the West Bank in 2002. After the invasion, Sistani was so involved in current events that media outlets often referred to him as "the most influential political figure in Iraq."[1] He was able to galvanize his followers behind political positions in a way that no other person could. Most famously, his fatwas of June and November 2003 called for direct elections as the way to determine the makeup of Iraq's transitional government and the body that would draft a new constitution. Later, Sistani insisted on a one-person, one-vote system for parliamentary elections. The popular protests inspired by these "democratic fatwas" derailed US plans for a controlled state-building process that would have excluded the majority of Iraqis.

In the wake of these interventions, Sistani attracted a great deal of Western media attention. Many US commentators were pleasantly surprised to see such gestures coming from a senior cleric in a traditional hierarchical structure. Thomas Friedman praised him highly for urging his followers not to retaliate for sectarian violence and for offering a vision of Iraq for all Iraqis.[2] Noah Feldman, a Harvard law professor who helped draft the Transitional Administrative Law that Sistani's fatwas rendered moot, likewise wrote that the ayatollah's interventions had wide appeal.[3]

At the other end of the spectrum, Sistani was depicted as having "quasi-Machiavellian qualities" in that he worked behind the scenes to maximize his personal power.[4] This was in part caused by the novelty of Sistani's political role, and these sorts of allegations led him to call for only pronouncements that included his "seal" and that originated from his office in Najaf to be deemed verifiable. There was also widespread confusion in the media about his new political role and suspicion about the new role that the clerics would play in post-Saddam Iraq. In one example, MP Izzat Shahbandar from the State of Law Coalition issued a few press statements in which he accused Sistani of "trying to take the place of the state's authority" by appealing to people's emotions. He was concerned about the enormous power that Sistani had maintained because of his financial resources, lack of public accountability, and monopoly over how the seminary's funds were dispersed. These statements were a reaction to Sistani's pronouncements and activism against corruption, the lack of security, and poor public services in Iraq after 2003.[5]

Strong residual suspicion of Shiite clerics remained after the 1979 Iranian revolution, when the "radical" religious views of Ayatollah Ruhollah Khomeini had "hijacked" the political process. To be acceptable, Muslim religious actors needed to be "moderate," meaning that they needed to demonstrate a commitment to pluralism and democracy.[6]

Both the positive and the negative views of Sistani were in part reactions to the novelty of his political interventions. His scholarship in the 1990s had eschewed politics altogether. In 2003 he began taking questions in writing from reporters, and the answers would then be published as official *bayans*. But no other evidence of a political vision appeared in his writings. It was therefore no accident that every reporter asked him about Khomeini's doctrine of *velayat-e faqih* (rule of the jurisprudent). Sistani persistently shunned that model, saying instead that he was a guide for his followers. Visser demonstrated that although Sistani offered a commentary on the doctrine of *velayat-e faqih*, he did not try to develop a "theory of state." His fatwas, delivered during the period

June 2003–November 2004, did not revolve around "politics" or the "state" in an institutionalized setting. They were responses to questions and reflected his ability to see how the *velayet* could play a broader social role.[7] Sistani was shrewd. His fatwas were broadcast across Iran, and as will become clear, the battle between Najaf and Qom drove his political behavior. When it came to answering whether the doctrine of *velayet-e faqih* was appropriate for Iraq, Sistani did not hesitate. In all of his fatwas, his answer was an unequivocal no.

His main function was to "provide believers with religious decrees regarding the affairs of individual and social life." After Saddam Hussein's regime fell, he had to be more active in order to "teach the ignorant, advise and guide the believers, and make peace among them." But he made clear that he did not "request a position of governance and authority and that men of religion should necessarily refrain from executive responsibilities."[8] Sistani continued in a later response to a journalist's question that the times required that he "follow continuously all aspects of Iraqi affairs" but that he would not intervene in the "details of political work" and would "open the way for the politicians entrusted by the Iraqi people for performing this mission."[9]

This prominent example illustrates the nature of the *hawza*'s engagement with politics since 2003. It was focused on state building and democracy, subjects that the ayatollahs were well positioned to address in Shiite-majority Iraq because of the special position they hold in Shiism. Without the ayatollahs' intervention, "democratic" measures that required widespread Iraqi participation might not have developed, at least not as quickly. But the ayatollahs also imposed clear limits on their political activities, leading many observers to conclude that they were religious scholars, not politicians—quietists, not activists.

In fact, it is too simple to posit a binary opposition between quietism and activism when it comes to the ayatollahs of Iraq. The misperception dates to the 1979 revolution in Iran, when Ayatollah Khomeini articulated a vision of an Islamic state with a cleric as absolute leader. This doctrine—which is still not characteristic of all Iranian clerics—nonetheless became generalized as "Iranian." The ayatollahs in Najaf today are not adherents of *velayat-e faqih,* nor are they forever buried in books in ivory towers. The proper way to understand their political engagement is the idea that political context can drive religious decisions.[10] The ayatollahs' positions, like those of Sistani on the US-designed political transition, were based on rational, strategic calculations about the Iraqi political milieu. The ayatollahs did not start with their religious or philosophical ideas and try to derive policy therefrom. All four of the ayatollahs considered in this chapter, Sistani, Muhammad Baqir al-Hakim (d. 2003), Muhammad Ishaq al-Fayyad, and Bashir al-Najafi, had political visions emanating from their analysis of what was desirable and achievable in the new Iraq.

Nonetheless, many scholars have continued to brand the ayatollahs of Iraq as quietists, by virtue of the fact that for most of their tenure under Saddam Hussein, they did not comment on political matters. For example, Yitzhak Nakash says of Sistani that he was reluctant to get involved in "worldly affairs." While acknowledging Sistani's pragmatism in dealing with the United States and his role in serving as a moral voice, Nakash identified all of the senior clerics as part of the quietist school. Many other scholars agreed with this classification, and some of them assumed that clerics were one or the other. The descriptions varied. Linda Walbridge wrote that Sistani "shunned all involvement" in politics. Faleh A. Jabar identified Sistani as "apolitical" when compared to Ayatollah Sadiq al-Sadr. In an updated version of "quietism," Muntazra Nazir referred to all of Sistani's political activities as "quietist," as part of the tradition of "minimum daily involvement in active politics." By this designation Nazir meant that Sistani wanted Iraqis, not the Americans, to determine the future of the country.[11] Robert Gleave labeled Sistani as "less aloof from community politics" than the other three ayatollahs of Najaf because of his willingness to engage the state and act as a broker among Shiite factions.[12] The other three grand ayatollahs were, in fact, not aloof from politics but were quite vocal and active in their political positions. Sistani is seen and heard because of his prominence in the hierarchical structure and the sheer number of followers he maintains.

The tension in naming the new political role was clear even after the first few years of Sistani's activism. Soren Schmidt, while acknowledging Sistani's political activism, labeled his philosophy as "essentially quietist."[13] Juan Cole traced the activities of Sistani and acknowledged his quietism prior to 2003 and his political activism afterward. Yet he argued that Sistani eventually retreated from politics.[14] In another example, Mohamad Bazzi referred to Sistani as a cleric "rooted in the 'quietist' school of Shiism," even if he "took on a more prominent role as a stabilizing force in the Shiite community."[15] In essence, Sistani's actions are viewed through the lens of Iran. His political engagement could move only so far on the scale of activism when compared to the extreme version next door.[16]

Quietism, based on the sixteenth-century notion of *irshad wa tawjih* (guidance and direction), was rooted in a deal with the Persian monarchy by which the clerics of the day opted to remain above the political fray. Although contemporary discussions tend to elide Iranian and Iraqi expressions, the roots of *irshad wa tawjih* date back to a complex history that blurred geographic boundaries prior to the rise of the modern nation-state. In addition to the quietist doctrine established with Persian monarchs, a long list of events would shape the nationalist discourse. After over a century of fighting over Mesopotamia (Iraq) between the Ottoman and the Safavid (Persian) Empires, for example, Iraq was permanently ceded to the Ottomans in 1639. This discussion over the blurring of nationalist lines continued to be debated by scholars.[17] However, it is unlikely that the ayatollahs were adhering to a centuries-old pact in the decades before 2003. They were more likely practicing a form of dissimulation, for opposition political activity in Iraq, by ayatollahs or anyone else, usually met with stiff penalties, including torture and death.

This chapter fleshes out the logic underlying the layers of activism by the ayatollahs after 2003. Through a study of the ayatollahs' strategic thinking, I add nuance to the concept of clerical activism—which does not have to be either *velayat-e faqih* or nothing at all. In fact, Iraqi ayatollahs have a long history of engagement with the state, but their engagement defies any neat categorization. Their political behavior after 2003 invites us to treat them as keen, strategic political actors with strong ties to society and a newly evolving role as public intellectuals. The ayatollahs have proven flexible and extremely adaptable to political context. They are keenly aware of the multi-ethnic and multireligious composition of the country and the need for a pluralistic attitude in political action. Despite some ayatollahs' desire for an Islamic state, their political savvy deters them from imposing their will or forcing a one-size-fits-all solution on the people. Yet their declaration that they should hold no political positions does not make them apolitical. Rather, their activism should be understood as a reinvented activism.

The proliferation of ideas in the post-2003 milieu reveals that there was no such thing as a single "Shiite" position or viewpoint. Rather, there were clear tensions among the highest-ranking ayatollahs about the course of state and nation building.

Nevertheless, the ayatollahs wanted to serve as a point of reference for the political process but not to be at the center of the official state structure. To some, this stance connotes quietism. Yet, as it turns out, the ayatollahs' "guidance" is quite active. The clerics derive their political clout from hovering around the system but never co-opting it. In fact, one can argue that becoming part of the official state system has a neutralizing effect, one that reduces the aura of power and dynamism that the ayatollahs have been able to maintain over the years, certainly when compared to the jaded, discredited politicians in the government.

Shiite activism is most often associated with Khomeini's construction of an Islamic state after his 1979 return to Iran from exile. Khomeini began speaking forcefully about politics after the relatively quietist Ayatollah Hossein Borujerdi, then the senior cleric in Qom, died in 1961. But he had been writing about the formation of an Islamic state with clerics at its head for some time. His thinking went as far back as the ninth century, when Twelver Shiism, the branch followed in Iraq and Iran, suffered a succession crisis. The Twelfth Imam, Muhammad al-Mahdi, disappeared in 874 without having designated a deputy. He was said to be in "greater occultation," from which he would return one day as earthly leader. In his absence the community was to follow the tradition of the imams. Against this backdrop, Khomeini reasoned that trained clerics should rule in the occulted imam's place. His book, *Islamic Government: Governance of the Jurist,* first published in 1970, became the basis for the Islamic state in Iran.[18]

But there was actually great debate in postrevolutionary Iran on this issue. Ayatollahs in Qom reached no clear consensus on the proper role for the clergy in politics, but Khomeini found himself in the minority. To consolidate his power, and mute clerical criticism, Khomeini created a special court for trying clergy and relaxed the requirements for his successor, believing that no qualified ayatollah would agree to succeed him. His decision to settle in Tehran rather than Qom reflected the tensions born out of that debate.

Iraq had a deeply rooted activist tradition as well. Najaf, a city 100 miles south of Baghdad, gained prominence as a center of Shiite thought in the mid-eighteenth century and rivaled Qom for preeminence. Its importance dates back to the death of Ali, the first imam, in the year 661. Imam Ali was buried in Najaf, and a mosque was built around his tomb. Shiite theologians subsequently flocked to the city to establish seminaries so they could be near the martyred *amir al-mu'minin* (commander of the faithful). In 1918, 6,000 students were in Najaf, many of them non-Iraqis. By 1957, the number of students had dwindled to 1,954, of whom 326 were Iraqis. There followed a brief golden age, when the number rose again to 3,000, before declining by 1979 to 600. After the eight-year war with Iran, only 150 students remained.[19] Saddam Hussein, ever wary of "Persian" influence, wanted to Arabize the *hawza,* but Arab students were too afraid to study in Iraq. Since the fall of Saddam, the seminaries in Najaf have staged a comeback.

Shiite activism focusing on the "state" and the role of the clergy began in Iraq in the 1950s, when the Da'wa Party's selected *faqih* (jurist), Ayatollah Muhammad Baqir al-Sadr, began to write extensively about Islamic rule, though not necessarily rule by clerics. The rise of the Da'wa Party came in part in response to the popularity of the Ba'ath Party and the Iraqi Communist Party. These mass parties explicitly rejected communal identities and old communal authorities. This context laid the foundation for the enmity between Saddam and Ayatollahs Muhammad Baqir al-Sadr and Muhammad Sadiq al-Sadr, both of whom were put to death under his regime.[20] Baqir al-Sadr, born in al-Kazimiyya, Iraq, in 1935, was the father-in-law of the widely known "firebrand cleric" Muqtada al-Sadr and the cousin of his father, Ayatollah Sadiq al-Sadr. After writing the main political platform for Da'wa, Baqir al-Sadr was deemed too controversial for Najaf because of his leftist leanings. Accordingly, he abandoned the party and focused on preparing for the role of ayatollah, or *marja'.* He enacted reforms that included the establishment of an academic curriculum, fatwas written in layman's terms for wider dissemination, and a focus on contemporary problems.[21]

Early on, Sadr was concerned with reforming the *marja'iyya* for the modern world. He acknowledged that each ayatollah was an individual with distinct viewpoints, leadership skills, and experience. But he wanted to transform the "individualistic *marja'iyya*" into an "institutional *marja'iyya,"* a formal organization akin to a government. He believed that without an institutional structure, decisions for each local community would be made locally. For the greater welfare, he wanted to shift power from the individual *marja'* to the office of the *marja'iyya.* Sadr spoke about a "consultative council" as well as various offices and courts. He envisioned a committee structure in which the whole religious establishment would be involved in decision making. Sadr believed that this structure would make the consultative process more objective, less arbitrary, and more rational.[22] It was to be a democratic form of Islamic government, one that incorporated the consent of the faithful, the consensus of clerics in choosing a leader, and a separation of powers between the clergy and the state, with both held accountable to the law. In the context of the Cold War, Sadr spoke of an Islamic "third way" that rejected both communism and capitalism.

Baqir al-Sadr's blueprint for an alternative Islamic form of government—a kind of political activism that was notably distinct from the Iranian model—was never implemented. However, it is clear that Sadr's philosophical and intellectual contributions influenced the Iranian system of dual government, featuring both the rule of the jurisprudent and Western-style elections.[23] Yet as Khomeini consolidated his power, he leaned less on the political thought of Sadr. Meanwhile, in Iraq, Sadr sensed that his life was in danger and asked Khomeini for asylum. Khomeini declined. Shortly thereafter, in 1980, Sadr was tortured by Saddam Hussein's regime and then allegedly burned to death.

The fate of Sadr is but one example of the tyranny and repression that Najaf was subjected to under Hussein's regime. The ayatollahs were not calling loudly for Saddam's overthrow. Many of them were more interested in competition with Qom and among one another.[24] But Saddam's goal was to demolish the *hawza:* In addition to Sadr, hundreds of family members of Grand Ayatollah Muhsin al-Hakim (d. 1970) were killed. Ayatollah Muhsin al-Hakim's grandson, Muhammad Baqir al-Hakim, fled to Iran in 1980 and continued to write against the Ba'ath regime until he returned to Iraq in 2003. The state worked hard to exclude "Shiite" political or communal expression. The state's strategies included the declaration that Shiites were really Persians, the orchestration of televised forced confessions by ayatollahs, and the assassination of grassroots leaders. Ayatollahs issued fatwas, delivered speeches, and offered guidance under severe constraints.

Before 2003, the content of clerical activism in Iraq could be summarized as follows: resistance to Saddam Hussein, discussion of Khomeini's formation of an Islamic state, and statements about the disenfranchisement of the Shiites in a state where they were always a majority yet explicitly told they would be ruled by Sunnis, whom British imperial policy maker Gertrude Bell deemed "less alien" in appearance.[25]

Perhaps the most dramatic figure was Ayatollah Muhammad Sadiq al-Sadr, who advocated a more revolutionary move toward an Islamic state. Sadr pitted himself against Sistani, whom he criticized as the "silent jurisprudent." In times of tyranny, he claimed, ayatollahs were obliged to play the part of "speaking jurisprudent" and inveigh against oppression.[26] Sadr was killed by the regime in 1999.

Naturally, Iraqi ayatollahs in exile were free to be more forthright in their condemnations of the regime. In July 2002, Grand Ayatollah Sayyid Kazem al-Haeri, who resided in Qom, issued a famous statement about the plight of the Shiites.[27] He recognized that the rights of Shiites in Iraq had been violated for a long time. He blamed the violations not on Sunnis but on "tyrannical governments" that trampled on the "majority Shia" and the "minority Sunnis" alike.[28]

Likewise, Ayatollah Muhammad Baqir al-Hakim wrote extensively on the role of Shiites in opposition to Saddam throughout the 1990s up to the invasion. Baqir al-Hakim wrote about Saddam's "confiscation of the legal rights of all Iraqi people, civil, cultural and political rights," without distinction between "Sunni and Shiite," for the regime sought to destroy the morale of all Iraqis.[29] Enjoying the safety of exile in Iran and influenced by its politics, Hakim came to think that some version of an Islamic state might be suitable for Iraq, despite its multireligious and multi-ethnic composition and its history of colonialism.

Saddam's removal in 2003 left a power vacuum. Ayatollahs who had been in exile or under house arrest were now free to act and speak. It was no longer necessary to speculate about whether ayatollahs were practicing dissimulation out of fear of retribution or they were pure quietists by choice.

The ayatollahs' discourses and calculations changed accordingly. Perhaps because they were socialized under authoritarian settings, the ayatollahs wanted to take a back seat to formal politics and to intervene only when necessary to keep the democratic process on track. The ayatollahs used their brand of activism in favor of popular sovereignty. The fatwas and decrees of Ayatollah Sistani and his counterparts brought protesters into the streets carrying signs that read "Yes, yes to elections! No, no to occupation."[30] Over and again, the ayatollahs would assert that they would guide Iraq in the right direction, in line with the will of the majority.

The ayatollahs shifted their focus to the specific problems of statehood, occupation, and new modes of sectarian strife. Their discourse in earlier decades reflected their status as a disenfranchised, oppressed majority. Post-2003 statements were consistent with their new status as an empowered majority, although they often spoke on behalf of all Iraqis and downplayed sectarian differences.

Their positions were crucial at a time when nonclerical Shiites were catapulted into the political process. Having destroyed the Saddam-era state, and bent on policies like debaathification that precluded working with most Iraqis who had lived in the country for the duration of Saddam's rule, the United States cast its lot with the Kurds and the formerly exiled opposition. Some of these exiles, like Ahmad Chalabi and Iyad Allawi, were secularists who happened to be Shiite, but the more powerful forces on the ground were Shiite Islamists such as the Da'wa Party and Baqir al-Hakim's Supreme Council for the Islamic Revolution in Iraq (SCIRI).

US advisers warned their Iraqi allies that Washington would not support the formation of an Islamic state.[31] After debaathification, enacted by CPA Order 1 on May 16, 2003, helped to push the Sunnis out of the political process, Vice President Dick Cheney expressed concern over the possibility that an ayatollah would take over. Ayatollahs were not incorporated into the state-building plan, nor did they request formal inclusion. Yet they issued a series of statements about the political situation, intervened when necessary, and sometimes affected the process by calling followers to action. One thing is certain: Their actions proliferated. Their abundant writings and activities established their place as a new class of public intellectuals, with a new brand of activism that defied the artificial distinction between quietism and Khomeinism. Yet the senior clerics did not completely agree on what that activism should look like or what it should push for. The next four sections will illuminate the ensuing debates through analysis of the statements of Ayatollahs Baqir al-Hakim (d. 2003), Sistani, Fayyad, and Najafi.

Ayatollah Muhammad Baqir al-Hakim

Ayatollah Muhammad Baqir al-Hakim returned to Iraq on May 12, 2003, after twenty-three years of exile in Iran.[32] Ten thousand supporters were there to greet him when he crossed the border. As Hakim's hundred-vehicle convoy entered Basra, crowds showered it with flowers, and men threw themselves at the ayatollah's own car.[33] The visual parallels with Khomeini's return to Iran after twelve years in exile were striking. In his first speech, Hakim condemned religious extremism, rejected any foreign-installed government, and made the case for Iraqi sovereignty. He also said that the role of the Supreme Council for the Islamic Revolution in Iraq (SCIRI), his political party, was to "realize the will of the Iraqi people" and to rebuild the country with that goal in mind.[34] He continued, "We will not take up arms against anybody to reach our objectives. We will pursue the path of dialogue and free elections." In that same speech he stressed that "all tribal, ethnic and religious groups should unite" to form a new government.[35] He stated explicitly that an "Islamic government" would not work for Iraq. He favored instead a "democratic state" that was based on "freedom, independence and justice." Hakim insisted on a "popularly elected government" that was grounded in civil society and represented all "ethnic, racial and religious groups."[36] On the eve of the invasion, he had spoken of his past and avoided making assumptions about his future role: "I started my resistance to the regime to save the Iraqi people from dictatorship, sectarian discrimination and racial discrimination. I have no desire to play a political role, but if they [the people] choose a role for me, I will accept."[37] Hakim would not have the opportunity to develop his ideas alongside the state-building process. He was killed by a car bomb in August 2003.

Hakim's disavowal of "Islamic government" and respect for interdenominational pluralism marked a clear break with his writings in exile in Iran. It was not only his writings; Hakim had also tried to implement his ideas for an Islamic state in Iraq after the 1991 uprisings that followed the Gulf War. The popular uprisings were in response to Saddam's brutality, and many of the Shiite conscripts defected to the rebel side, which was diverse and included Islamist groups, such as the Da'wa Party and SCIRI. Hakim's Badr Brigades crossed into Najaf and Karbala, and they concentrated their efforts on an Islamist agenda, filled with pro-Iranian symbols and slogans. This approach, which clashed with Iraqi nationalism, was widely unpopular. It alienated the population and led to widespread criticism of SCIRI, especially by the Da'wa Party. This competition resurfaced again after 2003, when scholars labeled the Da'wa Party as "centralist," committed to the nationalism of Iraq.[38] But already in 2002, Hakim had publicly abandoned the Iranian model and espoused an elected form of government, the precise shape of which would be left to the Iraqi people to decide. He was confident that "a government would be formed bringing together all strands of Iraqi society."[39] It was months before the wheels were set in motion for war.

While in Iran, Hakim wrote about the importance of an Islamic state. He argued that "the Islamic nation was unified by testimony of God's saying, 'And surely this nation of yours is one nation.' This nation has to have one general leadership." He reasoned that the "Islamic nation" was unified in purpose and doctrine, regardless of region, as outlined in the "primary principle of political Islamic theory."[40] On that basis, Hakim understood that the Islamic nation (of Shiites) as a "comprehensive movement and total attitude" had to be subject to "one international leadership" embodied in Khomeini's successor as leader of the Islamic Republic of Iran, Ayatollah Ali Khamenei.[41] Hakim continued that the Islamic nation was obliged to obey the decisions issued by this guardian. He also implied that there was "regional leadership" in the person of Khamenei, as he advocated for a more universal Shiism.[42] He did acknowledge a "fault" in his thinking: Although the Islamic nation was united, each nation-state within it had unique "political problems and cultural circumstances" that needed to be considered.[43] He reasoned that some countries, like Iraq, therefore required revolutions to account for their unique "purposes."[44] In 1980 Hakim had created SCIRI, which called for the removal of the Ba'ath Party. Hakim advocated that a "political and religious *marja*'" take up leadership of a movement to bring about Islamic revolution in Iraq.[45] This leader should possess characteristics in line with "Islamic recommendations," such as *ijtihad,* jurisprudence, justice, and legitimate guardianship. Political issues, he reasoned, should be addressed strictly from a "personal or democratic" point of view.[46] He also acknowledged that although Iraq was composed of three prominent ethnic groups (Arabs, Kurds, and Turkmen), such "secondary characteristics" would disappear under the proper Islamic leadership, as had happened in multi-ethnic Iran.[47] Here he operated on the assumption that opposition to Saddam Hussein in Iraq was overwhelmingly "Islamic." Islam, he said, was "the doctrine of the majority of the Iraqi people" and fostered a general religious culture in which "coexistence and harmony" were anchored in a way that no other "religion or political approach could achieve."[48] He referred to Iran as Iraq's "mother" and suggested that Iraq align with Iranian foreign policy, such as the bounty on writer Salman Rushdie for his novel *The Satanic Verses*.[49]

Hakim's thoughts on the role of the ayatollah were radical. He went so far as to split the institution between what he called *marja'iyya diniyya fiqhiyya* (legal religious leadership) and *marja'iyya diniyya siyasiyya* (political religious leadership): "Religious leadership in terms of giving fatwas and religious leadership in political action were two responsibilities that could naturally be distinguished, one from another." He went on to say that the *marja'* in political matters need not be the same person as the *marja'* on religious matters. Society was developing rapidly, and no single *marja'* could be expected to have the answers to all questions, political and religious. More importantly, political situations differed across the world, and each society would need its own voice of guidance.[50]

Hakim, of course, was aware of the existing hierarchy. He argued that the religious *marja'* would always need to be respected and followed above all, so, in essence, the political *marja'* could never rise above him. In this sense, Hakim was in support of *velayat-e faqih*. Khomeini was a high-ranking ayatollah, but the term was subsequently modified to reflect the understanding that people could follow a jurist who headed an Islamic state, even if he was not the most learned, as in the case of Khomeini's successor, Ayatollah Khamenei. Evidently, Hakim developed a theory of separation of powers between a political ayatollah and a religious ayatollah in order to carve out a position for himself in a future Islamic state in Iraq. Yet in light of realities on the ground, he abandoned these ideas.

Hakim had developed close ties to US-backed opposition groups, such as the Iraqi National Congress. Established after the Gulf War, the Iraqi National Congress was funded by the United States to allow opponents of Saddam Hussein to join forces. Hakim began attending conventions hosted by Iraqi opposition groups beginning in 2001. And by February 2002, during a convention in London, Hakim's new position was crystallizing.

He was turning toward Iraq. By the next year, referring to the "power of the convention," he invited Iraqis to be prepared as an opposition bloc to fill the expected political void after 2003, and to do so responsibly. On March 7, 2003, he gave a farewell speech to Iranians, in deep appreciation of the twenty-three years he had spent there and the "brotherhood" between the two peoples. It was clear from his language referring to Iran as a place for "scholars and martyrs" that Hakim was also ready to distance himself from the political program he had advocated for years. It was the realization that context matters that led him to this decision.

In his Basra speech after the invasion, Hakim stressed that Iraq would be saved by forming a "democratic national government" reflective of all the people. He repeated, "Our priority is a united word" and "We are here to serve the religious authority." He was setting the stage for a policy of noninterference in state building but importantly reserving a role for the *hawza* in the process.

Yet the *hawza* had no room for political parties and militias. This was the consensus in Najaf, as illustrated through a series of fatwas and speeches from the four grand ayatollahs over the years. Hakim, as he abandoned his role for an Islamic state, and worked his way back into the hierarchy of the *hawza* and the culture of Najaf, did not have the opportunity to redefine his party's platform within the new public sphere or to decide whether to disband it altogether. SCIRI, under the leadership of Hakim's brother Abd al-Aziz and, later, his son Ammar, would steer the political party toward policies that were not only highly interventionist but also controversial, as illustrated in chapter 3. Yet this was part of the reinvention of Najaf. Ayatollah Hakim, who was among the hierarchy of Najaf, was not his brother or his nephew. SCIRI would be redefined after 2003, and that task would not be Hakim's responsibility. It was clear from his triumphant return that Ayatollah Hakim was prepared to embrace the culture of Najaf. More importantly, his early language about democracy paved the way for the discourse of Sistani, whom I have previously described as the "guardian of the democratic process."

Hakim toured all the cities of the South, from al-Nasiriyya to al-Samawa, and then continued to Najaf days later. There he delivered speeches about forming a government involving free elections and conformity with Islamic principles. He warned that unrest would erupt if any form of government were imposed on Iraqis against their will. In Najaf,

Hakim became the imam for Friday prayers in the Sahen al-Hudairi al-Sharif, a position in which he served until he was killed.

Hakim developed a political vision for the "new Iraq" in the last fourteen speeches he delivered before his death. He made clear that he did not favor either a "Taliban state" or "Islam on America's terms."[51] Instead, he called for a parliamentary system grounded in Islam that also respected the rights of non-Muslim Iraqis. He insisted that, although at the forefront of the process, he would not seek a Shiite government: "Some say Shiites want to seize power in Iraq, but this is not true, although we are the majority. It was all Iraqis who sacrificed their blood. We do not want a tribal government."[52] Hakim intervened at a time when he was increasingly worried about the consequences of the power vacuum. Rather than leaving security to the United States, he determined that the ayatollahs would have a crucial role to play. In a sermon delivered on May 20, 2003, he said that instability required "scholars and religious authorities who have social presence to political power to stand up."[53]

Some analysts, such as Faleh A. Jabar, argue that parties such as SCIRI and Daʿwa have a purely majoritarian view: Because Shiites are the majority, electoral mechanisms will ensure that they rule.[54] However, my analysis concerns the ayatollahs as the highest-ranking religious leaders in Iraq. Their position in society, strategic thinking, and goals, as well as their institutional constraints, make them different from political parties that seek to gain formal seats in government. After 2003, Hakim tried to carve out a place for himself within the traditional hierarchy in Najaf and in so doing displayed thinking that was different from what he had displayed in Iran. This context-driven behavior, in which politics shaped his religious thinking, makes him similar to the other four grand ayatollahs who remained after his death.

On June 6, 2003, he spoke again about a future Iraq with a government chosen by the people through free and fair elections. He continued to stress that no one should be marginalized, regardless of sect or political orientation, and the need for a united Iraq, from north to south. He was widening the political discourse to allow a range of viewpoints, perhaps thinking back to the censorship and exclusionary practices of the former regime. He also warned of the dangers of sectarianism. He did not fit neatly into the categories of quietism and activism as he did not always speak of himself exclusively as a "guide," as the *hawza* in Najaf preferred.

But it soon became clear that the other senior clerics were crafty in their interpretation of "guide" in ways that also went beyond the binary opposition between being apolitical or passive on one end or revolutionary on the other.

Ayatollah Ali al-Husseini al-Sistani

Ayatollah Sistani was born in Mashhad, Iran, in 1930 and studied in Qom under Ayatollah Hussein Borujerdi. Sistani moved to Najaf in the early 1950s and settled there to build his career as a cleric. He lived through the secular Arab nationalism of the Ba'ath Party and then the consolidation of power by Saddam Hussein as military leader in the decade before he ascended to the presidency in 1979. Sistani never challenged the Ba'athist state, but he had years to observe the two extremes of Shiite clergy-state relations: In Iraq he watched the Ba'ath Party torture, exile, and kill clergy in order to silence them, and across the border in Iran he watched decades of what amounted to a failed Shiite theocracy, even from the perspective of ayatollahs within the system.[55] These factors influenced his advocacy for popular sovereignty and a pathway to democracy. In his first fatwa on the topic, Sistani stated that "men of religion shall not push roughly in administrative and executive affairs, but their role shall be limited to guiding and supervising the committees formed in order to administer affairs and provide security and public services for the people."[56] He stated explicitly that "it was out of the question" that he would have a "special place" in the future government of Iraq, unlike Hakim, who left the possibility open.[57] At the same time, like Hakim, he afforded space for Islam to enter the public discourse. In the early days of the war, Sistani spoke of the biggest threat to the future of Iraq as "the obliteration of its cultural identity, which is considered one of the most important pillars of Islam."[58] In his statements on the constitutional process that followed, he was clear that Iraqis should be entrusted to draft the constitution because only they would be able to "express their national identity." Sistani described Iraqi national identity as a "pillar of Islam," anchored in "noble social values."[59] He argued that the new government must respect Islam, the religion of the majority, and must not contradict its teachings.[60] Therefore, Sistani's language included Islam, yet it was about Islam as the moral foundation of society.

It is not that Sistani had no opinion on Islamic government. He wrote on the subject, but his vision was different from that of Khomeini, and he never developed a "theory of the state." Sistani was influenced by his predecessor, Ayatollah Abu al-Qasim al-Khoei (d. 1992), who accepted the political reality of a modern nation-state led by lay politicians, as well as by Muhammad Hussein Naini, who wrote on government accountability. Ayatollah Khoei had institutionalized the idea of religious tolerance and created a tolerant attitude in the *hawza* of Najaf that would be carried on after his death. These included the stopping of Quranic punishments such as stoning and the acceptance of equal rights for non-Muslims, such as the widespread use of holy books other than the Quran for oaths of allegiance in courts.[61] None of Sistani's writings on the relationship between jurists and followers rested on an institutionalized role for the jurist in a state structure.[62] After 2003, Sistani rejected the Iranian model on many occasions, saying, "Forming a government based on the idea of the absolute guardianship of the jurist was out of the question."[63] Iraq was too complex in its ethnic and religious makeup, and it had a complicated history of colonialism and minority rule by Sunnis. Iranians, on the other hand, were 90 percent Shiite and mostly Persian-speaking. If he were to ignore the political realities of Iraq, he would be out of touch with the needs of the people.

His approach was followed by the other three clerics of Iraq. In their bid to survive in this complex new political space, they understood that there was no room for clerical rule. They instead focused on making themselves relevant to modern discussions with the frequency of their statements so that they would serve as "guides," "watch the government closely," and "ensure that the will of the people would be pursued." They reasoned that if they were able to help cultivate a new political structure that was participatory and reflective of the will of the people, they would win on several fronts. First, they would be able to preserve the status and legitimacy of their hierarchical institution as new social actors emerged to challenge them. Second, they would appear in front of the political process as the leaders of an indigenous democratic movement. They would continue to forge ties with their followers on questions of democracy, voting, minority rights, constitutionalism, and human rights, and stand against corruption and sectarianism. Last, they would remain independent of the state. Their power could be summed up with Sistani's response when asked about the best type of government for Iraq: "We wish what the majority of the Iraqi people wish; the way shall be opened for them."[64] The ayatollahs would exert their power by hovering around the system and being "active" when they chose, not all the time, as heads of state would be obliged to be.

In the months following the US invasion, Sistani managed to carve out a unique position for himself as a powerful nonstate actor. He always refused to meet with US representatives but issued several statements about US policy in Iraq. In addition to his fatwas on elections and the constitutional process, he expressed "great unease over the goals of the occupation forces," indicating that Iraq should be a sovereign state, free of foreign intervention. As the violence in post-Saddam Iraq spread, he argued that regardless of who was behind the attacks on civilians, the "occupying forces" would be held responsible for the security of the country.[65]

Sistani's clout was such that he was able to steer the state-making process at times, but then he would recede from the spotlight, making only the occasional intervention. The tendency to adopt black-and-white, all-or-nothing views of clerical quietism and activism made the falloff in fatwas confusing to outsiders. Some assumed that fewer interventions meant that the ayatollah's power was declining or that he had ceased to follow politics. Reidar Visser has evaluated the proposition that Sistani "returned to seclusion" and a position of classic quietism. Indeed, from March 2003 to December 2004, Sistani issued a total of forty statements, fourteen of which contained commentary on the political transition under way in Iraq. From December 2004 to January 2006, the number of statements dropped to fifteen, with only three directly related to affairs of state.[66] Visser hypothesized that Sistani's interventions were "spasmodic," not "incremental."[67] Juan Cole also evaluated the thesis of Sistani's "dramatic decline." Rather than counting the number of fatwas, Cole was more concerned with the changing landscape in Iraq. He attributed Sistani's seeming decline to the rise of mass social violence and the new political parties that had filled the void after the fall of the one-party state. Cole recognized that Sistani nonetheless maintained widespread influence.[68]

Sistani's actions were in fact consistent with his most direct comments on politics, in which he said he would not meddle in the "details of political work." He said that Iraqis had entrusted politicians with this task.[69] Although he was not "in control," he could advise on the best pathways.[70] In his speeches, fatwas, *bayans,* and correspondence, Sistani was brief and seemed to answer queries with intentional vagueness. Many interpreted his stance as quietism. Yet political action is complex and layered, and sometimes informal involvement has more impact than action through formal channels.

Journalists were puzzled about Sistani's refusal to get bogged down in the intricate debates about federalism versus centralism in 2004 and 2005, even though these debates were crucial to the future of the state. He met every question on federalism with either neutrality or a pronouncement that it was up to Iraqis to decide by way of national elections and consensus. This position must be understood within the context of Sistani's broader vision for Iraq. He was concerned about the large, formative events that would establish the rules of the game. If he were to debate the details of federalism or discuss the Kurdish question, he would weaken Iraqi trust in his commitment to equality of all Iraqis and a nonsectarian stance. In his strategic way, he understood that any position he took would inevitably be perceived as sectarian, particularly in light of the enthusiasm of Shiite parties like SCIRI for the strong form of federalism that eventually was enshrined in the 2005 constitution.

Sistani's emphasis on the big picture was reflected as well in his dealings with Nouri al-Maliki, the country's first prime minister after the transition from the interim government. Maliki's time in office would last from May 20, 2006, when he was officially sworn in, to August 14, 2014, when he announced his resignation because of allegations of corruption and a host of other accusations that included inciting sectarianism among Iraqis.

In an April 2006 statement before Maliki took office, Sistani insisted on the need for a government composed of "efficient" administrative and staff members. He stressed the importance of integrity and reputation, and he said that the premier should protect the "higher national interest and ignore personal, party, sectarian and ethnic interests." The government, Sistani went on, should have a list of priorities. The first mission was to get a handle on the security of the country and end criminal acts, which included kidnapping, torture, murder, and daily explosions. He advocated that only government forces be allowed to carry weapons.[71] Months later, in September, he warned Maliki about the hazards of sectarianism, noting that if the government failed to provide security, "other forces will do it," which would be "very dangerous." The ayatollah urged Maliki to establish a state that left no room for administrative corruption, which he referred to as an "incurable disease," and to prosecute corrupt officials whoever they might be. Sistani stressed "social justice."[72] He was concerned, for instance, by the large discrepancies in pay for comparable jobs in government.

The steps Sistani outlined were intended to aid the restoration of political and economic sovereignty and to "remove the effects of occupation." If the government succeeded, all Iraqis would succeed. He assured Maliki that he would not intervene to "inflame" disputes over specific issues. However, he did intend to "monitor" the government's performance and point out faults *when necessary*. Sistani stressed that the premier's job was to give voice to the people, regardless of sectarian and ethnic affiliation.[73] He was telling Maliki, point blank, that he must work for all of Iraq. Maliki said he would form a government that met these criteria.

As time passed, however, it became clear that Maliki was building a state of partisan fiefdoms. Many of the security services were in effect militias aligned with paramilitaries out of uniform. Iraqis were more and more fed up with the ongoing violence, the high levels of corruption, the low quality of public services, and unemployment. On February 25, 2011, demonstrations swept across the country.

Sistani sometimes met with Iraqi officials at key moments of the state-building process, receiving them as guests in his home in Najaf. In 2011, however, immediately after a meeting with Maliki, Sistani announced that these consultations would cease. He cut off communication with the prime minister. The other three grand ayatollahs agreed, and they issued similar decrees in solidarity with the legitimate demands of the populace.

In 2014 sectarian violence reached a fever pitch with the ISIS conquest of Mosul and other major cities. With Maliki nonetheless preparing for reelection, Sistani made the strategic decision, along with the three other ayatollahs, to become active in formal politics again. They issued statements, and YouTube videos of their collective no-confidence vote in Maliki went viral. Although Maliki's Da'wa Party won a majority in the 2014 elections, he would not return as prime minister. He was replaced by Haider al-Abadi, also from the Da'wa Party.

In this episode, the activism of Sistani and the ayatollahs was keen and sustained. But Sistani had not developed an interest in the "details of political work." He was concerned about ensuring the government's broad commitment to national unity and anti-sectarianism. He would intervene only to keep progress toward those goals moving or if the integrity of the state was threatened. For eight years, he had watched Maliki foment sectarianism in the country and enact authoritarian measures that violated the law. Events required Sistani to modify his quietism. He called on Abadi to enact specific reforms to be implemented on a short time line. Sistani also had to learn from political experience.

Sistani is still often judged by scholars and journalists based on the power of his fatwas to bring people into the streets and to the polls. But his contribution was not about the volume of fatwas; it was about setting the terms of the debate as a key public intellectual. His reluctance to intervene made him more powerful because it conveyed the impression that he intervened only when necessary (and also allowed him to evade criticism he might have received had he been associated with specific policies). In authoritarian and immediate post-authoritarian settings, it is hard to measure the political power of nonstate actors, for the institutional legacy of authoritarianism lingers.[74] Sistani, along with everyone else in Iraq, was socialized to play by the authoritarian rules of the game. But he proved over and again to be "activist" in resisting the impulse to revert to authoritarianism. His moments of contentiousness happened only occasionally, and at critical junctures—to check the power of the United States, to ensure Iraqi participation in the political process, and to combat corrupt, sectarian practices in government.

A final motivation behind Sistani's brand of clerical activism in post-Saddam Iraq was that he had to act strategically to ensure his own political survival and that of his institution. He very much wanted to establish the importance of Najaf as a center of Shiism. In part in reaction to the rise of Sadr, Sistani worked to keep the *hawza* at the center of discussions. He first worked to dispel the myth of a "dispute among the leadership of the *hawza*." Sistani made clear that Najaf was open to all and that he was not a "party to any disputes," but was rather "above them" and a patron to all people.[75] He expressed hope that conditions would allow Najaf to be restored to its "golden age" without weakening the positions of other *hawzas*.[76] In a response to a reporter's question, Sistani's son, Rida, made clear that qualified persons would thrive and "outperform" in Najaf regardless of nationality, a reference to Saddam's goal of Arabizing the *hawza* and restricting its activities. Rida was careful not to pit Najaf against Qom. He acknowledged that Ayatollah Hakim had returned after years of exile in Qom and that perhaps Ayatollah Haeri would follow, but he made clear that there was room for both cities to be centers of excellence.[77] However, a rivalry between Najaf and Qom persisted, and much of Sistani's activism would be driven by it.

When asked about Iran's political role in Iraq, Sistani responded that all governments should respect Iraq's sovereignty. He went on to say that he would not "communicate with any foreign entities with regard to Iraqi affairs."[78] Ayatollahs in Lebanon, Bahrain, and Iraq fiercely maintained their independence from the Islamic Republic. Therefore, it is not surprising that every time Sistani was asked about Iran or the model of the Islamic Republic, his reactions ranged from dismissive to perplexed.

In order to preserve his status, Sistani was always on the lookout for Iranian meddling. His famous "jihad fatwa" of June 2014 that called on Iraqis to join the military to push back ISIS was an appeal to Iraqi nationalism without any sectarian sentiment, shying away from language that would conflate ISIS with Sunnis. Yet we can also view this fatwa through the lens of the rivalry with Qom and with Tehran. General Qassem Soleimani, commander of the Quds Force of the Iranian Revolutionary Guards Corps, had been coordinating with Iraqi politicians such as Prime Minister Maliki, as well as Iraqi military officers, in the fight against ISIS. Sistani was also concerned about the growing number of militias in Iraq that were affiliated with Khamenei, such as the League of the Righteous, the Badr Organization, and the Khorasani Brigades. These militias did not acknowledge Sistani's power and therefore needed to be kept at arm's length. So Sistani's overt support for the new prime minister, Haider al-Abadi, in 2014 and his call for reforms through constitutional and parliamentary processes should be understood as much as attempts to reverse Iran's encroachment into Iraqi politics as attempts to strengthen Iraqi democracy. Sistani also issued select fatwas on responsible government; the legitimacy of the military, and not militias; and trust in the legal authority. These decrees must have also taken signs of undue Iranian influence into account. After all, throughout 2015 portraits of Ayatollah Khomeini appeared in Baghdad and southern cities. Supporters of Khomeini renamed a street in Najaf after the Iranian ayatollah and plastered his name all over the walls. Iraqi nationalists immediately defaced the pro-Khomeini posters and graffiti.[79]

Sistani operated all along with the knowledge of Ayatollah Khamenei's desire to secure a foothold in Najaf after the fall of Saddam. Khamenei opened an official bureau in Najaf near Sistani's house, only to relocate soon after when he learned of Sistani's ire. Khamenei also started the process of determining Sistani's successor. Shiite doctrine requires that a grand ayatollah die before the informal, opaque succession process can begin. Yet Sistani was very much alive when Iran tried to pave the way for Ayatollah Mahmoud Hashemi Shahroudi to succeed him. Shahroudi, a cleric of Najafi origin, had risen in the ranks in Tehran after teaching Khamenei to become a grand ayatollah upon the death of Khomeini in 1989. In 2012 he began a campaign to attract followers in Iraq. He opened an office in Najaf and offered clerics stipends, housing, and other services. He began meeting with Prime Minister Maliki and made statements to politicians about positioning himself to be next in line.[80] Shahroudi's challenge was enormous; such a succession might lead the *hawza* away from the stance of clerical noninterference in democracy that Sistani had helped to mold. Rule of the jurisprudent would create all kinds of problems amid the complex ethnic and religious composition of Iraq. And Iran's proactive move came in part because of the ethnic composition of the *hawza* of Najaf itself. Fayyad is of Afghan origin, Najafi is Pakistani, and Sistani, of course, was born in Iran. It is unusual for non-Arabs to rise to such lofty positions. Saeed al-Hakim is of Arab origin but does not have a large following. Aware of this, Shahroudi and Khamenei have been importing Arabic speakers from Qom. This competition will set the tone for how the new generation of scholars in Najaf is educated, but it could also reorient Najaf along the lines of Tehran.

Given the historical record of brutality and the political milieu described in chapter 1, and given the new competition for power on a substate level, it was and remains wise for Sistani and the other three ayatollahs to be strategic in choosing their moments of intervention. In many ways, Iraq after 2003 was a free-for-all. Not only were the ayatollahs worried about the wrath of the state; they also had to contend with opposition from Shiite militias, Sunni insurgents, and others who scoffed at their once uncontested authority. The ayatollahs' connections to society were now more crucial than ever, as were their capacities to reinforce these ties, either by way of fatwas or more modern modes.

At the time of this writing, in 2017, Sistani looks like a great success. He has proven that he can issue a fatwa and have hundreds of thousands of people take to the streets in no time. He can stall a piece of legislation.

He can declare no confidence in a prime minister, prompting his resignation. He has used his activism for the promotion of democracy in Iraq, the prevention of sectarian violence, and the unity of the people. Iraqi politics often get read in relation to Khomeini's precedent, but Sistani's post-2003 actions defy a clear opposition between activism and quietism. He acts politically but is not a theocrat. He has made no calls for Shiite-led theocracy, partition of the country, or any other dispensation that would empower Shiites or the ayatollahs at the expense of other groups in Iraq. Sistani has displayed an enormous commitment to pluralism and human rights. His activism has been context driven.

Ayatollah Muhammad Ishaq al-Fayyad

Ayatollah Muhammad Ishaq al-Fayyad was born in Afghanistan in 1930 and moved to Najaf at the age of ten to begin his Islamic studies. He studied under Grand Ayatollah Abu al-Qasim al-Khoei, and after Khoei's death in 1992, he accepted a position as a leader in the *hawza*. Although his religious credentials rivaled those of Sistani, Fayyad knew that because he was not of Iraqi or Iranian descent, it would be hard for him to sustain a large following from the Arab world. Shiites who adhered to his school were mainly South Asian, although he did maintain a following in Iraq.

Fayyad, along with the other three grand ayatollahs of Najaf, remained committed to the "guides only" role after the 2003 war. Interestingly, his opinions about Islamic statehood and the proper role for an ayatollah meshed well with a more activist political stance. Yet he was predisposed to consider the atmosphere in Iraq and to conform to the prevailing position of a modified quietism in Najaf. His ideas would differ from those of Sistani, but he had reached a consensus with the other clerics. Fayyad understood the complexities of Iraq. His discourses were driven by his desire to remain relevant to contemporary discussions as a means of political survival.

To properly summarize the Najafi viewpoint on quietism, Haider Hamoudi coined the term "Najaf mantra" after meeting with the grand ayatollahs in November 2009. He quoted Ayatollah Fayyad, whom he said epitomized the mantra: "The role of the *marja'iyya* offers guidance for citizens and the state," and undertakes the task of "observation of responsible officials, to ensure they act in accordance with their duties to the people." Fayyad also spoke of the *marja'iyya*'s role in "unification of all of Iraq's population, Sunnis and Shiites and religious minorities." He warned that the *marja'iyya* was "not to play any direct role in the government."[81] The "Najaf mantra" was a direct and unambiguous refutation of Khomeini's doctrine of rule of the jurisprudent, yet it went against some of Fayyad's other ideas.

Ayatollah Fayyad believed strongly in the need for an Islamic state, but he was keenly aware of the imperative to follow the will of the people, despite his personal convictions. Like Hakim, he adjusted his religious thought according to political context. Fayyad reasoned that in the absence of the proper conditions and given the realities of Iraq, he would support a government structure born out of compromise. Fayyad and Sistani therefore represented two end points of a pendulum that met at the same point: The process of deliberation guided their thinking.

We can reconstruct Fayyad's ideas about quietism by reviewing his speeches and statements since 2003. In his early addresses, the Afghan ayatollah made clear that the job of the faithful was to "spread Islamic awareness" and "humanitarian, intellectual and moral values against all colors of corruption" and "foreign intellectual invasions." Islamic traditions could provide "great psychological energies" for combating what he perceived as the ills of encroaching Western culture. The country's newfound freedom was an opportunity to employ education to instill these proper "Islamic values" in society.[82] Fayyad believed that the *marja'* had a role in directing the government to "maintain the Islamic phenomena" and "grant people their freedom to preserve their dignity and rights within the boundaries acceptable to God and to stay away from Western cultures that were 'vulgar.'"

In his scholarly writings, Fayyad had gone considerably further, expressing a desire for establishment of an Islamic state. The conditions of the first Islamic state at the time of the Prophet could never exist again. The world had evolved. In any case, no "fixed system" was appropriate for "all of history and for every era." But there might be grounds for selection of a jurist with a mandate to rule if a "vacuum" existed in legislation and a jurist was needed to draft a constitution and complementary statutes to "fill the void."[83] However, such a state should conform to "the time the jurist lives in, and the best interest of the public."[84]

Fayyad did not think an Islamic state should be restrictive but rather should "implement justice and reserve people's rights." For example, he said that atheists should not be considered *kuffar* (infidels) but rather "lost" individuals who needed Islamic guidance and education. He was concerned that people not be "extreme and stick to limitations."[85] Islam—and not just the figure of the ayatollah—was to be the moral guide. This philosophy was in line with Fayyad's thinking that his Islamic state would create an "equal society." He argued that the state had the right to intervene in the private sector to ensure equal treatment. That power would render the government "honest" and keep it away from "embezzlement and administrative corruption."[86]

Fayyad's texts on Islamic governance stressed moderation, asserting that the seminaries were against "extremism and terrorism in all its forms and colors." Any state formed on the basis of "jurisprudence" or the "legislative independence" of Najaf would reject "bigotry."[87] That, in turn, would preclude problems such as sectarianism and civil strife. In his pronouncements on the violence in post-Saddam Iraq, Fayyad continued to emphasize the moderating role of the *hawza*.

Fayyad acknowledged that one of the biggest obstacles to forming an Islamic state was the presumed disapproval of the West and its "agents." Even Muslim intellectuals who were capable of forming Islamic systems were hesitant to do so for fear of backlash. He attributed this trepidation to "empty propaganda from the West" that refers to Islam as "extremist," "anti-freedom," and "anti-human rights." Fayyad wondered whether it was the growth of the global Muslim population that prompted this misinformation.[88] Islam did possess "humanitarian values," he went on, and could "balance between the layers of the nation" in a way that would "never harm the rights of others and would be commensurate with the limits of rationality and humanity."[89] Yet there was no room for this notion among Islam's detractors.[90] Fayyad wanted to combine the discourse on Islamic statehood, which he ultimately declared was unattainable in his lifetime, with language about human rights, moderation, and pluralism.

Despite his vision for an Islamic state, Fayyad knew that the people of Iraq were unlikely to vote one into being. So he supported Sistani's initiatives on state building. He urged Iraqis to support the 2005 draft constitution, for example, although it was "not cooperative with Islamic ideals." He even expressed a willingness to support the federalism model if it led to "social justice, and not sedition." In essence, he urged voters to participate in the various electoral exercises despite his "apprehension" that this course was "not commensurate with Iraq's Islamic status." He preferred that the word "Islamic" be added to the formal name of the republic, even if in an "honorific way," but reassured his base that this wish did not come from desire to establish a theocratic state like that in Iran. Rather, Iraq should be like "Mauritania and others who are known for their secular and liberal systems but rely on their Islamic constitution."[91] Fayyad had committed to being a "guide," but his role as an ayatollah required him to say what place Islam should have in state discourse. And that is precisely what he did.

Fayyad's brand of quietism crystallized as he focused attention on the importance of Najaf as a center of learning. He was insistent that Najaf maintain its independence, status, and prestige. He worried that the seminaries would be eclipsed by Qom or that they would lose their autonomy if ayatollahs insisted on interference in government. Distance was crucial. In a *bayan* dated June 18, 2008, Fayyad recalled that Najaf's prominence went back 1,000 years. The seminaries had graduated scholars from all over the world despite repeated efforts by the former regime to strip it of its importance and take control of it. Fayyad recalled the efforts of previous generations of scholars and *maraji'* who endured tremendous pressure, including physical abuse and campaigns to "defile their names." He attributed their survival to the fact that they were "unlinked to the government or to political parties, the educational system or economic structures."[92] Fayyad noted that Najaf's seminaries had never had to accept any financial aid from government. This independence meant that the ayatollahs did not need to toe the government line.

Fayyad illustrated this independence by recalling the seminary's most difficult years under Ba'athist rule. The goal of that "ominous" party had been to "demolish" the seminary and make it a "tool of the regime." He adduced the example of Grand Ayatollah Khoei, who was asked to support the regime during the 1990 war but refused. Fayyad said that acquiescence would have been a black mark on Khoei's record because it would have been equivalent to alliance with the "criminal Ba'ath." Yet Khoei remained steadfast in the face of the execution of his inner circle. It was incumbent upon Iraqis to emulate that historical precedent.

In 2008 Fayyad noted that Najaf was regaining its popularity, with more than 5,000 students enrolled in the *hawza*, all but 500 of them Iraqis. He said, "The beauty of the seminary was its moderation." A peaceful institution, its main role was to "keep order and spread Islam." Fayyad urged everyone to invest in "maintaining its level of purity" by way of monetary support.[93] It was a momentous statement. He did not advocate for a more activist or interventionist *hawza*. He was clear that, as "guides," the ayatollahs would be able to keep their distance from the state—and thus safeguard their independence and prerogatives. He was also signaling that the role of the *hawza* was to spread Islamic values but not impose them. In 2008, after sectarian fighting had turned into a civil war, the ayatollahs would be a source of moderation and peace. The violence on the ground had other roots.

Fayyad's elaboration upon quietism was not prompted by some theoretical question. He had been asked to comment on how the status of the clerics had changed after the fall of Saddam's regime. He responded that the ayatollahs were now "free" to guide the people and to educate them (without fear of retribution) with the "provisions of religion and humanitarian values, and to invite them to calm and stability." He believed the ayatollahs had a central role in "cooperating with government agencies to detect pockets of terror and to work on reinforcing the law" in an effort to "save the country." In this context, he viewed his role as one of an intermediary. When asked how the clerics should "deal with the people," he responded that the relationship was akin to how a "father treats his children."[94]

His mention of "cooperating with government agencies" must have caused confusion because it prompted the questioner to ask if the clergy sought a political role. Yet Fayyad's second reply remained the same, that "there was no practical role" for the ayatollahs in the government "internally or externally," but that their primary role was "guiding the government into taking the right path in its policies and getting it interested in serving people and providing security and stability." As such, the clergy's job was to ask the government (in the strongest possible terms) to "deal with terrorists, murderers, and the corrupt, and to unhesitatingly impose the harshest penalties on them, in front of the public, to be made examples of, because the blood of Iraqis that was spilled every single day was not cheap and worthless but there was great value to their blood."[95] Fayyad's statement aligned him with Sistani's comments that clerics should not be heads of state.

Indeed, although Fayyad advocated in the abstract for an Islamic state in his writings, he never called for one in Iraq when the new state structure was unveiled after 2003. News headlines nonetheless continued to appear asserting that the clerics wanted Islamic law in the constitution.[96] So Fayyad was given many opportunities to articulate his opinion on the proper relationship between state and religion. His answer was always similar.

In an undated fatwa, he stated that in the policies of current governments there was no connection to religion because "each government followed its own interest globally and regionally." The grounds of governance were for "God alone, but this kind of government does not exist in any country of the world." In another statement, Fayyad revisited his argument that the conditions for a "realistic Islamic state," based on the idea of the "governorship of religion," existed at the time of the Prophet but not today, not in Iran or anywhere else. He made this point in a speech to students at his seminary to warn them to steer clear of the state and political parties: "Affiliation of scholars with the state meant that the seminary would become the property of the state and political parties and a tool for implementing their goals." Also, the seminary did not need political terms of reference because religion contradicted the policies adopted by the countries of the world."[97] Given that the ideal role of religion in the state was unattainable, Fayyad stuck to his line that the seminary should maintain its independence and serve as a focal point for religion. Fayyad said that he would "keep an eye on the government," but he imposed restrictions on himself as well. He said that the role of clerics was like that of all political blocs, "to be in the service of the people," "to give up all self-interest," and "to take into account the interests of the country as a whole."[98] This logic would guide him away from ideals and toward practicality and Sistani's model of popular sovereignty.

The dearth of commentary on Fayyad's viewpoints among scholars and journalists may reflect a perceived disconnect between his belief in the necessity of an Islamic state and his commitment to clerical noninterference in government. This apparent contradiction between intentions and actions may make Fayyad look confused or inconsequential, but it is better understood as the consequence of rational calculation. Like Sistani, Fayyad demonstrated that he was not an aloof man atop an ossified hierarchical structure. Instead, he displayed a keen political awareness and an ability to recalibrate his stance when necessary. Above all, he showed that his religious views were not inflexible and rigid dictates that must determine his policy choices. In view of real-world circumstances, Fayyad could not allow a desire for the Islamic state to drive his decisions. He knew when it was time to recede into the background.

Ayatollah Bashir Hussein al-Najafi

Ayatollah Sheikh Bashir Hussein al-Najafi was born in 1942 in Jalandhar, a city formerly in British India, and moved to Pakistan after it declared independence in 1947. After receiving his early religious education in Pakistan, Najafi moved to Iraq in the mid-1960s and rose in the ranks of the Shiite clerical hierarchy. He is one of the few clerics of South Asian origin to be elevated to the status of grand ayatollah. Perhaps because of his ethnicity, he is below Sistani in the hierarchy, although he is technically the Iranian's senior in number of years of education. Like Fayyad, Najafi has a larger following outside Iraq than inside.

As is the case with the other ayatollahs of Najaf besides Sistani, there has been very little scholarly study or journalistic coverage of Najafi's output as an ayatollah since 2003. But Najafi has acquired a certain reputation for having a nonconformist attitude toward quietism. This reputation has come about because observers have heard passing comments by or about the ayatollahs, taken them out of context, and invested them with much more meaning than was intended. One journalist who interviewed representatives of the ayatollahs in Karbala surmised from vague evidence that Najafi is an advocate of *velayat-e faqih,* though perhaps not in the "extreme form" adopted by the Islamic Republic of Iran. The reporter further determined that Ayatollah Hakim is "Sistani's closest ally" because he shares Sistani's view that clerical authorities should steer clear of politics.[99] In fact, upon examination of his writings and statements, Najafi is broadly in line with the positions established by Sistani on the proper role of the *marja'iyya,* although he is more specific in his interventions and sometimes more strident in his opinions.

In a publication released in the summer of 2008, *Najaf, the Pioneer for* Hawzas *Around the World,* Ayatollah Najafi responded to a series of questions from his followers outside Iraq about the history of Najaf's *hawza* and the features that distinguish it from other *hawzas* elsewhere. He was explicit that a defining feature of the *hawza* is to train its students to spread its teachings "while avoiding political issues in its multiple forms." He went on to explain that "students are expected to not associate or confuse the *hawza*'s purpose with others." From this perspective, the role of the clerics is to "enrich minds" as believers await the "appearance of the Twelfth Imam *(ajf)*."[100] These words were written in 2008, five years after the US invasion and well into the experiment about what form that quietism would take under the leadership of the *hawza* in Iraq. Najafi had made some statements that praised the legacy of Ayatollah Khomeini as a leader, jurist, and protector of the *hawza*. In a 2012 speech in Khomeini's memory, he stated that the deceased leader of the Islamic Republic, like other clerics, had "fought against tyrants and served as an inspiration to others to revolt."[101] Like Fayyad, when interviewed by a Western journalist he also spoke of his "wish" to form an Islamic state but conceded that it was not possible until "foreign occupiers stop using Iraqis and stop trying to control Iraqi politics."[102] However, these seeming endorsements of Khomeinism cannot be taken out of the context of the actual state-building process in Iraq, lest Najafi's intent be misconstrued. Sistani himself has never said that Khomeini should not be praised for anything. More important, the overwhelming bulk of Najafi's statements and fatwas support the idea that ayatollahs should assume the role of "guide," especially with regard to the electoral process in post-Saddam Iraq. However, Najafi's style and tone are more in line with Fayyad's in that he names names and continually points to the dire consequences of inaction. He is like Fayyad, as well, in his insistence on safeguarding Iraq from cultural encroachment and his treatment of sectarianism. Many analysts and Iraq specialists have identified Najafi as the most vocal grand ayatollah on these pressing issues.

As early as May 2003, Najafi declared, "We do not participate in modern politics because it depends on lies and cheating and insincerity."[103] Yet that categorical statement was not so easy to apply in practice. As the post-Saddam political process unfolded, Najafi took a position similar to that of Sistani that the ayatollahs would exercise a unique brand of activism that rendered them guides to the political process. That stance notwithstanding, he was adamant that he wanted first and foremost a clear separation from Iran and guarantees of the independence of the *hawza* of Iraq. On the occasions that he was asked about Iranian domestic politics—for example, during the Green Movement protests following Iran's June 2009 presidential election—he remained silent. Through his son, Najafi stated, "We have no right to be in politics or government." He added, "There is complete separation between the government and the *hawza*."[104] The following year the French ambassador to Iraq, Boris Boillon, requested that Najafi intercede with Iran to persuade it to halt its nuclear research program. His response was swift—he would deny the request because "it was a political affair that concerned a sovereign state." Najafi also chided the French for their treacherous history of supporting the Ba'ath regime.[105] Likewise, in 2011, when the debate over US withdrawal surfaced, the *hawza* was in agreement that it was up to the people to decide by way of their elected representatives in Parliament whether US forces should remain in the country. Fatwas banning any extension of the US troop presence were issued by ayatollahs based in Iran, such as Ayatollah Haeri. But Najafi rejoined that "the religious authority will not interfere" because elected officials were positioned to settle the matter. He added, "We cannot make a crisis out of every matter in the country."[106] Here we clearly see Najafi making decisions in alignment with Iraqi national interests rather than some transnational Shiiism linking him to Iran or its clerics.

Despite his reputation for nonconformism, Najafi has very much been in step with Sistani's view of quietism. He had exhibited this predilection earlier, in 2006, when he issued a statement in support of the Iraqi government's effort at national reconciliation through a cabinet reshuffle intended to address the deterioration of the security situation and public services. Despite widespread resistance to the reconciliation efforts, Najafi affirmed the need to support the new government in order to "put an end to the bloodshed" and "enhance unity."[107] As the political process matured, he continued to assert his unwillingness to interfere and instead adhered to a position of neutrality during negotiations to form a new government or when the outcome of elections was in question. Najafi adopted a position similar to Sistani's in 2010, when Maliki and Allawi battled over the position of prime minister. Najafi said he would watch the election results closely but that it was not his place to interfere in the elections or the formation of future alliances. He "hope[d]" that a government would form, after a long impasse, but he limited himself to this general statement.[108] In accordance with the rule of law, even if there was strong evidence of electoral fraud or other such indication that Maliki should not have won, legal procedures still had to be followed. From this vantage point, Najafi seemed not to want to meddle in the details of the political process.

At the same time, Najafi has a fiery side. He was committed to the principles of guidance and neutrality in the electoral process, but he took his commentary further than did Sistani, referring directly to politicians and recommending particular courses of action. In December 2005, Najafi openly endorsed the United Iraqi Alliance, the coalition of Shiite Islamists that soon came to power, and he was the only one of the four grand ayatollahs to do so.[109] His endorsement came after much speculation as to whether Sistani had tacitly thrown his weight behind the coalition as well. Najafi did not cover up his endorsement but instead reasoned that it was an attempt to help the fractured bloc and that to do otherwise would "serve the enemies of Iraq."[110]

Over the years, Najafi was vocal about the need for politicians to remain morally upright and spoke loudly against rampant corruption and government inefficiency. He urged politicians to "rise above partisan differences," to address "administrative corruption," and to "shoulder responsibilities, spearheaded by preserving the religious constants of the people and devoting themselves to serve the interests of the Iraqi people."[111] He repeatedly called the Maliki government "deficient," "inefficient," and lacking in "qualified functionaries."[112] He also often made clear that conflict among political blocs had "negative consequences for services and security across Iraq."[113] The big picture was not lost on him.

Yet he often took his criticisms a step further. In preparation for the March 2010 general elections, for instance, Sistani issued a statement urging the *marja'iyya* to maintain strict neutrality toward the various candidates. This plea likely came in reaction to Najafi's withering verbal assaults on key Maliki allies who were up for reelection. Rather than bow to Sistani's wishes, Najafi continued to call out these politicians by name: Education Minister Khudayr al-Khizai, who he said had "betrayed the country," "stolen public money," and helped to create "sectarianism." He also named the acting commerce minister, Safi al-Din Muhammad al-Safi, who was responsible for the ration card system, and the oil minister, Hussein al-Shahristani.[114] In a sermon to his followers, not only did he urge Iraqis to vote for the most deserving candidates, but he also warned people not to reelect "advocates of sectarianism," again denouncing politicians by name.[115]

Najafi was relentless in his critical monitoring of government performance. When Maliki was running for a third term in 2014, amid social unrest and widespread disappointment with his tenure, Sistani fell silent. By contrast, Najafi issued a fatwa that called on the public "not to elect any party that has even one single minister in the government."[116] Sistani urged people to vote and vote wisely. Najafi admonished citizens that "boycotting the elections would usher in new dictatorship" and "allow corrupt officials to retain power."[117]

In his most unprecedented move, Najafi singled out Prime Minister Maliki for opprobrium, going beyond focusing on corrupt politicians from the lower echelons of government. Sistani wanted Maliki to step down in 2014 but endeavored to stay behind the scenes. After Maliki received a no-confidence vote from his own party, Sistani wrote a lukewarm letter to the premier. By contrast, Najafi issued a fatwa that explicitly called for large and broad participation in the elections, directing scathing criticism at the Maliki government and urging voters not to vote for him or his list. Instead, Najafi endorsed the Citizen Coalition, headed by Ammar al-Hakim.[118] Days before the polls opened, Najafi intensified his attack on Maliki by outlining all of his failures. His speech went viral on YouTube.[119] Sistani had pointedly condemned Maliki's actions over the years and insisted that the premier address the legitimate demands of protesters. Yet Sistani, cognizant of the potential harm of intervening, chose to allow the political process to unfold. Najafi, by contrast, did not mince words. He feared that the system would revert to authoritarianism and tyranny. Perhaps these speeches, delivered with noticeable fire in the belly, are what led many commentators to liken Najafi to Khomeini. The analogy in style notwithstanding, Najafi showed no sign of bowing to the doctrine of rule of the jurisprudent or to Tehran's wishes.

A final point on the basic conformity of Najafi to the *hawza* of Najaf: As demonstrated earlier, Sistani helped to lay the groundwork for a civil state (*dawla madaniyya*) in Iraq. The term can take on many meanings. It was first used by a Lebanese cleric, Ayatollah Muhsin Shams al-Din, who argued that Shiites were better off organized into territorial states and that the state should not assume a religious function. After 2003,

Sistani demonstrated that the state, rather than drawing upon Islamic law, should be formed on the basis of equal citizenship and a regulated relationship between religion and politics. Over the course of his involvement in the political process, he advocated for an inclusive process of reconciliation to see this process through. In fact, all the grand ayatollahs—Najafi included—remained committed to this platform of equality as a foundational principle. In 2010 Najafi objected to the introduction of a new high school textbook that described the different rites of Sunni and Shiite Islam. He rejected overtly sectarian teaching in the school system. At the time, Najafi declared that he would not be silent in his role as an ayatollah unless people wanted to "go back to the era of Saddam Hussein."[120] Likewise, he reacted sharply to the personal status law proposed in 2014 to set out rules for marriage, divorce, and inheritance. Opponents worried that the bill before Parliament represented a step backward for women's rights in that it reduced the age of marriage to nine. Critics also felt the bill could harm the fragile cross-sectarian ties in the country by granting autonomy in matters of personal status to various religious groups. Najafi issued a fatwa against the bill, stating that it had several "legal and doctrinal" problems and asserting that no credible scholar would agree with its provisions.[121] Najafi blamed the Virtue Party, and its spiritual leader, Muhammad al-Yacoubi, for bringing such a bill to the national assembly.[122] He made clear that the grand ayatollahs were not involved in the process. Ultimately, like his peers, Najafi maintained a commitment to the general principle of guidance and a recognition of political circumstances in his religious decrees.

Overall, the clerics of Najaf tended to follow Sistani's cues on major issues pertaining to the formation of government. They agreed that the proper role for ayatollahs was to "give advice and guidance." They all wanted the democratic process to unfold without their direct intervention, which they feared would render it illegitimate. But inaction in this context was action. Even in instances where the *hawza* adhered to a "position of neutrality," the term favored by Najafi, the ayatollahs' refusal to interfere in the outcomes of negotiations was a powerful statement. The ayatollahs agreed that they would watch the political process "closely." But the *hawza* responded to all allegations of electoral fraud with insistence on seeking redress through legal avenues. Fraud was not a pretext for the ayatollahs' intervention because the "religious authority cannot intervene in every detail."[123]

This mode of engagement was certainly far from the rule of the juris-prudent preached by Khomeini. Yet neither was it quietism as classically understood. The ayatollahs of Iraq, prudent and strategic, practiced a dif-ferent type of activism. It was an activism that freed them from the chains of state accountability yet allowed them to remain connected to the streets and their followers.

5

LOCAL AND REGIONAL SECTARIAN NARRATIVES

The 2003 invasion and the subsequent policies of the United States and its Iraqi allies effectively changed the structure of the Iraqi state. Nominally, before the war Iraq was a secular republic; in fact, it was a dictatorship controlled by Saddam Hussein and small circles at the top of the Ba'ath Party. Nominally, after the war Iraq was also a secular republic, but in fact it became an amalgam of fiefdoms allocated among former opposition parties according to a confessional logic. The change in state structure was framed in terms of representative democracy, the idea being that Iraqi communities that had been excluded or oppressed under Saddam would find redress. But the new state structure was widely perceived both in Iraq and the region as altering the basis of formal politics to ethno-sectarian affiliation as opposed to ideology or political program. More ominously, many Sunni Arabs in Iraq, as well as neighboring Sunni regimes, saw the change as empowering Shiites (and, to a lesser degree, Kurds) at the expense of Sunni Arabs. These perceptions were exacerbated by US policies such as the dissolution of the army officer corps and debaathification, whose costs were disproportionately borne by Sunnis.

Sunni Arab leaders in Iraq increasingly came to think of themselves, and even describe themselves, as Sunni rather than Iraqi. An example of this is the Association of Muslim Scholars, which was formed on April 14, 2003, four days after the US-led invasion. That group spoke of a "Sunni *marja'iyya*" and developed a theory of jurisprudence.[1] They encouraged a mass Sunni boycott of the January 2005 elections, which gave Shiite Islamist parties a large plurality in the transitional assembly that was to draft a new constitution. Violence escalated that year, with insurgent groups battling both the US military and the nascent security forces of the new Iraqi state. Already in 2004, King Abdullah of Jordan had coined the term "Shiite crescent" to connote the possible formation of a Shiite coalition of power stretching from Iran through Iraq into Lebanon. The rulers of Saudi Arabia and Egypt picked up the theme, warning of a Shiite bloc dominated by Iran that would threaten the regional balance of power. By 2006, as the fighting in Iraq intensified further, a new regional discourse revolved around this notion of "threat" from a "Shiite rise."

This discourse, in turn, helped to generate the parallel notion that the conflict in post-Saddam Iraq was sectarian in nature. The embittered Sunni Arab minority, in the common telling, was resisting the attempt of the Shiite majority to rule with the aid of the Kurds. In the West, and particularly in the United States, the sectarian view of the war dovetailed with long-standing ahistorical understandings of Iraq as a uniquely artificial state "cobbled together" from disparate communities who did not—and could not—make up a nation. This view does not consider the contribution of the US-led invasion and the policy choices that led to the communal discord. It was easier to assert that the best model for Iraq was a sectarian one, based on the flawed assumption that only the iron fist of someone like Saddam Hussein could keep these warring religious factions from one another's throats.

The ayatollahs tackled this rhetoric head-on. They rejected both the sectarian interpretation of Iraqi history and its implications for Iraq's present and future. Far from dreaming of a "Shiite crescent," as they were accused of doing, they appealed to pan-Iraqi unity and nationalism.

In the simplest terms, sectarianism is discrimination or hatred—institutionalized or informal—that arises from attaching importance to perceived differences between subdivisions within religious or political groups. The discourses of the ayatollahs that proliferated after the war supported the claim, consistent with good historical research, that sectarianism in Iraq was a construct, a prophecy with a false premise that nevertheless was self-fulfilling.[2] By 2005, there was indeed horrendous sectarian violence in Iraq. Yet these conflicts, however real, were not built upon 1,400 years of inborn hostility between Sunnis and Shiites, and did not represent a continuous historical record of ongoing fighting between these sects in Iraq. To call the sectarian fighting a construct, as I do in this chapter, is to point instead to the role of historical contingency in the post-2003 conflict. That is, sectarianism was not inevitable or intrinsic to Iraqi culture; it was the result of specific policies pursued by various state and nonstate actors in the interest of their own power.

As this chapter demonstrates, the ayatollahs challenged the construct of sectarianism and worked hard to undo the narrative that held Iraq to be a "patchwork" of incommensurable groups. They instead offered a counter-narrative of unity and harmony and issued decrees about the harm of communal violence. Most importantly, the ayatollahs wrote extensively about the need for a centralized state and a redefinition of citizenship away from sectarian notions.

Yet the ayatollahs had a much harder time dealing with the sectarian crisis than they did with any other single issue with which they were confronted, including voter turnout and Paul Bremer's constitutional plans. The reason was simple: The stakes were too high. Sectarianism in post-Saddam Iraq was about life and death. Entire families were being exterminated. The ayatollahs were very aware of the dire situation. Their fatwas were plentiful, filled with warnings and in many cases direct and vivid references to the Quran and imagery of heaven and hell. But where people were likely to follow the ayatollahs when it came to voting and legislative issues, they did not necessarily listen when it came to matters of existential urgency. The ayatollahs, despite their repeated pleas, were not able to stop the violence in the streets.

That is not to suggest that the ayatollahs lacked clout or that they failed. They could not possibly have gained control of the sustained and indiscriminate violence. Nor does their inability to rein in Shiite militias suggest that the ayatollahs' thinking on the matter ran contrary to the impulse and spirit of their followers. Rather, although it was started by the policies of state actors, the violence eventually took on a life of its own. My concern here is the proliferation of the ayatollahs' counter-narratives. As public intellectuals, they were setting the parameters for the proper discourse, correcting misinformation, calling out local and regional leaders, and setting moral examples for society. The ayatollahs' activism and political contribution formed a counter-discourse that directly refuted what their enemies imputed to them.

In many ways, as the last section of this chapter explores, we cannot understand the proliferation of the sectarian conflict talk throughout the region without contextualizing its origins in the formation of Iraq as a confessional system that would be perceived as a "Shiite state." The ayatollahs were aware of Iraq's ripple effect in the region. They wanted to make sure that the "Shiite crescent" narrative did not itself become a self-fulfilling prophecy, for they, too, were keen not to magnify Iran's power over Iraq and its clerical class. The ayatollahs' nonsectarian stance in the regional discourse underscored their fierce independence and their ability to distinguish their own voices from those of ayatollahs under the thumb of the Islamic Republic next door. For Najaf to be subsumed under Qom, and for Baghdad to be enfeebled at the hands of Tehran, would go against the grain of their defense of Iraqi nationalism.

Iraq had been dealing with "sectarian" violence since the start of the war, as clashes between Sunnis and Shiites became daily occurrences. At the peak of this violence in 2006–2007, Iraq was commonly described as experiencing a civil war[3] and was labeled a "collapsed state."[4] The February 22, 2006, bombing of the al-Askari Mosque in Samarra, one of the holiest sites for Shiites, marked a turning point in Iraq. It unleashed unprecedented sectarian retaliatory violence that ripped through the country. Al-Qaeda in Mesopotamia, which later morphed into ISIS, was waging an explicitly anti-Shiite war against the security forces of the government in Baghdad and associated militias. The Ministry of Interior, controlled by the Shiite party then called the Supreme Council for the Islamic Revolution in Iraq, ran death squads that targeted Sunnis.

The intercommunal tensions had not come out of nowhere. The Ba'athist regime had stirred up anti-Shiite sentiment on several occasions as part of a strategy of divide and rule. In the wake of the 1991 war, Saddam's forces used anti-Shiite slogans during the brutal repression of the uprising in the South. Many of the victims of that repression were found in mass graves unearthed after 2003. The tensions were fueled after Saddam's fall by the dissolution of the army and debaathification, policies of the US occupation authority that took away jobs, pensions, and state sub-sidies from tens of thousands, many of whom were Sunni Arabs.[5] But the scale and intensity of the sectarian fighting from 2006 to 2007 was with-out precedent in modern times. Even more alarming was what happened after that convulsion was thought to be over—the fragmentation of Iraqi territory along sectarian lines when ISIS began to capture towns in 2013.[6] ISIS proceeded to take major cities in 2014, although by December 2015 the Iraqi Army had recaptured Sunni-dominated Ramadi, the capital of Anbar province, eighty miles west of Baghdad.

To observers with a superficial grasp of Iraqi history, it was hardly sur-prising that post-Saddam Iraq would erupt in sectarian violence. These ob-servers were in the grip of the artificiality thesis, which holds that communal tensions in Iraq are timeless and ready to explode at any moment. The artifi-ciality thesis maintains that modern-day Iraq was "cobbled together" from three Ottoman provinces (*vilayets*)—Baghdad, Basra, and Mosul—by the British in 1921. Iraq was a "patchwork," as Gertrude Bell, a British colo-nial official at the time, lamented.[7] She entrusted King Faysal, whom she imported from Arabia, with the keys to the kingdom. Faysal lacked any con-nection with the indigenous population and repeatedly expressed his disdain for them. The creation of Faysal's kingdom, supported by a heavily Sunni Arab bureaucracy and army officer corps, effectively continued the Otto-man tradition of rule by the Sunni minority over the Shiite majority.

The artificiality thesis rests on the premise that the three provinces of Mosul, Baghdad, and Basra had no political connection to one another. The link of this thesis to sectarian analysis is the understanding that these provinces were populated by Kurds, Sunnis, and Shiites (in that order) and that these groups had experienced chronic conflict. The artificiality thesis was convenient for defenders of the US invasion who sought to explain the high levels of violence in Iraq after 2003. If Iraqis had always been fighting one another, no wonder they were doing so again. It was also convenient for critics of Bush administration policy such as Senator Joe Biden, who advocated a "three-state solution" loosely tracking the boundaries of the Ottoman provinces.[8] If there was no good reason for Iraq to be together in the first place, there was no reason for the United States to back a strong central government in Baghdad.

But the artificiality thesis was most consequential in the formation of actual policy by Bremer and the Coalition Provisional Authority, which effectively constructed the new state along confessional lines, as in Lebanon. In Lebanon the arrangement is de jure; in Iraq it is de facto, but the effects on politics are similar.

The artificiality thesis lives on in textbooks, popular histories, and media coverage.[9] But, oddly for a thesis purporting to be grounded in Ottoman history, it is not based on primary sources from Ottoman archives.[10] Reidar Visser, working from those archives, offers the most compelling rebuttal of the myth of the unique artificiality of Iraq. It is fairly common among historians of Iraq to assert that all states are artificial, according to the framework of Benedict Anderson's classic *Imagined Communities,* and to view Iraq as akin to every other modern nation in this respect. For example, Sami Zubaida offers a sophisticated application of such theory to the Iraqi case by drawing out the complexities of subnational identities. He argues that the tripartite description of Iraq is a "caricature," one that obscures the presence of modern civil society in twentieth-century Iraq, which included the active participation of all communities. He gives several examples. The famous 1920 rebellion against British occupation was composed of a coalition of interest groups such as the Shiite clergy, Ottoman officials, and tribes. More-contemporary political parties such as the Communist Party of Iraq and the National Democratic Party have included Shiites, Christians, Jews, and Kurds. Zubaida notes that in all instances of political activism, the identity of Iraqis was expressed using the modern vocabulary of "nations, representation, and constitutions."[11]

By contrast, Visser offers a deep historical analysis of Iraqi identity that traces a long line back to Baghdad. He demonstrates that Mesopotamia has a rich history of a vibrant political life that included the three provinces, with a political center in Baghdad, dating back hundreds of years. He shows the presence of a strong precursor of statehood prior to the actual formation of the state in 1921. His analysis is meant to show that the territorial and political unity that defined the identity of Iraqis predates the emergence of the concept of the nation-state.[12] Iraq's story, in his telling, is thus more than the simple, if correct, narrative that "all states are artificial and imagined" and "states build nations."[13]

Visser demonstrates that all of the assumptions about Iraq's artificiality and sectarian origins are, to put it bluntly, historically incorrect. For one thing, the *vilayets* of Iraq had no particular or unique sectarian coloring. For example, there were always more Shiites in Baghdad than in Basra in the South. Mosul, defined as home to the Kurds by the terms of the artificiality thesis, was in fact a mixed province of Arabs, Kurds, and a half dozen other groups. The heavily Kurdish regions are only one part of Mosul. Politically, all three provinces were Sunni Arab–dominated. Moreover, British plans to divide the *vilayets* of Basra and Baghdad were based not on a sectarian calculation but more on the strategic importance of Basra as a gateway to India, rendering the "tripartite division of Iraq as ahistorical." The division of Iraq into three *vilayets* was present in 1914, but that had been the case for only thirty years. Previously, there had been a great variety of administrative divisions, oscillating between establishing more than three *vilayets* and a structure that looked very much like the Iraq of today.[14] Historians who popularized the artificiality thesis were therefore studying the immediate history only, rather than taking the longer view.[15]

Visser talked about Baghdad as the undisputed capital of Iraq for most of the time between its foundation in 762 and the Ottoman conquest in 1534. He investigated the various subunits that emerged in Iraqi administrative history and that were consistently nonsectarian and nonethnic in character, especially during the Ottoman era. Holy cities such as Najaf were no exception, and it was hard to conceive of the Shiites outside of Baghdad's political jurisdiction. Accordingly, there was no such thing as a purely Sunni or Shiite administrative entity. All such entities were mixed. More importantly, the Ottomans used the concept of Iraq in an administrative sense in the nineteenth century, as did many local writers at the time. History shows the durability of the territorial and conceptual framework of Iraq.

To make the case that unity was a likely historical outcome, Visser pointed to the absence of major separatist movements that we would expect to see historically if there were indeed deep divisions in society and fragmented administrative structures. The famous Basra movement for the creation of a separate Gulf state in the 1920s, which Visser highlights in his work, was nonsectarian. It was composed of a range of political and economic elites, and headed by a coalition of Sunnis from Najd, Christians, Jews, and a few wealthy Persians, with the Shiite Arab majority of Basra uninvolved in the movement. Visser conceded that sectarianism did emerge from time to time, but it was the exception, not the norm.

If we fast-forward to events such as the 1979 revolution in Iran and Ayatollah Khomeini's attempt to export that revolution by inviting Shiites to unite to overthrow the Iraqi regime, we learn that the majority in Iraq did not respond. They chose Iraqi nationalism and local identity over the call for Shiite universalism. The same can be said of the war between Iran and Iraq from 1980 to 1988, when Khomeini again invited Shiites to secede from the state, and they again chose their Iraqi identity over his call. The long historical record in Iraq demonstrated that Iraqi identity was solid and that the unity was grounded in factors that transcended and bridged religious differences. In fact, religious differences were not part of the calculations of Iraqis as they navigated their political community historically. The historical record contains little evidence of an "ancient sectarian battle." The Kurds are perhaps a separate case, having rebelled against both the British and the independent Iraqi state. But, as far as religious differences among Muslims in Arab Iraq go, the record is more consistent with long-term coexistence. In fact, there is evidence that Iraqis transcended the categories of "Sunni and Shiite" that were imposed on them in 2003.

The Ayatollahs' Responses

The grand ayatollahs are among the most outspoken critics of the sectarian model, and indirectly their opinions supported the conclusions of scholars on Iraq who challenged the artificiality thesis. They wrote extensively about the need for a centralized state to maintain the integrity of Iraq. They tried to calm the violence with fatwas, speeches, and letters to counter the delegitimization of the Shiites and calls for their destruction. They argued that Iraqi identity should be inclusive of all sects rather than defined by a power-sharing agreement that favored one sect at the expense of others. Most interestingly, this reality ran counter to the popular perception that religious leaders were the primary source of sectarian thinking, as claimed, for instance, by the malicious Abu Musab al-Zarqawi, leader of al-Qaeda in Mesopotamia. This finding is perhaps counterintuitive, given that the ayatollahs operate from a traditional religious institutional setting that is often considered to be more conservative in orientation.

A sampling of the ayatollahs' writings suggests that they had reasonable, calculated responses to the US initiatives on the ground. Their statements and rulings were progressive and enlightened in comparison to both the "colonial-style" policies of the United States and the policies of Iraqi allies of the United States, which fueled sectarianism. The ayatollahs renounced violence and stressed the need for Iraqi unity at this critical juncture in the country's history.

After 2003, sectarianism was among the most widely discussed topics in Iraq by those concerned with rebuilding the state or preventing its fragmentation along the confessional lines of the US blueprint.[16] Radical Sunni Islamist insurgents, led by Zarqawi, raised the sectarian stakes with indiscriminate attacks against Shiites, hoping that reprisals, chaos, and civil war would expedite the withdrawal of US forces. Zarqawi's anti-Shiism was so bloody that the international al-Qaeda leadership to whom he had pledged allegiance later disavowed him. He wrote extensively about a two-front battle: one against the United States and the other against the Shiites. He described Shiites as "the insurmountable obstacle, the lurking snake, the crafty and malicious scorpion, the spying enemy, and the penetrating venom."[17] He also maintained that Shiism was riddled with atheism, polytheism, and infidelity. Zarqawi argued that the problems between Sunnis and Shiites were age-old and could not be reconciled, leaving only the option to "drag them into battle."[18] The US policies contributing to communal divisions were fodder for Zarqawi, who wanted to see the two main branches of Islam perpetually at war with each other.

This radicalism brought a strong response from the ayatollahs. Fatwas to counter this narrative envisioned a nationalism that included Sunnis, Shiites, Christians, Arabs, Turkmen, and Kurds all under one state. The ayatollahs wrote repeatedly that the killing of Muslims, regardless of sect, was a hateful act. Ayatollah Ali al-Sistani went so far as to declare that his fatwas were binding on all Muslims, not just Shiites. His effort to embrace all Muslims, not only the fraction of Shiites who followed him, was unprecedented and quite noteworthy. It shows that, contrary to standard narratives that portrayed him as focused solely on matters of Shiite theology and ritual, he sought to reach a broad national audience.

Ayatollah Kazem al-Haeri, a grand ayatollah who resided in Iran after his exile from Iraq in the 1970s, also declined to blame Sunnis as a group for sectarian violence. The senior cleric argued that Islam did not differentiate between sects and that both were equal, regardless of demographics. Most importantly, he argued that attempts to divide Iraq along ethno-sectarian lines did not accurately depict the reality on the ground, as those lines were blurred. Haeri was writing about the sectarian problem well before 2003. His thoughts were best summarized in a statement he made in July 2002, in which he attributed the problems in Iraq not to "our Sunni brothers" but to "tyrannical governments" that effectively trampled on the rights of both Shiites and Sunnis. He declared that all Muslims enjoyed "equality of rights under the mantle of Islam," with recognition of the rights of other national minorities "in parallel" to the Arabs of the state. He therefore argued that it was not proper to advocate that power "be shifted" from Sunnis to Shiites because the "scholars of Islam had all agreed that Islam does not differentiate between the rights of Muslims, irrespective of their sects."

Haeri was a signatory to the "Declaration of the Shia of Iraq," a statement that received widespread support from leading scholars and jurists in the summer before the invasion. That document attributed the problems in Iraq to the "conduct of an overtly sectarian authority determined to pursue a policy of discrimination solely for its own interests of control, a policy that has ultimately led to the total absence of political and cultural liberties." Because of this history, it would not be possible for Iraq to emerge out of the crisis "without the complete banishment of official sectarianism from any future political construct, and its replacement by a contract premised on a broad and patriotic definition of citizenship that is far removed from sectarian calculations and divisions."[19] The statement continued that Shiites wanted this contract as much as anyone else and that any solutions based on the "division of the spoils according to demographic formulae" would create conditions that would result in "sectarianism becoming a social and political reality rather than a manifestation of an unscrupulous state authority."[20]

With this statement and others, Haeri and the other grand ayatollahs declared that the lessons from Iraq's history were clear: The Shiites had at no point sought to establish their own state or unique political entity. Haeri summed it up best by saying that when the opportunity was afforded to them, the Shiites had participated "enthusiastically in nationwide political movements and organizations, ever conscious of the need to maintain national unity."[21] Generally speaking, the ayatollahs of Iraq chose to identify with their fellow citizens in political, not sectarian, terms. This choice was all the more compelling because scholarship on the Middle East has often erroneously attributed the formation of political identities among people in the region to religion and ethnicity. Scholars had argued that Muslim communities could not envision modern nation-states because their association with one another was organized around an *umma*, a religious community that transcended geographic borders. It has even been said that Arabs cannot entertain modern notions of "nation" and "state" because these words did not exist in the Arabic language, at least not as exact corollaries to usage in the West.[22] This thinking was derived from faulty assumptions made about Muslim societies, based on incomplete and nonauthoritative history texts. Roger Owen deconstructed some of the major arguments made by scholars in the interwar period. These were assumptions about "Islamic culture" and how it divided societies between "ruler and ruled." The culture, based on a literal reading of the Quran, was "absolute," requiring an authoritarian leader to contain factionalism. These "Islamic societies" were purely religious societies in which the "theory of the caliphate" or sharia law were seen as reflective of the real world. Owen critiqued the work of Gibb and Bowen's *Islamic Society and the West,* a late-eighteenth-century study of Ottoman and Arab society. This interwar study was never completed, but its major arguments have resonated in scholarship over the years.[23] Despite the fact that Owen's critique of scholars during the interwar period was written in 1976, the arguments about Muslim societies continued to be repeated. Crucially, it was the modern discourse that the ayatollahs embraced directly, working to dispel these hackneyed myths in progressive and modern ways. Religious actors, not secular ones, were at the forefront of the process.

Each of the grand ayatollahs approached the issue of sectarianism in his own way, addressing the violence and the policies of the United States and the Iraqi government in a unique style. However, all of the ayatollahs were clear from the beginning that the violence was not to be tolerated, as they were perhaps wary of the consequences of a quietist position for the integrity of the state. This basic stand inspired a broad shift in the ayatollahs' attitude toward the Iraqi government: In 2011 the senior clerics broke off communication with the government in response to the corruption described in chapter 4, and by 2014 they were issuing fatwas in support of the military's campaign to push back ISIS. The pragmatic shift, reflective of their rational calculations, was an important collective statement. The existential crisis threatened not only individuals in Iraq who were at the heart of the sectarian fighting but also the nation-state at the heart of their discourse.

Grand Ayatollah Ali al-Husseini al-Sistani

The output of Ayatollah Sistani rebukes the conventional wisdom that Iraq is composed of warring factions whose impulses can be suppressed only by a strong leader. From the very beginning of the war, Sistani was asked if he feared the onset of sectarian strife in Iraq. He replied, "No, we do not have such fears if foreign parties do not interfere in Iraqi affairs."[24] On many occasions he was asked to comment on the US intervention and occupation. In all instances, he opposed the notion that Iraq should be saved by outsiders. He was also adamant that Iraqis should be free to choose their own leaders and form of government, although he was never explicit about exactly which form of government that should be. His line was usually that Iraqis should decide these matters through a national dialogue and elections. In response to a question about his vision for Iraq, Sistani summarized these points: "His Eminence ensures the principle stating that governance in Iraq must be for Iraqis and free of any authority or foreigner; Iraqis have the right to choose the system applied in Iraq without any intervention from foreigners."[25] When the sectarian state structure was unveiled, which favored the Shiite Islamist and Kurdish parties allied with the United States, many thought the mass of Shiites would embrace the initiative. Reporters flooded the ayatollahs with questions about what they imagined would be the "Shiite" position. But Sistani disappointed them. In response to a question about whether the Shiites in Iraq were more unified after the invasion, for example, Sistani responded, "If foreign hands do not interfere in Iraqi affairs, the people of all sects in Iraq will be more harmonized and converged."[26]

Sistani contended that sectarianism was a foreign creation and that sectarian violence was a symptom of this construct. Accordingly, most of his assessments of the security situation described acts of violence simply as "criminal acts." His explanation of the violence was always linked to the occupation, which he said bore "all the responsibility for what Iraq witnesses, including the breakdown of security and the increase in criminal operations."[27] He refused to answer questions about Iraq without reminding his audience of the conditions under which he was questioned. A seemingly innocent question that asked his opinion about the proper duration of US occupation usually got an abrupt answer: "How can we support the existence of occupation forces in Iraq?"[28]

Consistent with his description of sectarian attacks as crimes, Sistani tried to give al-Qaeda in Mesopotamia as little attention as possible in his speeches and pronouncements. Rather than calling the group by its name, Sistani preferred to refer instead to its acts as "threats" from a "deviant class."[29] As the most widely followed ayatollah in the world, Sistani refused to give Zarqawi and his overtly sectarian discourse free publicity.

Although Sistani made clear his disdain for Saddam Hussein, he was equally adamant that it had not been "his desire to change the despotic regime by invasion and occupation." He lamented the tragedies that followed, which included the "lack of security and stability."[30] Sistani emphasized commitment to the rule of law, and he eyed cautiously the growing and increasingly dangerous militias. When asked if individuals should carry weapons for self-defense, he embraced the Weberian idea that the state has a monopoly on the legitimate use of physical force. Accordingly, "[A]ll weapons looted by the country are the possession of the country," and no one else should be "carrying weapons" or "shooting bullets."[31] He was asked about the rise of Muqtada al-Sadr, who not only had his own militia, Jaysh al-Mahdi, but also sought to collect money from looted property to establish offices. Sistani repeated that under no conditions would militias be allowed, "not even in exceptional cases to protect the *hawza* or to monitor or maintain public ethics."[32] He refused to acknowledge Sadr by name, usually offering a response of "no comment" when asked about the young cleric's actions.[33] If the question sought to elicit a comparison between Sadr and Sistani, he would comment that his own vision for Iraq was clear and that he "did not take into consideration what others mentioned regarding these issues."[34] Long before the death squads and the unleashing of al-Qaeda in Iraq, Sistani was setting up the principle of the legitimacy of the central authorities and warning about what would come with the rise of militias.

Sistani warned that if the central authorities did not assert control, "serious problems would occur in the future, and this would not be due to the Shiites."[35] He worried that, as the majority in the country, the Shiites would be blamed. Accordingly, he repeatedly warned about the interference of "foreign parties" in Iraqi affairs. He spoke of himself as "keen since the first days of the occupation" to help Iraqis endure this critical time without "falling into the trap of sectarian and ethnic sedition."[36] He argued that he was aware of the "plans of strangers" to destroy Iraq.[37] The words "foreign" and "strangers" have two plausible meanings as used by Sistani. The first was a historical reference to the disenfranchisement of the Shiites by the process of state formation under British colonial rule. Much of the sectarian strife at that time was caused by British meddling. The analogy to the role of the United States after 2003 was obvious. The second reference was to Sunni extremists who were not indigenous to Iraq among the insurgents. For example, Zarqawi was from Jordan. Moreover, some of the Shiite militants who were inciting sectarian violence in Iraq had been in exile in Iran under Saddam, fought on the Iranian side during the eight-year war, and still had the sponsorship of Iran's Revolutionary Guards. Sistani laid out a narrative whereby the violence in Iraq was born outside of the country's borders.

As the violence devolved into full-blown civil war, it was clear that Sistani could not control the various factions. He could issue fatwas calling for calm and then remain steadfast that tit-for-tat reprisal was prohibited, but the violence continued in the streets. In his fatwas he pleaded with citizens to put their trust in the courts to administer justice for the wrongs they had suffered. He argued that vigilante action "was not permissible."[38] In a statement released after the uncovering of a group of mass graves, Sistani insisted, "Retribution was a right for the guardians of the slain only after the crime had been proven in a legal court."[39]

Although Sistani was unable to halt the violence, he tried to drown out the sectarian discourse with an alternative narrative. Sistani typically began his narrative by showing years of cooperation between Sunnis and Shiites, and he decried the "ignorance" of those who downplayed that historical reality. He highlighted the collaboration among Iraqis in "the 1920 Iraqi revolution, confronting the British occupation, and defending their country whenever it had been attacked."[40] He waited a long time before he even used the term "sectarianism." Throughout 2005 he referred to the violence as "organized crime."[41] By the middle of the following year, however, he did acknowledge "sectarianism" and lament that despite his best efforts, "there was no deterrent."[42] Sistani's statement in mid-2006, filled with commentary about "heart-wrenching news and pain," was reflective of the statistics. That year was the deadliest one for civilians in Iraq between 2003 and 2014, with the largest number of fatalities occurring in July.[43] Still, Sistani called on Iraqis of "all different sects" to "throw away hatred and violence and substitute love and peaceful dialogue in order to solve all disputes." He referred to all Iraqis as "brothers of humanity" and "partners in the motherland."[44] His emotional appeal followed the months of violence after the February 2006 bombing of the al-Askari Mosque in Samarra.

Sistani's anti-sectarian discourse was consistent with his overall emphasis upon nonviolent collaboration among Iraqis to end foreign intervention. On March 31, 2003, the *New York Times* asked Sistani about direct calls for resistance to the American occupation: Would he call on his Shiite followers to heed them? Sistani's message, reiterated on several occasions, began with the exhortation to "follow peaceful methods for accelerating the process of restoring Iraq's sovereignty."[45]

When asked if a "schism" had developed on the issue of resistance against the United States, Sistani objected to the term, calling it the result of the "thinking of a few people." Sovereignty, according to the ayatollah, would "prevent the development of matters according to this trend."[46] He understood the power of constructive narratives: No deep-seated differences existed historically or even at the time, but the "trend" of a schism could become another self-fulfilling prophecy if foreign intervention continued. Therefore, Sistani's rejection was not a blind denial of the events on the ground. Much like Visser asserting that sectarianism in Iraq was a construct, Sistani acknowledged that although its roots were artificial, sectarianism was quickly becoming a reality as the post-Saddam state was institutionalized. In addition to the role of foreign intervention, Sistani made connections between a sectarian state and sectarian fighting. He argued that the majority of Iraqis agreed that "it is necessary to establish a new regime which adopts the principles of justice and equality among all people."[47] He commented upon how corruption in government was linked to sectarian fighting. In a statement to Prime Minister Maliki, Sistani urged him to "take care of the higher national interest and ignore personal, party and sectarian interests." He warned that he would "monitor the government's performance" and "support the voices of the oppressed regardless of their sect."[48] These steps would be necessary to ensure a sovereign and unified Iraq.

In essence, Sistani offered a consistent reminder of cause and effect regarding the events under way in Iraq. His interpretation of the cause explains his counter-narrative—his consistent commitment to the rule of law and his position on militias. He always said there was no place for the formation of "special armies" by either men of religion—including himself—or by other groups outside of the structure of the state. He also declared the Iraqi Army to be the "national army."[49] Sistani saw the armed forces as the key to intercommunal peace and continued to warn over the years that the security forces needed to remain neutral, free of both militias and political or partisan interference.

When asked if he was willing to engage in a dialogue with the Sunnis of Iraq, Sistani immediately referred to them as "brothers" and urged direct meetings because Sunni and Shiite views were similar on most of the primary issues. If a dispute existed, direct dialogue was the best method to resolve it.[50] For Sistani, the key to ending the sectarian conflict was a state built on the principles of justice and equality for all people, in addition to his earlier points about pluralism and respect for the opinions of others.[51]

Sistani was often asked if he believed that the Shiites were more unified and collaborative than the Sunnis. He viewed this question as a divisive one that hinted at Shiite superiority. Usually, he stayed away from answering such questions phrased in the abstract. That would be dangerous essentialism. His line was that if foreign hands did not intervene in Iraqi affairs, all the people of Iraq, all religious sects, would be "harmonized and converged."[52] In the category of foreign hands, he included neighboring countries, likely a nod to Saudi Arabia and Iran.[53] Again, Sistani was careful in his semantics and was slow to use the word "sectarian" freely. While many Western commentators saw sectarianism as a legacy of Iraqi history, Sistani and the ayatollahs recontextualized it as a legacy of the invasion and of the commentary itself.

When Ayatollah Muhammad Baqir al-Hakim was killed months after his return to Iraq in 2003, Sistani issued a series of statements calling the dead cleric a martyr. He referred to a series of "brutal crimes" committed by foes of security and stability in Iraq, who wished instead to sow discord among its people. Sistani was confident in his communiqués that the people of Iraq were cognizant of this "fact" and would stand united so the enemy would not achieve its goals. He also held the occupation forces responsible for the security breakdown in the country.[54] His ideas meshed with critical thinking on terrorism that makes a connection between foreign military presence and the rise of insurgent activity.[55] There was no al-Qaeda in Iraq prior to the US invasion.

Of course, when Sistani downplayed the Sunni-Shiite conflict, he was trying to counter the influence of those who looked for, or assumed, deeper historical roots to explain sectarianism in Iraq. Clearly, he had a fear of the crisis escalating into something bigger. He warned of the dangers on many occasions. In one instance, he said that the Iraqi Army needed to act quickly to "strengthen its forces, confiscate the unlicensed weapons from the armed groups, and provide security and stability."[56] If these steps were not taken, he said, the Shiites should not be held responsible.[57] Sistani meant that because the Shiites were the majority and Shiite parties had been entrusted with the state, it would be easy to blame Shiites as a group for Iraq's problems.

In the early days of the conflict, Sistani's language was intended to contextualize the conflict and stress that there were no inherent religious conflicts among Iraqis. By 2005, Sistani was using the term "civil war" to describe what was happening on the ground in Iraq—to provoke such strife, he said, had been Zarqawi's goal.[58]

By the beginning of 2006, it was commonplace to refer to the civil war in Iraq as "sectarian." Sistani referred often to his earlier speeches in which he had warned Iraqis of the trap of ethnic and sectarian sedition. He acknowledged the cumulative effects of the violence upon the unity of the people. He pointed to the "strangers" who had "plotted these crimes." Sistani understood that whatever doctrinal differences did exist among Iraqis were magnified by acts such as the bombing of the shrine of the two imams in May 2006. He talked about the "blind violence" all over the country as something that was happening under false pretexts.[59] Sistani called on all Iraqis to "discard hatred and violence in favor of love and peaceful dialogue," however challenging that task. The violence required that people loyal to Iraq—politicians, religious leaders, and tribal heads—collaborate in putting a stop to it. Iraq, he said, would come "fully out of the current impasse" when "all partners decide to prohibit the spilling of Iraqi blood and end all forms of violence."[60]

Sistani reminded Muslims that they should "model the Prophet and that they must value the souls of the innocent," regardless of their feeling for the sect to which they belong. He quoted the Prophet: "Whoever helps to kill a believer, even with half of a word, will meet Almighty God with the word written between his eyes. He has no hope of mercy from God."[61] As for those who targeted civilians, he quoted famous lines from the imams: "If you have no religion and are not afraid of the day of judgment, you are free in your life and may return to your families."[62] He used religious language in an attempt to appeal to those who were using a religious argument for the attacks. He deplored the targeting of innocent people who had no role in politics, saying, "If your religion does not prevent you from committing these acts, may your humanity prevent you." He expressly included non-Muslims (Christians and Sabeans) in his comments and declared that the spilling of any and all Iraqi blood was prohibited. He contrasted scenes of "car bombs, random executions in the streets, and forced displacements" with visions of "constructive dialogue that is based on justice and equality." He warned that the violent acts would "reignite authoritarian tendencies and policies for sectarian and ethnic control."[63] He understood that the balance between security and liberty was delicate, and he repeatedly mentioned security alongside his support for free elections and democracy.

Although he acknowledged the real problems on the ground, he never referred to the violence as a Sunni-Shiite religious conflict. In response to reporters' questions about the role of religious leaders in a solution to the "Sunni-Shiite conflict," Sistani vehemently rejected the sectarian categorization, saying that no such religious conflict existed. He said it was a political conflict, used opportunistically to mold a sectarian conflict. He stated clearly that "there was no Sunni-Shiite religious conflict in Iraq, but there was a political crisis and some parties used sectarian violence to achieve political gains and create a new balance of power." As a result, "new parties got involved in the sectarian conflict," and "outsiders, whose intentions were clear," fueled the conflict between the sects.[64]

As al-Qaeda in Iraq declined by 2007, Sistani increasingly turned his attention to the stability of the state and the ability of leaders to pursue anti-sectarian policies. He saw a clear link between state policies and the violence on the ground. His statements were focused on corruption and the responsibility of the government to provide goods and services to the people. He gave the prime minister repeated warnings about the consequences of taking this responsibility lightly. Sistani had always talked about "keeping a close eye on the government" in his role as a "guide."

On February 21, 2011, after a period of silence on the subject, Sistani issued a fatwa calling on people to take to the streets in protest of the government's corruption and its failure to meet their basic needs. Thousands of protesters responded with a "day of rage" in seventeen cities throughout Iraq. The demonstrations were mostly peaceful. These protests occurred shortly after the uprisings that unseated the presidents of Egypt and Tunisia and at the same time as the turmoil in Libya, Syria, and Yemen. Yet the popular revolts in the region, which aimed to topple regimes, were distinct from the protests in Iraq, which were calls for reform.

Sistani praised Iraqis for their ability to "protest in a peaceful and civilized manner," while noting that those who did not protest "had their own hidden agendas." The Iraqi protesters' demands were for improved public services, clean running water, proper sewage, and "the abolishment of unacceptable privileges given to current and previous members of Parliament." Sistani continued that these protests were important to pressure the government of Prime Minister Maliki to step up reforms: "The *marjaʿ* has always stressed the importance of working to achieve the demands of the people."[65] Yet the response from Maliki, who dismissed the protesters as "extremists," offered no room for negotiation.[66] Maliki had become increasingly sectarian in his policies, which in turn fueled sectarian fighting on the streets. In his bid to centralize power, for example, he purged the security forces so that they were loyal to him personally. Behaving like militias, the security forces selectively targeted his Sunni opponents.[67] Sistani had warned nonstate actors against this tactic, but as Maliki consolidated his power, the state, too, was behaving in a sectarian manner.

After years of patience and calls for restraint, Sistani seemed to lose faith in the ability of the government to maintain security and refrain from inciting sectarianism within society. Sistani's call for protests was one such indicator. His characterization of the renewed violence was another. As he saw the fighting on the ground morph and sectarianism take a new form in ISIS, Sistani recalibrated his discourse.

Sistani referred to ISIS as "strangers" and "disbelievers," and all his statements and proclamations were addressed directly to the people, an "invitation that sees no sect." Sistani expressed concern that ISIS was "targeting anything their hands could reach" and had the "goal of killing all who disagree with their opinions." Sistani reminded Sunnis that they were "not only our brothers, but a reflection of ourselves," and called on politicians to work to preserve the rights of all Iraqis, equally. Yet because the circumstances now involved the fragmentation of the country and the loss of territory at the hands of the "strange terrorists," action was needed. Sistani, now using the word "terrorism," called for an immediate end to "extremist positions of politicians in speeches to the media." He argued that these hard-line positions eventually worked their way to social media, where they were expressed in the form of "racism" within society. Sistani declared that the "new greatest danger" to Iraq was the "divided reality of its future." The solution, Sistani continued, was a domestic political one in which politicians would move beyond "ego," "jealousy," and "rivalry." He wanted constitutional durations to be heeded and new governments formed according to proper rules and regulations.[68] Sistani was concerned about the connection between increased authoritarianism and the sectarian crisis on the ground. He saw corruption in the government as a cause of the rise and spread of ISIS. Still a conformer, Sistani made requests for Iraqis to volunteer for the armed forces in order to protect Iraq from the new terrorist threat.

Sistani argued that this threat was grave and that action was "everyone's responsibility." He issued a fatwa to that effect: "Citizens who are able to take up arms and fight terrorists in defense of their country must volunteer and join the security forces."[69] Sistani made clear that ISIS was not Sunni and that there was no sectarian basis for the fatwa because "all of his pronouncements over the years had proven, even in the most harsh circumstances," that there was no historical basis for sectarianism. It is clear that in this case his fatwa had a major impact. By June 2014, the time of the fatwa, ISIS had taken approximately one-third of Iraqi territory. His fatwa brought tens of thousands of volunteers to the Iraqi Army. Three years after Sistani had cut all ties with the government, with one fatwa he effectively helped the government rebuild its forces. He was also effective on the issue of unity. His fatwa propelled Shiite militias, Sunni tribal men, and Christian and Yazidi armed groups to be organized under the single umbrella of the Popular Mobilization Forces (PMF).[70] This organization was supervised under the authority of the new commander in chief, Prime Minister Haider al-Abadi. That these groups responded to Sistani's fatwa was a sign of two things. First, his fatwas had a reach beyond his segment of Shiite followers, a statement he had made about his fatwas from the start of the conflict. Second, he was offering support to the new prime minister and telling the Iraqi people that they, too, should back Abadi. His influence as a political figure was that great.

Grand Ayatollah Muhammad Saeed al-Hakim

The other ayatollahs followed Sistani's lead in subverting the false construct of sectarianism. Grand Ayatollah Muhammad Saeed al-Hakim (b. 1934) seemed to understand many of Sistani's cues when it came to his general position on sectarianism. When the regime in Baghdad fell, he issued a directive to the people in which he spoke of a moment of "historical joy" caused by an end to "injustice, tyranny, arrogance, recklessness, and the underestimation in values of a bygone regime that was extended" past its time. Hakim included several pages of quotations from the Quran and flowery religious language—a style that Sistani did not normally engage in—as he addressed the realities facing Iraqis. He spoke of the violence of the previous regime and assured his followers that God was "on the lookout for the wrongful," quoting from the Quran: "And we will surely let them taste the nearer punishment short of the greater punishment that perhaps they will repent" (Surat al-Sajda, verse 21).[71]

First on Ayatollah Hakim's agenda was the fact that Iraq was composed of sects of people from different religions, creeds, nationalities, and affiliations. Hakim said this diversity was not a feature unique to Iraq. And because this reality was accommodated and successfully managed in the structure of other nations, it could be in Iraq as well. He argued that diversity in society "must be admitted to and coexistence should be maneuvered with prudence and discretion, to keep all people away from serious complications." If "intense disputes" should arise between groups and sects, it would be unwise for some groups to infringe upon the rights of others. This approach would do injustice to the country's foundational truths. He warned that "fanaticism on the part of the neglected party" would "preclude the chances of convergence, rapprochement and dialogue." He also urged calm because the "flaring of emotions" would be "conducive to bloody conflict" and "destructive to the nation." Most importantly, he spoke about a "loophole from which ambushing enemies could enter, those opportunists who live in swamps and fish in turbid waters." He made the connection to the recent past in his acknowledgment that Iraq was a "country of tragedies and destruction," with many historical lessons to be learned.[72]

Hakim did not address any particular law or leader—he was more poetic in his language and inclined to speak in code. Many of his speeches and fatwas were riddled with admonitions from the Quran and sayings from the imams. He wanted to instill fear in the people and thereby induce compliance. Sistani seemed to address concrete issues in a calmer manner, with clear and simple edicts. He addressed the people directly, not leaving it up to them to make sense of the context. Yet Hakim was clear, like Sistani, when he spoke of sectarian hostility and hatred, in all its forms, as conducive to bloody conflict and lethal to national unity. Hakim acknowledged that state formation was a product of negotiation, so he embraced the diversity within Iraq as a natural phenomenon. He did not try to deny differences. Very early on, like Sistani, he warned of the interference of outsiders, who might capitalize on divisions within society to pursue their own interests.

As for sectarianism, Hakim was less interested than Sistani in the careful delineation of terms. For him, the message was simple: Sunnis and Shiites were the two largest communities in Iraq, with common origins in religion and "common goals." That "makes it incumbent upon them to respect property and blood" and, among other things, "rais[e] the word of Islam, hold back machinations of enemies, unite their line and forget their divisions." He said that Sunnis and Shiites must "cooperate seriously in pursuit of that goal," especially given the dire circumstances.[73]

Hakim was convinced that "people of sanity should behave rationally in coexistence, dialogue and collaboration." Prudent people are all around, he commented. Intercommunal conflict, he said, is not unique to Iraq or to Muslims—the "same happens in most ethnic affiliations"—but the job of Iraqis is to alleviate its acuteness. So, like Sistani, Hakim took the nonsectarian angle that the fighting was not an expression of innate hostility between Sunnis and Shiites. Rather than take Sistani's approach of debunking the artificiality thesis, Hakim compared Iraq to other countries. He argued that, far from a unique Iraqi problem, ethno-sectarian diversity was a near universal and normal condition of states.

Hakim defined sectarianism in Iraq as the "infringement upon others, usurping their rights, and preventing them from their practices and strangling their freedoms therein." He connected these practices very closely with "racial intolerance," which he called "loathsome." It was "not sectarian to stick by your group," Hakim continued, but it was a greater commitment to religion to interact with other religions. He drove home his points with verses from the Quran: "That is so. And whosoever honors the symbols of God indeed is from the piety of hearts" (Surat al-Hajj, verse 32).[74] Again, Hakim talked about the universal condition of religious and ethnic diversity, drawing constant analogies to the outside world that made Iraq seem less strange.

As Hakim saw things, it should be expected that Iraq, given its composition and historical circumstances, would be home to "divergent views," "contradictory streams," and "acute conflicts." The issue was how to deal with them. Each party should respect the view of the other and rely on argumentation that is "calm, sober, and logical." He called for the avoidance of violence even if there was mistrust. He cited Abu Jafar Imam al-Baqir's saying: "The messenger of God, peace be upon him, said: Mercy when placed in a thing would beautify it and when removed from it would disfigure it."[75] He also quoted the Quran: "But whoever kills a believer intentionally—his recompense is Hell, wherein he will live eternally" (Surat al-Nisa', verse 93). The speech then gave examples of punishment for such acts. He warned that "clashes and the use of force" would result in "a lasting sedition that would burn everything and destroy this torn country."[76] Hakim's message was that restraint was the top priority. He asked his followers to have faith in God instead of taking matters into their own hands, even if justice was on their side, because the consequences were too great.

Unlike Sistani, who worked more like a practical politician, Hakim spoke almost exclusively from a religious perspective, appealing to the pious and those attracted to the texts of theology and jurisprudence. Hakim did note that although the verses and hadiths on intercommunal discord were numerous and Muslims were in general agreement on the topic, there was also a general sentiment that it was a human issue. Those who transgressed were "criminals and brutes."[77] He, too, was interested in the human rights aspect of the problem.

Hakim recalled the legacy of authoritarianism and warned against recreating anything like Saddam Hussein's regime. Throughout the world, he said, tyrants have committed crimes against the people and then contrived excuses. The oppressors eventually coaxed society to believe that the excuses were valid justifications. Therefore, society bore some responsibility for the actions of tyrants as well.

Hakim was describing Saddam's regime and the factors that explained the regime's longevity and brutality, a matter he deemed "too lengthy and painful to discuss." However, his point was that this "experiment" should not recur. He was urging the people not to collaborate with the tyrants who might rise to power in the future. He was also warning them never to pardon a tyrant's oppression. Such de facto participation, he argued, was why the consequences ended up being so "disastrous."[78]

Hakim, like Sistani, wanted citizen accountability in the face of the mounting obstacles. Where Sistani focused on voting and respect for the judiciary, however, Hakim spoke of the duty not to aid and abet authoritarian leaders.

Hakim wanted to see Iraqi citizens take ownership of a pluralistic structure and warned that otherwise they might face "the wrath of God." In the case of Saddam's regime, of course, the complicity that Hakim denounced was not true support of the regime, but rather a survival strategy for individuals within the system. The alternative to cooperation was often death.[79] Hakim therefore put a great amount of faith in the wisdom of citizens in a democratic setting. He warned over and again that the "past experiment should never recur."

Hakim was asked what he saw as the main difference between Sunnis and Shiites. Specifically, he was asked by his followers, in light of the ongoing conflict, to comment on whether the differences mainly concerned beliefs or worship. He described the primary split over the succession of Ali ibn Abi Talib, the fourth caliph for Sunnis and the first imam for Shiites. Hakim said that the sects nonetheless agreed on the principles of Islam: "monotheism, prophethood, and destiny." They disagreed on the subject of the imamate and the designation of the imams but had "no substantial difference in jurisprudence." He acknowledged the richness of tradition and practice created by the diversity of opinions within each branch; because of the structure of the religion, in fact, it was common practice for scholars to "come to differ."[80] Hakim was commenting on his own institution, whose multiplicity of fatwas is a testament to the diversity of legal opinion. Although the Sunni tradition is not hierarchical, the same is true for the legal opinions of scholars therein. Orientalist literature, which sometimes made the case that Sunni legal thought was frozen in time, referred to the phrase "the closing of the gates of *ijtihad*." This phrase means that after Sunni law was codified in the ninth century, scholars simply practiced *taqlid* (imitation). This negative view has been refuted by scholars who revealed that Sunni law continued to be updated over the centuries. The discourses of the ayatollahs were a constant reminder to help undo myths and stereotypes.

Grand Ayatollah Muhammad Ishaq al-Fayyad

On June 21, 2003, Ayatollah Muhammad Ishaq al-Fayyad gave one of his first long speeches, called "a word of guidance to the beloved people of Iraq," to address the recent invasion and the plans to reconstruct the country amid the violence and chaos of its aftermath. He addressed all the people, scholars, preachers, and intellectuals, urging them to work hard in the "sensitive circumstances" and to seize the "precious opportunity": "First, fear God who is the standard of human dignity according to the verse in the Quran which says, 'The most honorable to God among you are the most righteous.'" Fayyad urged his followers to "maintain security, stability and tranquility in the country, particularly in these circumstances, careful not to abuse or bypass others." This injunction included restraint in raising "sectarian and racist issues that would lead to divisions among Muslims."[81]

Fayyad was thus not afraid to use the word "sectarian" from the beginning, but he took a strong stand against the phenomenon of sectarianism. He issued warnings about the consequences for people who chose to participate in civil strife. He often spoke of how a person's rights were tied to his or her actions: "I remind you of the need to be vigilant; be careful not to waste your rights, and to maintain your Islamic identity."[82] As the years passed, Fayyad left little or no room for reintegrating miscreants into society. He was tough in his interpretation of the role of the courts, and unlike the other senior ayatollahs, he tended to brand the insurgents as terrorists. He had harsh prescriptions for punishment as a way to deter future aggressors. His method differed from the others, but it was in the same spirit of linking the security situation to legitimate elections and the hope of ending the occupation.

In his early speeches, Fayyad merged the word "racism" with sectarianism. He was the only ayatollah to use the word explicitly, and he did so deliberately. He, like the others, was making clear that the sectarian conflict was constructed and that it had a strong connection to foreign incursion, but he put a unique inflection on this argument. In his first fatwa after the US invasion, Fayyad equated the plight of Iraqis with that of Muslims everywhere at the hands of the West: "In such a tragic situation as experienced by our brothers in Palestine, all Muslims worldwide, of all languages and nationalities, should close their ranks, renounce their differences, unify their position, and save the holy Islamic lands from the usurper terrorists." He made the case that those who defended their property, land, and honor from invasion were not terrorists, for self-defense was a right "acknowledged by all religions and international conventions." "The terrorists," he said, "were those who usurped the land of others."[83] In connecting Iraq to the Palestine question and the plight of all Muslims who had suffered as a result of colonization, Fayyad demonstrated that the invasion of Iraq illustrated a glaring international double standard. The Geneva Convention forbade the Israeli military occupation and settlement of Palestine; the UN Charter proscribed unprovoked invasions such as the US invasion of Iraq. But although Palestinians and Iraqis both have international law on their side, not much can be done to halt the aggression against them. In essence, prejudice, discrimination, and antagonism are directed at "Muslims everywhere" based on the belief that they are inferior. Although Fayyad did not categorize Palestinians and Muslims as a "race," the discriminatory acts against them were similar, which allowed Fayyad to make clear that foreign intervention is a "racist act." Indeed, literary critic Edward Said argued that racism was involved when people in the developing world were colonized, objectified, and reified.[84]

Fayyad's language about racism was by far the strongest among the grand ayatollahs. Yet it was clear that all the ayatollahs were on the same page about the importance of dispelling the sectarian myth of timeless Sunni-Shiite hatred and substituting an explanation rooted in classic colonization.

Fayyad, for his part, offered some constructive suggestions for combating the "foreign incursion." He argued that it was the "job of the faithful" to "spread Islamic awareness among diverse people and to spread humanitarian, intellectual, and moral values against all colors of corruption and immoralities, especially when they are foreign intellectual incursions." In these instances, "[I]t is important to maintain Islamic traditions and culture because they provide a person with great psychological energies in the face of any foreign or intellectual invasion, like a firm mountain that can't even be moved by storms."[85] Here Fayyad is talking about something akin to the earlier Islamic slogan "Neither East Nor West," used by Iranian ideologues in the prelude to the Iranian Revolution in 1979. It describes the feeling that using foreign-born or borrowed ideologies to help legitimize identities or political movements eventually fails or proves empty. Such borrowings lack an authentic connection with the population. Fayyad is not saying exactly that "Islam is the solution," but he is saying that Iraqis should be true to themselves and should look to their own steadfast culture and roots for their own solutions. If we recall Charles Taylor's discussion of Muslim idiom in chapter 1, the ayatollahs were guides as Iraqis navigated the new modes of political and religious expression in the post-Saddam order.

That new terrain came with big responsibilities. The newfound post-Saddam freedom had "positive and negative effects on the people of Iraq." The positive aspect was the opportunity to establish rituals of "the doctrine," to disseminate Islamic ideals and religious culture, and to claim their rights.[86] Here, Fayyad did not specify Sunni or Shiite thought when he talked about religion. He was talking in general about religion as a guiding principle for moral decision making.

As for the negative aspect, Fayyad pointed to the new factors that created opportunities for "moral corruption and the foreign cultural and intellectual invasion." To combat these forces, those who were qualified must give guidance as to "Islamic values, moralities, and religious ideas because those values equip a person with the virtues to create a perfect person and safe society."[87] Fayyad contrasted this pious virtue with Western culture, as he feared that the new freedom could lead people astray. He shared some of the same concerns as Hakim, namely that individuals would need to assume personal responsibility for their behavior in the new political milieu, part of which was the perceived "cultural onslaught" from the United States. Therefore, it was essential that Islamic thought and religious and moral awareness be the focus of education, especially at college and universities, in conjunction with the important lessons of humanitarian values and other righteous virtues. Fayyad, like Hakim, used Islamic discourse much more than Sistani, yet he managed to harmonize this narrative with one about participation and humanitarian values. He was not speaking only about Islam.

In his 2003 writings, Fayyad addressed the sectarian issues that he already saw in the country. From the outset, he thought that intellectuals from each sect needed to establish "committees of notables" from every province in order to demand that the "rights of the sect that had been neglected during the time of Saddam be redressed." However, this coordination had to occur without trampling on the rights of others because this claim was "at the heart of a democratic, free country where all the rights of the sects and doctrines are preserved, as well as the rights of minorities."[88] Whereas Sistani was careful about the term "sectarianism," Fayyad seemed not to mind it. Yet he was keen to encourage a democratic, egalitarian impulse for moving forward in a new Iraq.

Fayyad spoke regularly about the correct way to move forward with regard to "the policies on the sects," basing his view on what he saw as past errors. He posited that the doctrines and history of the Shiites should be taught in all schools and universities where the Shiites were a majority. It was "strange" that the Shiites were 65 percent of the population, yet in the past they were taught the dogmas of others. He advocated for freedom of religion, arguing that "no country or movement had the right to impose dogma on followers of another religion."[89] Accordingly, he wanted Sunnis to have freedom of thought under the system. Fayyad had one caveat: He argued that all religious schools and mosques should remain under the supervision of the Shiite committee of scholars on the grounds that they are not connected to the government. Fayyad was advocating for the continued separation between the religious class and government in Shiism, a long tradition maintained over the centuries, in contrast to the Sunni tradition, in which the government and the schools of law were connected. Fayyad feared that with the changeover of power the ayatollahs might lose their autonomy as the Sunnis did at the turn of the twentieth century.

In his April 1, 2005, *bayan,* "Statement on the success of the elections," Fayyad spoke about the security situation. All the clerics made the connection among successful elections, government stability, and a reduction in sectarian conflict on the ground. He framed the conflict as one in which Iraqis triumphed "under the hard circumstances of terrorist threats." He talked about how the "ground was now paved for the path of consensus and unity for the people of all sects and classes." He also spoke of the need for the Iraqi government to have sole responsibility for the safety of citizens. Fayyad did not refer directly to militias, but his message conveyed his rejection of them when he recommended standing with intelligence officials against "terrorists, criminals and the corrupted." Fayyad spoke a lot about the need to curb terrorists, "destroying their hiding places and cleansing the country of them." His ultimate goal was to push "harm and evil away" from the "generous people of Iraq and to unite them." Fayyad's opinions about the perpetrators of sectarian conflict were clear. Unlike Sistani or Hakim, he did not leave room for individuals to find their way. He did not issue statements about individual responsibility. There were no warnings that sectarianism was a trap. For Fayyad, there were no gray areas. There were "terrorists," and they should be hunted down and destroyed. They should be delivered to the government, where the justice system should "bring down the hardest punishments on them, as examples for others." He argued that to deal with them compassionately would be a "reward."[90]

By September 2005, Fayyad escalated his requests to Prime Minister Ibrahim al-Jaafari, urging him to eliminate what he perceived to be state sponsorship of "terrorists and killers." He made a specific request for the government to declare a state of emergency. He asked the national assembly to issue an "exceptional law" to outline the punishments for terrorists who confessed their "heinous crimes." He urged "speedy action, since prison was a reward to them." He went on to criticize state institutions for using "gleaming slogans" such as "democracy," "freedom," and "human rights" because those slogans could have meaning only in a more stabilized country.[91] He perceived that only the terrorists were benefiting at the moment, with Iraqi citizens as the victims.

Fayyad observed that Iraqis, including intellectuals, were criticizing the government as weak in its response to horrific events. People were starting to resent the government more with each day. People felt "worthless." Their "dignity was destroyed"; they were being "killed and raped daily by terrorists," without any of the terrorists "being killed or slaughtered or hanged." Fayyad honed in on the matter of retribution. Significantly, he was speaking of the terrorists as the perpetrators of sectarian violence, at a time when scholars had labeled the violence on the streets a civil war. Fayyad expressed dissatisfaction with the courts that were issuing sentences of approximately five years. This light punishment, he argued, showed the courts' "lack of integrity" and would "take the country down to a disaster." "Nothing good would come of it," he concluded. Fayyad lamented the slow pace in which the courts deliberated. He also wanted those found guilty to be publicly hanged. Fayyad claimed that in addition to a "government that called for democracy and human rights," the majority of Iraqis wanted a government that was able to deliver security as a top priority.[92] He believed that security would give people a sense of social justice and restore legitimacy to the government. In essence, Fayyad had a zero-tolerance policy. Like Sistani, he understood the devastating implications of sectarian fighting for Iraqi society. Yet Sistani repeatedly receded to the background, allowing the courts to do their jobs. Fayyad wanted to tell the courts exactly what to do.

Fayyad linked his discussion of terrorism to the notion of national reconciliation. He argued that the success of national reconciliation depended on "the real intentions of the parties involved" as well as their ability to meet the goal of "saving the country from the tragic situation."[93] He argued that the previous government had "failed miserably" in dealing with the issue of terrorism. This failure had helped to increase criminal acts. He conceded that Iraqis had witnessed only "useless condemnation, denunciations and fatwas that prohibited the killing of Iraqis, and sharp rhetoric without serving maximum penalties" on the perpetrators. Conceding that even the fatwas from the *hawza* were "useless," he opted for a set of methods that were "more powerful and cruel, because treating the problem of terrorism can only be addressed with firmness and rigor." He assured the prime minister that "people of all sects and classes want the government to use force" and that a prime minister who represented his people with a "will of iron" would find "people from all segments of society" standing behind him. Fayyad repeated over and over that people were tired of listening to calls for "democracy and human rights." Going by what he had "seen, heard and read," Fayyad said that the people wanted a "strict and strong government." Any delays in trial and sentencing would mean that "Iraqi blood was taken for granted."[94]

Although Fayyad held this position on punishment, he nonetheless urged a high degree of transparency so that "the process not be undertaken behind closed doors." He urged the government to consult with believers, intellectuals, members of the national assembly, and others "to save the country from the spiral of terrorism and administrative corruption." To this end, trials of the former regime members must be expedited, Fayyad urged, because some of these men were carrying out acts of terrorism in hopes that they might come back to power. Fayyad was critical of the legal process by which international lawyers were representing members of the former regime. He commented that for Saddam to get a legal defense was an injustice itself, and a "violation of the Iraqi human being." Fayyad said that Saddam was being treated as if he were "Mandela." He preferred an immediate death sentence for Saddam, as he foresaw "unstoppable chaos" should the deposed dictator only be imprisoned.[95]

Fayyad did not get into the sensitive issue that the former regime was, for the most part, composed of Sunnis. Historically, there had been many Shiites in the Ba'ath Party, but over time, and particularly under Saddam, the upper echelons were purged so that they were composed mainly of Sunnis. Fayyad's first concern was dealing with the violence on the ground, but his prescriptions were risky because he could appear sectarian.

Interestingly, Fayyad's interventionist language regarding the issue of terrorism might, at first glance, seem to go against his quietist impulses or his decision to defer to popular sovereignty despite his preference for the formation of an Islamic state. In the first instance, Fayyad always declared that the role of the ayatollah was to serve as a "guide" to the people, in consensus with the *hawza* of Najaf. He made clear on several occasions that "there was no practical role for the *marja'* in the internal and external politics of government, except in guiding the government to take the right path in policies and serving the people."[96] Yet on the issue of terrorism, he added a function that was echoed many times: "to cooperate with the government agencies to try to detect the dens of terrorists and to enforce the law in order to save the country from this tragic situation."[97] This call for a "state of emergency," despite the caveats about transparency, broke with the other clerics in its seemingly undemocratic language. Fayyad was calling for a strong executive, with the expectation that liberties would have to suffer for the sake of security. Inaction, in his view, was not an option. He took the position that after "three years of failure," the government needed to change course. Fayyad's recommendations were probably in line with much of public opinion. They also came in strong reaction to the growing refugee crisis in Iraq. At the time of his statements, there were four million Iraqis who had fled their homes, including approximately two million internally displaced persons within Iraq.[98] From Fayyad's perspective an immediate intervention was necessary, especially in light of how the conflict evolved after the rise of ISIS.

When asked about Sunni-Shiite conflict, Fayyad's response was to deny the validity of the sectarian construct. He insisted that Sunnis and Shiites had been "living in Iraq for hundreds of years, like brothers in one house without repulsion and disgust, with a relationship filled with love and affection," consistent with the historical record outlined by Visser, Nakash, and others. Sunnis and Shiites used to intermarry and live in neighborhoods side by side, he explained. After the fall of the regime, "enemies of the Iraqi people from abroad, and Saddam's men from the inside," started to create division between the two sects. Both groups fueled the war. He gave credit to the efforts of the *"marja'iyya* of al-Najaf al-Ashraf and some wise politicians" to bring attention to this matter and "uncover this malicious conspiracy." In his calculations, the "probability of a sectarian war in Iraq does not exist." He reduced it to "hateful" people. Fayyad was careful to separate the issue of terrorism from the issue of Sunni-Shiite relations and rebuked the media for their conflation of the two, calling it "unrealistic" or "poison."[99] He had blamed the media for the fact that by this time, the sectarian crisis had taken on a life of its own. The ayatollahs were now battling to remind Iraqis that "sectarian violence" was not the norm but was a product of past state policies, foreign intervention, and occupation.

Fayyad was asked about the biggest threat to Iraq. Ever confident of the long history of nationalism and unity in the country, he answered that Iraq faced no real danger. Yet he acknowledged that "there was a malicious plot internally and externally to create sedition and division, and to prevent the country from remaining stable and secure." He was confident that this conspiracy would not last once Iraqis were aware of it. Overall, Fayyad had faith in the Iraqi people. He was sure of the shallowness of sectarian discourses and the strength of the will of the people. He saw the occupation—and not an ancient history of sects—as the roadblock. On the US presence, Fayyad said, "The occupation is disliked by every single Iraqi with no exception. No one would ever accept it even for one hour." The only remedy to occupation was "unity."[100]

The ayatollahs tirelessly combated the false but compelling sectarian narrative, each in his own way. However, all of them would have to grapple with the growing influence of that narrative not only within Iraq but increasingly throughout the region.

Sectarianism and the Regional Ripple Effect: The Shiite Crescent and Beyond

King Abdallah of Jordan was not alone in seeing the post-Saddam dispensation in Iraq through a sectarian lens. Saudi Arabia, ever suspicious of Iranian intentions, increasingly framed its entreaties to Washington in terms of protecting the Sunnis in Iraq. The Saudis repeatedly warned that premature US withdrawal from Iraq would result in disaster for the Sunnis. Even leaders of Arab countries far from Iraq began speaking in this way. In 2006 Hosni Mubarak, president of Egypt, stated that the Shiites of Iraq were loyal to Iran. Top politicians in Iraq held a news conference to repudiate Mubarak's remarks.

The growing talk of a "Shiite crescent" attracted the Iraqi ayatollahs' attention as well. They were very sensitive to the regional ripple effect of the contrived sectarian narrative. Sistani, addressing Mubarak directly, said he was "puzzled" because an assessment that "Shiites are not loyal to their own country" meant that by Mubarak's logic, the patriotism of millions living on the Nile was also in question. He continued that this "vision" ignored clear, basic facts about countries such as Iraq, Lebanon, Kuwait, and Bahrain. He referred to the historical nationalist struggles of these countries, regardless of sectarian makeup. He warned Mubarak that his comments about Iraqi Shiites discounted the nationalism of prominent leaders who had crucial roles in "liberating and developing" their countries. Sistani told the Egyptian leader that the "data" behind his statement were "incomplete."[101]

Sistani also admonished Mubarak about the danger facing the region because of "sensitive and complicated conditions," in which attempts were made "to break up countries and to fuel sectarian and ethnic conflicts." The most dangerous aspect of Mubarak's rhetoric, he argued, was that it "reduced" citizenship to presumed religious attachment. It was an "abridgement of fixed citizenship rights" and a denial of the historical record. There were complex cultural, political, intellectual, and social forces at play that were not factored into Mubarak's calculus. Following such a narrow vision, according to Sistani, created an environment that would invite further bloodshed and impede regional development. Sistani saw that "black-and-white thinking" about sectarianism was perilous not only for Iraq but for the entire region.[102]

In his usual diplomatic manner, Sistani praised Mubarak for his otherwise skillful leadership in the past and his serious attention to regional matters. He therefore urged the Egyptian president to rethink his position on this question. After all, the region depended on Egyptian leadership, which was known for its "insight" and was "qualified to play an important role" in the region.[103]

In keeping with Sistani's views about sectarian conflict itself, his language in replying to Mubarak was consistently about "Iraqis of all sects and ethnicities." "Shiites and others," he said, "are unified in demanding the respect of their will to self-determination and rejecting foreign plans for their political, economic and social future." This unity included a wholehearted rejection of alliance with Iran and an absolute proclamation that Iran, like all governments, "shall respect Iraq's sovereignty and the will of its people."[104] Sistani wanted to continue to banish the image of all Shiites of the region as a unified bloc. He wanted to keep the Iraqi unity narrative alive.

When the ayatollahs talked about the regional sectarian narrative and the direct role of outside actors in fueling it, they often referred to how this narrative has played out in other countries besides Iraq. Fayyad pointed to the example of Bahrain. Like many other countries, Bahrain had an uprising during the spring of 2011. Shiites in that country called for greater political freedom and equality for the majority population. Protesters included a call for the monarchy to end its deadly raids upon the largely Shiite villages surrounding the capital of Manama. Bahraini leaders were able to crush the peaceful demonstrations with the help of troops from Saudi Arabia and the United Arab Emirates. Bahrain instituted martial law and declared a state of emergency. This policy involved further persecution of the Shiites, which included more midnight raids into the villages, denial of access to medicine and resources, mass imprisonment, and other tactics of intimidation.[105] However, the case of Bahrain did not receive the same widespread media attention as did Egypt or Syria.[106]

Fayyad sympathized with the Shiite population of Bahrain, which perhaps reminded him of the historical plight of Shiites elsewhere. In a *bayan* dated March 16, 2011, Fayyad described the origins of the Bahrain crisis, which began with "peaceful demonstrations for legitimate rights and stolen dignity." At least initially, the regime seemed to meet the demonstrations with dialogue and promises of comprehensive reform. Fayyad then moved to his "surprise" at the entry of "foreign troops" (the Saudis) into the country, at the request of the Bahraini government, "using force to suppress unarmed protesters" and "destroying their dignity."[107]

Fayyad invited all Bahrainis, of all sects and factions, to unite, despite this turn of events, and to work for peace in the spirit of moderation and reason. It was important to "demand legitimate rights and to leave violence and confrontation in all its forms."

He talked about the imbalance created when the Arab League, the United Nations, and Western countries toppled Muammar al-Qaddafi in the name of defending the Libyan people, while not only turning a blind eye to the aggression against the (largely Shiite) Bahrainis but also (in the Saudis' case) sending troops to suppress a defenseless people. Fayyad called this turn of events the "strange duality of the Arab Islamic countries." He stressed the importance of equal treatment from the international community. He asked the international community, the Arab League, religious scholars, and Muslims in all countries to stand with the Bahraini people as they strove to achieve their legitimate demands.[108]

In this and other instances Fayyad served as a public intellectual, intent on standing against the dangerous ripple effect of the sectarian narrative beyond Iraq and into the entire region. He made the analogy between Iraq and Palestine on the eve of the 2003 invasion, with a stern condemnation of the international community that stood idle as Palestinian rights were violated. He was concerned in 2003 that Iraq would suffer the same fate, and in 2011 he reiterated these concerns when it came to Bahrain.

By 2012, sectarian fighting in Iraq was commonplace, and many also saw the fighting elsewhere in the region as sectarian in provenance. The ayatollahs did not stop commenting on these connections. In one example, Iranian parliamentary speaker Ali Larijani, who was in Iraq with a visiting delegation, held a meeting on November 27, 2012, with Ayatollahs Hakim and Najafi to discuss the Syrian crisis and other regional issues. Both clerics said that the conflict was caused by the interference of outside actors, not by sectarianism. They agreed that all disputes should be resolved domestically. Hakim said specifically that "religion does not teach the use of violence to further interests."[109] They were talking about Syria, yet they could have been talking about Iraq, where for the longest part of their lives they had known nothing but one form or another of outside intervention, culminating in years of US occupation. Events after 2003 added new pages of violence to the record, which required a domestic solution comparable to the one required in Syria. The ayatollahs' references were littered with imagery that reminded their followers of the impact of colonialism and the repercussions of foreign intervention. All of their pronouncements about cooperation and unity in order to end the occupation were a testament to that position.

Over the years, the ayatollahs continued to issue statements to combat sectarian polarization. Sistani, for one, had been trying to dodge the proliferation of forged statements and fatwas in his name that flooded the media and the political scene. Some of these forgeries appeared to have Sistani making government appointments in a number of ministries, government institutions, and the army. He immediately called for the investigation and prosecution of such acts, and continually stressed the need to look for his seal of approval. He insisted that he would never interfere in the workings of government,[110] a reminder of his brand of quietism. He reiterated that such forgeries could increase sectarian strife.

Sistani, acknowledging the enormous challenge ahead, urged Muslims to close ranks and avoid sectarianism and ideological differences. He advised that "ideological differences were centuries-old," could not be resolved to the satisfaction of everyone, and "should not affect the fundamentals of Islam or the pillars of faith" because everyone believed in the one and only God and the message of his Prophet. All Muslims should focus on these "true foundations of Islamic unity" to tighten the "bonds of love and affection between the sons of the nation and to settle for no less than living together peacefully."

Yet, Sistani continued, it was undeniable that some entities were dedicated to deepening sectarianism among Muslims. They had increased their efforts after the escalation of political conflicts in the region. "Since the conflict for power was greater," he concluded, "the attempts to stoke sectarianism were renewed and strengthened with new tactics and techniques."[111]

The ayatollahs were constantly drawing the connection between regional sectarian rhetoric and domestic Iraqi politics. The sectarian crisis was not limited to the fighting on the ground. It took on a whole new dimension with the framing narratives that the media deployed. Sistani, for one, identified the role that various media—satellite TV, the Internet, magazines, and other outlets—played in issuing "weird" fatwas in his name that offended Islamic doctrines in an attempt to increase sectarian tensions. He assured the community that all Muslim blood was worthy, and he forbade the shedding of any of it. He rationalized that his methodology was good for all Muslims and that if it had been followed, the level of "blind violence" would not be where it was.[112]

Everyone, after all, could be a target of arbitrary communal discrimination. The Shiites had a long history of being included in the state, and then were shunned, and then included again, depending on the whims of Saddam Hussein. Their loyalty was always in question, and their citizenship always on the verge of being revoked. The same was true for tribes. The 1968 Ba'ath Communiqué 1 was a rejection of tribalism in no uncertain terms. Sheikhs were purged, jailed, or killed, and the use of tribal names was banned. Then that policy was overturned, based on Saddam's survival needs, during the Iran-Iraq war. Saddam revived tribalism so that it became the center of political life up until the invasion.[113] Then there was the questioning of loyalty on ethnic grounds. Sistani himself was attacked at times for his Iranian birth.

Overall, the narrative on sectarianism stressed its importation from outside and the foreign elements involved. Sistani and the other ayatollahs may not have been successful in preventing violence with their pronouncements in the same way that they had a tangible impact on other arenas of state building, yet they made a real contribution in correcting the false narrative of unique artificiality and deep-seated sectarian conflict. The ayatollahs exposed sectarianism as a false construct within Iraq and in the region as a whole. Their differences in personal style revealed the delicate balance, echoed in the debates surrounding quietism, between intervention and reticence for these self-proclaimed "guides." Sistani and Hakim opted for a policy of less interventionist guidance, while Fayyad, fearing the worst from his earlier pronouncements, opted for a more aggressive approach. The ayatollahs' methods differed, yet their narratives intersected in the most powerful ways.

Conclusion

Rethinking Religion and Politics

The relationship between religion and politics in the Arab world has been studied for decades. In this book I have attempted to make sense of this interplay through analysis of the discourse of the four grand ayatollahs of Najaf in post-Saddam Iraq.

In the Western experience, the Protestant Reformation resulted in the formal separation of church and state—and religion became, in large part, a private, personal matter. In the Arab and Muslim world, no such defining event took place, and although generations of Islamic scholars engaged in interpretation of the proper relationship between the two, religion remained a main source of political identity. In the modern era, religion remained a key building block of nationalism.

Modern Iraq is no exception. Upon taking Iraq from the Ottoman Empire, the British attempted to separate religion from politics, at least nominally, despite the Iraqi will at the grassroots level. The secular monarchy formed in 1920 carried out this vision, as did the series of rulers who replaced the king after 1958. But the effort to build a state in which religion was a private matter coincided with authoritarian practices by which the rulers actively suppressed opposition, often that of religious actors, in order to bolster state power. The tension between the state and the religious establishment loomed large in Iraq with the fall of Saddam Hussein in 2003.

Since then, the national discussion about the relationship between religion and politics has continued to be plagued with uncertainty because religious actors moved to the forefront of the democratic state-building process, causing confusion for Iraqis and outside observers alike. In particular, the emergence of the grand ayatollahs as political actors served to entwine religion with politics in new and important ways. The post-Saddam state did not relegate religion to ostensibly apolitical status as a matter of individual faith. The ayatollahs walked a fine line: Even as they maintained their role as leaders of the *hawza,* offering guidance on spiritual and personal matters to their Shiite followers, they stepped out of their traditional quietism into more active intervention in worldly affairs. At the same time, there was continuity with the recent past. The post-2003 state-building process brought into the open what had long been the practice of Iraqi political leaders: the calculated use of religion as a tool for achieving strategic goals.

From 2003 onward, the grand ayatollahs played a vital role as the very notion of "Iraqi-ness" was thrown into question. They reached into history to make the case for pan-Iraqi nationalism and reached out to their Sunni coreligionists to make the case for Iraqi independence from the rule of the United States. In offering a counter-narrative to both the United States and the various violent insurgencies on the ground, the ayatollahs carved out a place for themselves in the free-for-all that was US-occupied Iraq. These religious actors, deeply entrenched in society, could have chosen to call for an Islamic state along the lines of the one formed in neighboring Iran after the 1979 revolution. Instead, they called for a civil state, demanded Iraq's sovereignty under international law, insisted on direct elections, and served as "guides" to the political process as it unfolded. This choice must be understood in the context of the complex relationship between religion and politics in the Arab and Muslim world.

Although they held no formal political position, the grand ayatollahs were able to reframe the prevailing narratives about Iraq in order to address the issues of the time, such as sectarianism, democracy, and state building. The country was and remains in transition. It may take a few steps toward national reconciliation and democracy, and then several steps back. One major challenge at present is the rise of ISIS, which began to conquer territory from the central government in 2014. As of late 2017, the Iraqi Army had recaptured Ramadi, Tikrit, and Mosul from ISIS, but there was no guarantee that the extremist group would not retreat and resurface in one of its previous strongholds. The cycle of conquest and reconquest may continue. Another lurking uncertainty lies in the advancing age of Ayatollah Ali al-Sistani (eighty-six at the time of this writing), who has led the way in formulating the political interventions of the senior clergy in Najaf. When Sistani dies, the *hawza* may take a different position on the relationship between religion and politics. But there are strong indications of a settled consensus not to follow the Iranian model. To date, the actions of the ayatollahs have been a stabilizing factor: They have demonstrated that political circumstances drive their religious thinking. Their contribution during this crucial transitional period—indeed, this foundational moment—was simply to assert that central religious actors in the informal public sphere would shape the political discourses in the post-Saddam era. These discourses, powerful as they are, have served as checks on the political system when it moved away from the guiding principles laid out by the ayatollahs.

This book has argued that because the ayatollahs are so embedded in society and because their hierarchy and function are so entwined with the relationship between state and society, their courses of action in post-Saddam Iraq show a deep democratic process at work. The hierarchical system itself and its dependence on the acquiescence of the people, or the popular will, meant that the *hawza* had a structural advantage over rival political actors. The ayatollahs also benefited from the particularities of post-Saddam Iraq. The ayatollahs had always issued fatwas. But with the new public realm that allowed for new public demands, they were able to reinvent themselves. In the power vacuum a traditional religious institution needed to be at the center of modern discussions to remain relevant. The grand ayatollahs did just that. Over the years, they issued fatwas that rejected reliance upon militias that would sow further social division. They decreed that the public welfare was more than the needs of their Shiite constituents. Time and again, they made clear that their fatwas were to apply to the general population, irrespective of sect or identity, as they worked to push the state-building project forward.

But the ayatollahs' role was more substantial. The state had become increasingly weak and unable to provide basic protections and services. Protests had been the norm for years because of corruption, decreased government accountability, and Prime Minister Maliki's sectarian policies, all exacerbated by the ascendancy of ISIS. As the government lost credibility and control, the holy cities gained power. Despite the fact that the ayatollahs stated that they did not intend to rule, especially not in the way found in Iran, Iraqis increasingly turned to the ayatollahs for more than guidance and advice. One example is the provision of housing, sanitation, and medical care to internally displaced persons (IDPs) who fled their homes ahead of the sweep of ISIS across northwestern Iraq in 2014. These services would normally be a government responsibility, but for a short period, the shrines shared the costs with the state. By 2017, support for the IDPs came entirely under the management of the shrines. To cover the costs, the *hawza* drew on donations from around the world, as well as revenues from the increasing number of pilgrimages to Najaf and Karbala, and dividends from a sizable and well-managed investment portfolio. They invested in businesses, took government contracts to pave roads and build airports, and oversaw a vast network of charities, such as hospitals and orphanages. Their presses printed the textbooks for the country's schools. In essence, the *hawza* was able to fill the gaps in the social, political, and economic spheres during a national emergency. At a time when the state was weak, the shrines "assume[d] the functions of the state."[1]

This state-like role, reminiscent of what Hezbollah has been able to do in Lebanon for years, has a few implications for the relationship between religion and politics. As in Lebanon, the religious actors in Iraq have provided services when the state falls short. They are thus granted legitimacy, which is premised on the idea that they are an organization rooted in society, with a moral purpose. They are distanced from the corrupt institutions of the state. This political role, reinforced by their own narratives, interventions, and overall political action, is in line with their claim to be not only moral guides but also providers for the state. It remains to be seen if this de facto assumption of state functions will continue to render the *hawza* immune from the criticism routinely directed at politicians. As time goes by, the expectations of their constituents are bound to rise. They risk disappointing their followers if they do not take a stand on a given issue. Eventually, citizens will want them to intervene—simply because they can.

Second, the entrenchment of the grand ayatollahs is a strong indication of the resiliency of the religious establishment in Iraq. It lays to rest the question of whether Iranian ayatollahs will be able to replace Sistani with one of their own. Many observers have asked these questions: Will Sistani be succeeded by Ayatollah Muhammad Saeed al-Hakim, who shares his view that clerics have an advisory role only? Or might Sistani's successor advocate the doctrine of *velayet-e faqih,* by which the clergy becomes the supreme legal authority? The answer is clear at this point. Despite a concerted effort, clerics associated with Iran have not been able to rise in the religious ranks in Najaf. Several pro-Iranian propaganda campaigns have been launched in Najaf, but they have all failed. Some of these campaigns tried to merge the image of Sistani with that of Ayatollah Ruhollah Khomeini. In one such instance, a book titled *My Leader Khomeini* was circulated. It contained an endorsement falsely attributed to Sistani: "Always walk behind Sayyid Khomeini and support *wilayat al-faqih.* Today, the reputation of Islam depends on the reputation and dignity of the Islamic Republic."[2] All of the evidence from the last decade and a half, from grassroots protests to the shape of legislation, indicates that Iraq will not follow the Iranian model. There is little room for any external actor to introduce new religious traditions in Najaf. Iranian attempts to implant clerics in the seminaries were viewed with disdain by Sistani, who maintained more than 600 representatives throughout Iraq as a bastion against Khomeinist influence. Muqtada al-Sadr, who is increasingly in line with Najaf, has become more and more critical of Iranian meddling in Iraqi affairs, including that of ayatollahs he once viewed favorably. And even Saddam Hussein struggled to force Najaf to toe his line, as studies of Ba'athist archives from the Iran-Iraq war period have revealed.[3] Najaf maintained its independence from all manner of external influences, including the central government in Baghdad, during the bloodiest years of modern Iraqi history.

Beyond their ability to penetrate the state structure, the ayatollahs have managed to tap into the ongoing conversation about Iraqi nationalism. The background to this achievement is the decades of authoritarian Ba'athist rule, which in its structure and implementation made it incredibly difficult for genuine cross-ethnic and sectarian political alliances to form. Saddam Hussein's divide-and-rule tactics ensured that the upper ranks of those loyal to the Ba'ath Party, largely but not exclusively Sunni

Arabs, benefited from the perpetuation of authoritarianism, often at the expense of marginalized groups, notably the Shiite majority. The Iraqi variant of Ba'athism was originally linked to pan-Arabism, and even after its regional ties became wholly rhetorical, it did not accommodate any form of indigenous nationalism rooted in Islam, especially not one that originated in the Shiite community. The social and political fragmentation was severe, and it worked its way into the discourse of the Saddam-era opposition groups, which were positioned to reproduce it after they re-turned from exile in 2003. Thus, Kanan Makiya, recalling the marginal-ization of the Shiites, repeated many times that because of their culture of "victimhood," the Shiites would be righting the wrongs of history by assuming majority status. Indeed, some Shiites looked back to the rise of Shiite Islamism in Iraq in the 1950s as a restoration of their core identity and values. After 2003, many Shiite Islamists, including those in Maliki's party, found in sectarianism a default strategy for building the social base they could not build in exile. Identity politics, derived from a narrative of victimhood, increased the likelihood that Iraqis would be further polar-ized into "Sunni" and "Shiite" camps, distant from a pan-Iraqi national project.

Crucially, the grand ayatollahs did not embrace this culture of victim-hood in their narratives after 2003. The clerics of Najaf, setting themselves apart from their counterparts in Iran, laid out a place for themselves in the new political arena that was a modification of the traditional quietist school of thought. After a long period of stagnation under Ba'athist rule, these clerics came to the forefront of the political process. Not only did they counter the new sectarian narratives and the older, subtler ones that had been embedded in the state structure since 1920; they also worked to offer a new vision for collective identity. The ayatollahs rejected the tripar-tite view of Iraq, whereby the country was divided into zones of "Sunnis," "Shiites," and "Kurds," and the confessional state model that this view produced. In essence, they served as conduits for the emergence of a new, civil nation-state after the demise of Saddam Hussein. They sought to pre-vent the institutionalization of communal identities by flagging a history of cooperation among various sects and ethnicities in order to demon-strate that sectarianism was in fact a constructed narrative. Throughout this process, however, the ayatollahs continued to say that they were guides only. They needed to maintain a reasonable distance from the state in order to ensure that their communal identity did not contribute to sectarianization at the expense of preserving the national democratic project.

However, questions remain unresolved about the religio-political arrangements established after 2003. The default discussion among Westerners about the relationship between religion and politics in the Arab and Muslim world is often exclusively about sharia, or what is sometimes simply called Islamic law. We saw illustrations of how this discussion often proceeds in early 2003 when the mere possibility that religion could play a part in the post-Saddam Iraqi public sphere elicited panic from journalists and pundits. Even Juan Cole, who went on to write extensively about the meaningful ways in which the ayatollahs would contribute to the state over the years, said, "Sistani and the other grand ayatollahs will press for as much Shariah—or Islamic law—as possible in Iraqi law. They can afford to be patient if they can't push through everything now."[4] Commentators and regional specialists alike focused on "sharia": The clerics could certainly never be "Jeffersonian democrats," and Islamists would inevitably form "illiberal" democracies. We often read that Islamists, however they come to power, inevitably want a "strict interpretation of sharia." This idea, popularized by Fareed Zakaria in 2003, emphasized that more and more countries were choosing to be democratic because of democracy's basis in popular sovereignty and government accountability to the public. According to Zakaria, however, democracy did not necessarily sit well with liberalism, which emphasized personal rights and freedom. Through this lens, Islamists in post-2003 Iraq would be suspect because of their adherence to sharia and Islamic principles. They would have a hard time marrying Islamic law to the concepts of liberalism and democracy. Still other scholars have lauded the benefits of including Islamists in the political process because it moderates their political behavior.[5] What exactly does this debate mean when the term "sharia" is so poorly understood?

Whether in theory or in practice, for believing Muslims sharia is "the ideal realization of divine justice—a higher law reflecting God's will," as defined by Noah Feldman. But this "higher law" is not a rigid set of injunctions that are written down in one place and universally agreed upon. When Muslims talk about sharia, they are generally referring to a wide range of options for what is expected from them in their daily practice. Throughout Islamic history, religious scholars and ordinary Muslims have spent a great deal of time interpreting God's will. In essence, sharia is simply the consensus that Muslims are, on the most basic level, religious believers. How they want to exercise this belief in practice is another matter entirely—one that is constantly negotiated in Iraq just as it is elsewhere. Feldman differentiates between sharia and *fiqh* (jurisprudence), the interpretation and application of sharia in the real world.[6] This distinction is important because not even the most qualified, highly trained religious scholars can say with certainty what Muslims should do in real life to attain the fullest expression of God's will. Yet the notion that sharia is immutable black-letter law appears over and over in debates among non-Muslims about Islam and democracy, often yielding absurd or extremist conclusions.

In post-Saddam Iraq, indeed, the discussions about sharia in the political order largely deployed the term to refer to general guidelines with substantial room for interpretation, both by legislators making laws and by jurists applying the laws to particular cases. The grand ayatollahs, of course, were far from the only Shiites (let alone the only religious figures or the only Iraqis) involved as debate began over what kind of state should replace Saddam's regime. In the early days after Saddam's fall, Muqtada al-Sadr and other proponents of political Islam wanted to form a government that conformed to dictates of Islamic law, although what they meant by this term was vague. For example, debates about the personal status law, involving such matters as divorce and child custody, almost always included a discussion of the Quran and the moral example of the imams, fused and supplemented with contemporary legal and administrative regulations. With the memory of Saddam's era fresh, a high priority in the debates among Shiites was the preservation of autonomy for Shiite thinkers.

The same was true of the public debates surrounding the draft constitution in 2004 and 2005. The grand ayatollahs did not directly oversee the constitution-writing process. Nor did they spearhead the arguments that called for a fusion of a modern legal structure with classical Islamic law. Yet when "Islamist" politicians demanded that no piece of legislation "violate classical Islamic law," the ayatollahs seemed to agree. They reasoned that there was no contradiction in stating that although everyone was equal under the law, Islam should nonetheless be a source of legislation. However, their viewpoints were usually delivered by way of fatwas, *bayans,* or commentary rather than direct involvement in the "details of political work."

The language about Islam in the 2005 Iraqi constitution did wind up being vague, too much so for liberals seeking to enshrine the separation of mosque and state. Scholars were concerned as well with contradictions in the text of the constitution, its inability to guarantee full equality, and its inadequacies on gender issues. However, it is important to note that no constitution by itself guarantees the protection of personal freedoms envisioned by liberalism or, for that matter, the preservation of democracy. The US Constitution guarantees the protection of civil liberties through the Bill of Rights, but these protections are not unlimited, and they can be amended or repealed by majorities. And as illustrated best by the history of civil rights in the United States, all democracies face struggles as they negotiate the relationship between popular sovereignty and liberalism. Democracy is an ideal, and it is perpetuated by practices that over time become the norms of a political culture committed to the survival of the system. These norms, in turn, can erode or be overridden entirely in times of perceived crisis. As we have seen during the young presidency of Donald Trump, the US political system remains susceptible to illiberal tendencies. Two months into his presidency, Trump had already made two attempts to subvert established principles of freedom of religion by way of executive orders restricting entry of certain foreign nationals that amounted to a "Muslim ban." The courts blocked implementation of both orders, but the legal battle over White House prerogatives in this domain is far from over. As a presidential candidate, Trump exhibited utter disregard for other liberal democratic norms by suggesting that he might order the killing of the families of terrorists, by encouraging violence against his political opponents, and by insinuating that he might not accept the outcome of the 2016 election.[7] Similarly, many of the potential problems that observers foresee being caused by the illiberal tendencies of Islamists in Iraq would happen outside the purview of the constitution. And these problems would have less to do with the constitution itself than with failure to establish the norms that the ayatollahs hoped to strengthen via their political discourse in the post-Saddam milieu. As Haider Hamoudi has argued in his defense of the flexibility of the language in the Iraqi constitution, it is unlikely that legislation will pass that is outside the mainstream of the existing political culture. In this regard, as well, Iraq is not exceptional.

Prior to the drafting of the 2005 constitution, the highest-ranking religious authorities of the majority Shiite population—the grand ayatollahs—had called repeatedly for a civil state. But the constitutional process was not about strict application of the religious ideas of Sistani, Fayyad, Hakim, or Najafi. It was about politics—significantly, the ability of other actors, such as the Supreme Council for the Islamic Revolution in Iraq (SCIRI), as the group was known at the time, to advance policy that was religious in nature though not necessarily derived from religious doctrine or endorsed by the ayatollahs. SCIRI figures such as Abd al-Aziz al-Hakim and Jalal al-Din Saghir, both elected to Parliament in 2005, are clerics but not in the sense that the four grand ayatollahs are. They are considered to be "lay" politicians rather than religious leaders. As members of SCIRI, they operated as a conservative Shiite political party. Many of their proposals, such as the push for explicit mention of Islam in the constitution and the federal structure that they hoped would favor the Shiite majority in the South, were based neither in sharia nor in jurisprudence, but in plain old identity politics. In this sense, they were acting more as conservatives than as Islamists. Yet SCIRI overreached and lost first momentum, then credibility, and, eventually, votes.

In many ways, the debates among Shiite thinkers and politicians in post-Saddam Iraq are an example of what Nathan Brown has referred to as a "post-Islam discussion."[8] In 2003 and beyond, the ayatollahs were well aware that voices other than theirs were willing and able to fill the vacuum. There was a disconnect between the ayatollahs' religious interpretations and the laws and policies being passed and pursued by the central government in Baghdad. The ayatollahs were trying to make new connections with their followers as moral guides and, at the same time, as promoters of a civil state that could guarantee rights to all Iraqi citizens. But their statements and jurisprudence were not the only important interventions in Iraq after 2003, not even within the realm of what one could define as political Islam.

The political Islam of the ayatollahs does not fit neatly into the category of political Islam that scholars conventionally use, for the ayatollahs are not primarily concerned with the acquisition of power. The ayatollahs' political weight in Iraq rather derives from what Shiite Islam is and the fact that they are its highest-ranking moral figures. The situation may be compared to what the Frenchman Alexis de Tocqueville observed about US politics during his visit to America long ago. He noted that Protestant Christianity played a crucial role in setting the moral boundaries within which political discussions unfolded in the United States. Therefore, although religion per se was not rooted in the political structures, it was an important political institution, one valued for its own sake, that had become entrenched in the political system over time.[9] Islam served this same function in the discursive field in Iraq, among competing voices and demands. Islam, as Sistani argued in his statements, was rooted in the culture of the people, but he never took the additional step that it had to be enshrined in the constitution or the state.

The grand ayatollahs tried to revive their institution, after years of enfeeblement under Saddam Hussein and the decline of Najaf relative to Qom. The ayatollahs engaged in a type of activism that allowed for them to move from the domain of ritual to that of politics. They played an oversight role in the political process—one well short of the Iranian model, but one that was meant to mold public discourses in line with their thinking. They emerged as the country's most powerful arbiters, often intervening in ways that were not publicly understood or acknowledged. Over the years, we learned what the ayatollahs thought about a civil state, the role of Islam in the constitution, and the moral basis of a state. The senior clerics were not operating on the basis of sheer altruism. Their motivation was to ensure the legitimacy of the state. They saw it as their role to help define the nature of the state and to guarantee popular sovereignty through elections. These elections would, they thought, deliver a legitimate government to Iraqis and also reverberate in the region and the international community. In Sistani's communications with the United Nations, he sent a message to the world about the importance of Iraq's independence. He would deliver this message over and over, drawing attention to both the missteps of the US administration and his own democratic credentials.

Another side to the ayatollahs' consequential vocal interventions was that their silences were just as telling. On issues such as federalism, few if any fatwas or speeches emanated from Najaf. Often, when the ayatollahs' followers looked to them for answers, the clerics felt that inaction was action. That pendulum, swinging from the public to the private sphere, always landed them as the custodians of popular interests, prepared to intervene when they deemed it necessary. They had no prescription, as in the case of defining Islamic law, for what exactly necessitated intervention. Over the decade and a half after the US invasion, however, they chose the rule of law over chaos and grounded their opinions in concrete political circumstances rather than abstractions. They did not allow their religious teachings to shape their political narratives. They had a unique ability to step in at decisive moments in the political process without losing legitimacy at the grassroots. The seminal moments of intervention were the demand for an elected body to write the constitution, the insistence upon direct elections rather than caucus-based ones, the rejection of delay in elections, and the opposition to any measure that would curtail the sovereignty of the Iraqi people. These interventions, instances of *irshad wa tawjih* (guidance and direction), fell in line with Sistani's original idea that the ayatollahs should serve as counselors and not take a direct role in government. Perhaps the original principle of *irshad wa tawjih* has been modified as the relationship between religion and politics has developed in the post-Saddam era. But the concept, pliable both in its inception and its application during this time period, may well serve as the groundwork for future modifications over time.

But overall the grand ayatollahs cared most for the good of the majority, underscored by their insistence upon popular sovereignty. They positioned themselves as the protectors of a pan-Iraqi identity and worked to reconstruct that identity every time it was attacked, whether by external meddling or domestic sectarianism. Without interfering in the state-building project, engaging in sectarian maneuvering, or trying to build clerical rule, the grand ayatollahs remained relevant and vital to the political process, endowed with considerable credibility and a relentlessly critical eye on those politicians who were corrupt and those insurgents and terrorists who were sowing the seeds of sedition.

At the same time, the ayatollahs would have a hard time maintaining their monopoly over religious interpretation for the Shiite community. They would see challenges not only from competing Shiite groups such as the one led by Muqtada al-Sadr, but also from lower-ranking ayatollahs who have differing viewpoints about the relationship between religion and politics and the role of clerics in the state. Clerics such as Muhammad al-Yaqoubi have repeatedly called for more political intervention on the part of the ayatollahs. We may expect to hear more from this newer generation in the years to come.

Like Islamists or religious actors elsewhere in the region, the ayatollahs have learned that their position as sole arbiters of a social and political vision grounded in Islam is no longer unquestioned. For example, clerics in Qom have constantly interfered in Iraqi political affairs, despite the clear wishes of Iraqis that they refrain from doing so. In February 2017, mass demonstrations swept across Baghdad and the southern provinces to demand that the electoral commission be overhauled immediately. Shiite clerics close to the Iranian regime watched these protests closely, with an eye on the *hawza* succession. They issued several fatwas against the protests. Kamal al-Haydari, a high-ranking cleric, stated that "institutional reform cannot take place through begging in the streets."[10] Sadr and others reacted to this and other statements with great dissatisfaction, indicating that Iran should remain impartial because it lacked knowledge of Iraqi internal affairs. These comments were also directed at Ayatollah Kazem al-Haeri, a Qom-based cleric of Iraqi origin who once gave religious and political protection to Sadr when he formed his Mahdi Army in resistance to US occupation forces.

The grand ayatollahs were not heavily involved in this particular conversation, even though it at least tacitly involved them. At that moment, the political process required something more than what the traditional hierarchical institutions were able to supply. The ayatollahs left the field to Sadr despite their continued centrality, as evidenced by their ability over the last five years to rein in Sadr, rendering him a conformer who will likely follow in their path, albeit in his own shoes and with his own stride. Given the limits the ayatollahs have placed on themselves and the fluidity of the relationship between religion and politics in Iraq, the public sphere will continue to expand. However, one thing is likely to remain steady for some time: The grand ayatollahs will have a towering moral presence and a secure place in Iraq from their base in Najaf.

NOTES

The majority of the statements made by the grand ayatollahs are available on their personal Web pages. When I cite these sources, I do not include a link to the statements. For additional sources, I have added the URLs. Although the websites have versions in several languages, only the Arabic site has extensive material. The websites can be found by accessing the following links: Ayatollah Sistani at www.sistani.org/arabic; Ayatollah Saeed al-Hakim at www.alhakeem.com/arabic; Ayatollah Najafi at www.alnajafi.org; and Ayatollah Fayyad at www.alfayadh.org. A website dedicated to Ayatollah Baqir al-Hakim, who died in August 2003, has an extensive archive. It can be found at http://al-hakim.com.

Introduction

1. Makiya left Iraq in 1968. He returned briefly between 2003 and 2006 but then left for an academic position at Brandeis University. See Samir Al-Khalil, *The Republic of Fear: The Inside Story of Saddam's Iraq* (New York: Pantheon, 1990).

2. Edward Wong, "Critic of Hussein Grapples with Horrors of Post-Invasion Iraq," *New York Times,* March 24, 2007.

3. Tim Arango, "Advocating a War in Iraq, and Offering an Apology for What Came After," *New York Times,* May 13, 2016. In addition to reviewing Kanan Makiya's *The Rope: A Novel* (Pantheon: 2016), Arango quotes from an extended personal essay that was published in Arabic. It explains Makiya's reasons for writing the novel.

4. David A. Snow and Robert D. Benford, "Master Frames and Cycles of Protest," in *Frontiers in Social Movement Theory,* eds. Aldon D. Morris and Carol McClurg Mueller (New Haven, CT: Yale University Press, 1992), 137.

5. Ariel I. Ahram, "Symbolic Frames: Identity and Legitimacy in Iraqi Islamist Discourse," *Rhetoric and Public Affairs* 11, no. 1 (2008): 116.

6. Rajiv Chandrasekaran, "Iraq's Shiites Renew Call for Militias; Armed Men on Guard Day After Shrine Attacks," *Washington Post,* March 4, 2004.

7. Ahram, "Symbolic Frames," 116.

8. Ayatollah Mohammad Baqir al-Hakim (d. 2003) is included in the discussions although he returned to Iraq from Iran shortly after the war. He was killed in August 2003. Previous ayatollahs, ayatollahs residing in Iran, and lower-ranking clerics are also considered in order to establish lineage and relationships.

9. For a lengthy discussion of this process, see Yitzhak Nakash, *The Shi'is of Iraq* (Princeton, NJ: Princeton University Press, 1994), 243–44.

10. Mehdi Khalaji, *The Last Marja: Sistani and the End of Traditional Religious Authority in Shiism* (Washington, DC: Washington Institute for Near East Policy, Policy Focus #59, 2006), 12.

11. Ibid., 6. Shiite pilgrimages are organized by local clerics, whose jobs are to track Hajj (pilgrimage) codes and laws. They also field questions related to rituals and oversee a highly technical process, which helps to tally the number of followers that each ayatollah maintains.

12. Oudai Hatem, "Muqtada al-Sadr Ignores Fatwa Against Secularist Candidates," *Al-Monitor,* June 4, 2012. Najaf, Iraq, rose to prominence in the middle of the eighteenth century. Qom, Iran, began to challenge Najaf for preeminence in the late nineteenth century. The rivalry continues today. See, for example, Augustus Richard Norton, "Al-Najaf: Its Resurgence as a Religious and University Center," *Middle East Policy* 18, no. 1 (2011): 134.

13. Mehdi Khalaji, "The Future of the Marjaia: How Will the Leadership of the Shiite Community Evolve in the 21st Century?" *Majalla,* April 3, 2012: 2.

14. Nakash, *The Shi'is of Iraq,* 246–47.

15. Khalaji, "The Future of the Marjayia," 3.

16. Ibid., 2.

17. Quintan Wictorowicz and Suha Taji Farouki, "Islamic NGOs and Muslim Politics: A Case from Jordan," *Third World Quarterly* 21, no. 4 (2000): 688, as quoted in Laila Alhamad, "Formal and Informal Venues of Engagement," in *Political Participation in the Middle East,* ed. Ellen Lust-Okar and Saloua Zerhouni (Boulder, CO: Lynne Rienner, 2008), 43–44.

18. Holger Albrecht, "The Nature of Political Participation," in Lust-Okar and Zerhouni, *Political Participation,* 15.

19. Alhamad, "Formal and Informal Venues," 40–41.

1. The Ayatollahs and the Struggle to Maintain Legitimacy in the New Public Sphere

1. For a more extensive discussion on how this historical process unfolded, see Yitzhak Nakash, *The Shi'is of Iraq* (Princeton, NJ: Princeton University Press, 1994).

2. Yitzhak Nakash, *Reaching for Power: The Shi'a in the Modern Arab World* (Princeton, NJ: Princeton University Press, 2006), 6.

3. For example, Ayatollah Khorasani of Iran was a crucial player in Iran's 1905 Constitutional Revolution.

4. Nakash, *Reaching for Power,* 72.

5. Ibid., 36–38.

6. Nakash, *The Shi'is of Iraq,* 66–72.

7. Nakash, *Reaching for Power*, 77.

8. T. E. Lawrence was a military officer and diplomat during the Arab revolt against the Ottomans from 1916 to 1918. He decided that placing Faysal in power was easier than dealing with the tribal revolts that were taking place at the time, reasoning that indirect rule was better than direct rule. See, for example, Martin Walker, "The Making of Modern Iraq," *Wilson Quarterly* 27, no. 2 (2003): 29–40.

9. Nakash, *Reaching for Power*, 86.

10. See Youssef Cohen, *The Manipulation of Consent: The State and Working Class Consciousness in Brazil* (Pittsburgh, PA: University of Pittsburgh Press, 1989). He studied how elites in Brazil tried to instill in the lower classes the beliefs, values, and attributes that might justify their subordinate position in the social order. Other works have addressed the issue of reception. In *Ambiguities of Domination: Politics, Rhetoric and Symbols in Contemporary Syria* (Chicago, IL: University of Chicago Press, 1999), Lisa Wedeen argues that citizens in authoritarian settings transgress individually when they can, in meaningful and creative ways. In recent scholarship on the so-called Arab Spring, Marc Lynch, author of *The Arab Uprising: The Unfinished Revolutions of the New Middle East* (New York, NY: Public Affairs, 2013), makes sense of why a generation of youths lost their fear and broke their silence. He explores the new generation of activism and protest in the region.

11. Nakash, *Reaching for Power*, 87–88.

12. Ibid., 90. See also Ofra Bengio, *Saddam's Word: Political Discourse in Iraq* (Oxford and New York: Oxford University Press, 1998), 100–02.

13. Bengio, *Saddam's Word*, 87–120.

14. Nakash, *Reaching for Power*, 76.

15. Frederic Volpi and Bryan S. Turner, "Making Islamic Authority Matter," *Theory, Culture and Society* 24, no. 2 (2007): 4–5.

16. Ibid., 4.

17. This is not an argument about "stagnation" in Sunni versus Shiite thought. A rich intellectual tradition continues in the Sunni establishment despite the fact that the Sunni law schools were codified centuries ago. It is not an argument about the "closing of the gates of *ijtihad*," as some early Orientalist scholars had alleged. They made the case that Sunni Muslim leaders could no longer use *ijtihad* (independent reasoning) to solve problems. They supposedly had to use analogies from tenth-century texts, as if questioning new contexts was a dangerous practice. The closing of the gates, as the expression goes, ostensibly took place sometime in the ninth century, according to Joseph Schacht. H. A. R. Gibb went on to say that the "gates were closed, never to be reopened." See Wael Hallaq, "Was the Gate of Ijtihad Closed?" *International Journal of Middle East Studies* 16, no. 1 (1984): 3–41. My argument merely suggests that the decentralization in Sunnism more readily helps the rise of lay Sunni groups.

18. For a discussion of how lay trends influenced the revolution in Iran, see Nikki R. Keddie, *Modern Iran: Roots and Results of Revolution* (New Haven, CT: Yale University Press, 2003).

19. Sistani response to *Washington Post* questions, October 23, 2003.

20. Charles Taylor, *Varieties of Religion Today: William James Revisited* (Cambridge, MA: Harvard University Press, 2002), as quoted in Volpi and Turner, "Making Islamic Authority Matter," 4.

21. See Sami Zubaida, "Islamic Reformation?" *Open Democracy*, January 5, 2016, https://www.opendemocracy.net/north-africa-west-asia/sami-zubaida/islamic-reformation.

22. Melani Cammett, *Compassionate Communalism* (Ithaca, NY: Cornell University Press, 2014), 192–94.

23. Marc Santora, "Iraqi Government Officials Reach Out to Shiite Leaders," *New York Times,* December 24, 2006.

24. Amatzia Baram, "Religious Extremism and Ecumenical Tendencies in Modern Iraqi Shiism," in *The Sunna and Shi'a in History: Division and Ecumenism in the Muslim Middle East,* ed. Ofra Bengio and Meir Litvak (New York: Palgrave, 2011), 118.

25. "Peaceful Iraq Protests Spark Clashes; 50 Reported Dead," cnn.com, March 25, 2008, http://www.cnn.com/2008/WORLD/meast/03/25/iraq.main/index.html.

26. Yoav Peled, "Restoring Ethnic Democracy: The Or Commission and Palestinian Citizenship in Israel," *Citizenship Studies* 9, no. 1 (2005): 97.

27. See Juan Cole, "The United States and Shi'ite Religious Factions in Post-Ba'thist Iraq," *Middle East Journal* 57, no. 4 (2003): 543–66.

28. Oudai Hatem, "Muqtada al-Sadr Ignores Fatwa Against Secularist Candidates," *Al-Monitor,* June 4, 2012. Haeri had a history of issuing fatwas to the Sadrists. In 2010 he issued a "loyalist fatwa" that compelled Sadr to support Prime Minister Maliki for a second term.

29. Ibid.

30. See Mohamad Bazzi, "Commentary: The 'Bad Boy' Cleric Poised to Be Iraq's Next Kingmaker," Reuters, May 3, 2016, www.reuters.com/article/us-mideast-iraq-commentary-idUSKCN0XT1SJ.

31. Mushreq Abbas, "Sadr's Sudden Retirement Shakes Up Iraqi Politics," *Al-Monitor,* February 17, 2014.

32. Zygmunt Bauman, *Globalization: The Human Consequences* (New York: Columbia University Press, 1998), 58, as quoted in Robert Gleave, "Conceptions of Authority in Iraqi Shi'ism: Baqir al-Hakim, Ha'iri and Sistani on *Ijtihad, Taqlid* and *Marja'iyya,*" *Theory, Culture and Society* 24, no. 2 (2007): 60.

33. Anthony Giddens, *Runaway World: How Globalization Is Re-shaping Our Lives* (London: Routledge, 2000), 54–68, as quoted in Gleave, "Conceptions of Authority," 59.

34. See Gleave, "Conceptions of Authority," 59–78.

35. Ibid., 61.

36. The official website of the Association of Muslim Scholars can be found here: www.heyetnet.org/eng.

37. John Ehrenberg, J. Patrice McSherry, Jose R. Sanchez, and Caroleen Marji Sayej, eds., *The Iraq Papers* (Oxford and New York: Oxford University Press, 2010), 258–64.

38. See www.heyetnet.org/eng.

39. Ali Allawi, *The Occupation of Iraq: Winning the War, Losing the Peace* (New Haven, CT: Yale University Press, 2008), 183.

40. Seyyed Vali Reza Nasr, *The Shia Revival: How Conflicts Within Islam Will Shape the Future* (New York: Norton, 2006), 207.

41. Abu Bashir Tartousi, "Hawl al-Harb al-Ta'ifiya fi al-Iraq," *Tajdid al-Islami,* September 17, 2005, cited in Nasr, *The Shia Revival,* 209.

42. See chapter 2 for a full discussion of the chronological transition and post-transition phase that began with the temporary constitution and then continued with the permanent one. The Sunnis took issue with several of the terms put in place, including the disproportionate power given to the Kurds and the proposed federal state structure.

43. See Ariel I. Ahram, "Symbolic Frames: Identity and Legitimacy in Iraqi Islamist Discourse," *Rhetoric and Public Affairs* 11, no. 1 (2008): 113–32.

44. As reported by Ahram, the Council of Muslim Clerics published its letter in the official magazine of the Kuwaiti Muslim Brotherhood, *al-Mujtama'.* Eleven days later, another letter was addressed to Brahimi in *as-Sa'ah,* the official newspaper of the UPM.

45. Nakash, *Reaching for Power,* 25.

46. Juan Cole, *Engaging the Muslim World* (New York: Palgrave Macmillan, 2010), 87, 91–93.

47. Letter from Abu Musab al-Zarqawi to Osama bin Laden, July 2005, cited in Ehrenberg et al., *The Iraq Papers,* 252–57.

48. See Myriam Benraad, "Iraq's Tribal 'Sahwa': Its Rise and Fall," *Middle East Policy Council* 18, no. 1 (2011): 121–31.

49. Richard Barrett, "The Islamic State," Soufan Group, November 2014, 8, www.soufan group.com/the-islamic-state.

50. Thomas Erdbrink, "As Sunni Militants Threaten Its Allies in Baghdad, Iran Weighs Options," *New York Times,* June 12, 2014.

51. See "Foreign Fighters: An Updated Assessment of the Flow of Foreign Fighters into Syria and Iraq," Soufan Group, December 8, 2015, http://asiawe.org/foreign-fighters-an-updated-assessment-of-the-flow-of-foreign-fighters-into-syria-and-iraq. ISIS was savvy in its recruitment tactics. It released "greatest hits videos" and relied on recruits willing to engage in gruesome public executions. These people, according to Dexter Filkins, were "psychos and sociopaths." Filkins was interviewed by Terry Gross, host of WNPR's *Fresh Air,* on June 25, 2014. The full interview can be accessed at www.npr.org/2014/06/25/325503790/journalist-dexter-filkins-explains-bitter-consequences-of-iraq-war.

52. "In Their Own Words: Reading the Iraqi Insurgency," International Crisis Group, Middle East Report No. 50, February 15, 2006, www.crisisgroup.org/middle-east-north-africa/gulf-and-arabian-peninsula/iraq/their-own-words-reading-iraqi-insurgency.

2. Sistani, Guardian of the Democratic Process

1. See Rajiv Chandrasekaran, *Imperial Life in the Emerald City: Inside Iraq's Green Zone* (New York: Vintage, 2010), for a full description of the process.

2. There were some slight differences among them. They may have made statements in support of federalism, for example, in cases when Sistani had fallen completely silent, but those statements were usually qualified—for instance, "as long as it was in the interest of the national unity," as Fayyad had declared. Also, in 2014 Najafi agreed with Sistani that Maliki should not seek a third term, but he also called on his followers to support Ammar al-Hakim in the elections.

3. See Sarah Childress, "Ryan Crocker: Our National Security . . . Is at Stake Right Now," *PBS Frontline,* July 29, 2014, www.pbs.org/wgbh/frontline/article/ryan-crocker-our-national-security-is-at-stake-right-now. Empirical studies also show that it takes approximately fifty years to consider a transition fully consolidated. See, for example, Bruce E. Moon, "Long Time Coming: Prospects for Democracy in Iraq," *International Security* 33, no. 4 (2009): 115–48.

4. Sistani fatwa on the mechanism of forming a constitutional council, June 26, 2003.

5. Sistani fatwa in response to Associated Press questions, May 3, 2003.

6. The HBO documentary series *House of Saddam* has many notable quotations attributed to Saddam Hussein. This was among the most memorable ones.

7. Chandrasekaran, *Imperial Life,* 70–71.

8. Ibid., 70.

9. See Fareed Zakaria, "Islam, Democracy, and Constitutional Liberalism," *Political Science Quarterly* 119, no. 1 (2004): 1–20. This cautious discourse was prevalent in US circles.

10. Edward Wong, "Leading Shiite Clerics Pushing Islamic Constitution in Iraq," *New York Times,* February 6, 2005.

11. Marc Plattner, "Liberalism and Democracy: Can't Have One Without the Other," *Foreign Affairs* 77, no. 2 (1998): 174.

12. Ibid., 171–80.

13. Sistani response to *Los Angeles Times* questions, July 2, 2003.

14. Sistani response to French newspaper questions, July 14, 2003.

15. Sistani response to *Washington Post* questions, June 20, 2003.

16. Sistani response to Japanese newspaper questions, July 19, 2003.

17. Quoted in Sistani's condolence letter to the secretary-general of the United Nations on the assassination of the representative in Iraq, Sergio Vieira de Mello, August 20, 2003.

18. Sistani response to *Le Nouvel Observateur* questions, August, 29, 2003.

19. Sistani response to *Polish Weekly* questions, September 26, 2003.

20. Sistani response to *Kzata Hiebauracha al-Belenah* questions, August 25, 2003.

21. Sistani response to *Japanese Economy* questions, July 28, 2003.

22. Sistani response to *Le Nouvel Observateur* questions, August, 29, 2003.

23. Ibid.

24. Jolyon Howorth, "France: Defender of International Legitimacy," in *The Iraq War: Causes and Consequences*, ed. Rick Fawn and Raymond Hinnebusch (Boulder, CO: Lynne Rienner, 2006), 49. After the war began, France pressed the case for UN legitimization and oversight of the process of transition to democracy in Iraq.

25. Sistani response to *Der Spiegel* questions, February 15, 2004.

26. Sistani response to Associated Press questions, May 3, 2003.

27. Bremer's plan entrusted the council to craft a "basic law" that would lay the groundwork for the formation of a transitional government. Moreover, each of Iraq's eighteen provinces would hold conventions to elect members to an interim parliament. This parliament would elect a prime minister, based on a proportional system of representation. The IGC would hold elections for constitution drafters, as Sistani's June fatwa dictated, followed by formal elections, the turnover of power to a new government, and the transition from the interim constitution to the permanent one. By this time, the CPA would be dissolved, although the US military would remain on Iraqi soil.

28. Sistani response to *Indian Pioneer* questions, August 14, 2003.

29. Sistani repeated versions of the need for direct elections to reporters on different occasions: response to *San Francisco Times*, July 14, 2003; response to *Asahi*, July 19, 2003; response to *Japan Times*, July 28, 2003; response to *New York Times*, July 28, 2003; response to *Los Angeles Times*, August 2, 3003; response to *Indian Pioneer*, August 14, 2003; response to *al-Hayat* and *LBC*, August 17, 2003; response to *Le Nouvel Observateur*, August 29, 2003; This is just a sampling of the international appeal of and interest in Sistani's position.

30. Sistani response to *Washington Post* questions, November 27, 2003. For discussion of this fatwa, see also Anthony Shadid and Rajiv Chandrasekran, "Cleric Renews Calls for Iraq Elections," *Washington Post,* November 29, 2003.

31. Pamela Hess, "Iraqi Sovereignty on Ambitious Schedule," United Press International, November 17, 2003, www.upi.com/Iraqi-sovereignty-on-ambitious-schedule/90261069111918.

32. Sistani response to CNN questions, January 5, 2004.

33. Sistani statement on the report issued by the UN International Commission assigned to retrace the facts in Iraq, February 25, 2004.

34. Dexter Filkins, "Iraq Council, with Reluctant Shiites, Signs Charter," *New York Times,* March 4, 2004.

35. Sistani response to Associated Press questions, October 16, 2003.

36. Sistani statement on the TAL, March 7, 2004.

37. Sistani letter of response to Lahkdar Brahimi, March 18, 2004.

38. Ibid.

39. Sistani message to the International Security Council: "A Warning to Refrain from Referring to the Law of Administration for the State in Security Council Resolution 1546," March 18, 2004.

40. Andrew Arato, *Constitution Making Under Occupation: The Politics of Imposed Revolution in Iraq* (New York: Columbia University Press, 2009), 176–79.

41. Sistani response to *Der Spiegel* questions, February 15, 2004.

42. Sistani response to *Asahi*, July 19, 2003. Similar questions and answers were repeated over a two-year period regarding this process.

43. Sistani response to *New York Times* questions, July 28, 2003. This is one of many examples of Sistani's resistance to the formation of militias, even when he was asked about the formation of "special armies for the protection of the *hawza* or to monitor and maintain 'public ethics.'"

44. Sistani response to *Le Nouvel Observateur* questions, August 29, 2003.

45. Sistani referendum on registering the names in the voter records, October 10, 2004.

46. Reidar Visser, "Sistani, the United States and Politics in Iraq: From Quietism to Machiavellianism?" (Working Paper 700, Norwegian Institute of International Affairs, March 2006), 13.

47. The UIA won 140 of the 275 seats in the National Assembly of Iraq, with 48 percent of the vote. A majority required 138 seats.

48. Sistani had also issued statements around this time that warned his associates not to interfere in the elections. Additional evidence suggests that he did not offer his support because of the high volume of reporting that he was participating in events that had actually not taken place. He reiterated that no opinions attributed to him should be followed except those that were issued, signed, and stamped by his office in Najaf. Sistani had issued messages like these in the past in which he corrected information that the media had attributed to him. He reminded his followers that without his stamp of approval, the information circulated was likely fraudulent. Sistani often needed to issue statements of this nature because politicians and media outlets tried to feed off of his political prominence or wrongfully attributed statements to him.

49. Sistani's detailed explanation can be found at www.sistani.org/arabic/in-news/887.

50. Sistani delivered a statement, "A Referendum on Posting His Eminence's Pictures," in response to questions from his followers, April 16, 2005.

51. See, for example, Sabrina Tavernise, "Aiming to Reduce Violence, Shiite Hints at Wider Voting Role for Sunnis," *New York Times*, June 28, 2005.

52. Arato, *Constitution Making*, 198.

53. For an analysis of Kurdish gains in Iraq's political process, see Kenneth Katzman, "The Kurds in Post-Saddam Iraq," Congressional Research Service, October 1, 2010, https://fas.org/sgp/crs/mideast/RS22079.pdf.

54. For a discussion of the context of Hakim's announcement, see Juan Cole, "Federalism Issue Bedevils Constitution," *Informed Comment*, August 11, 2015, https://www.juancole.com/2005/08/federalism-issue-bedevils-constitution.html.

55. Arato, *Constitution Making*, 228.

56. Soft partition meant that Iraq should be fragmented into three regions rather than be governed by a central government. For a detailed explanation, see Edward P. Joseph and Michael E. O'Hanlan, "The Case for Soft Partition in Iraq" (Analysis Paper Number 12, The Saban Center for Middle East Policy at the Brookings Institution, June 2007), https://www.brookings.edu/research/the-case-for-soft-partition-in-iraq. Reidar Visser argued that SCIRI was not representative of the range of Shiite political parties and did not have wide appeal to

the Iraqi electorate. SCIRI had a long history of operation in exile in Tehran and was suscepti-ble to Iranian influence. The UIA was also composed of seventeen other parties with divergent viewpoints on a range of issues. Visser suggested that ignoring 75 percent of the UIA would empower "Iranian clerics in Iraq." Reidar Visser, *A Responsible End? The United States and the Iraqi Transition, 2005–2010* (Charlottesville, VA: Just World Books: 2010), 47.

57. Iraq specialists understood the diverse voices within the UIA. For example, follow-ers of Muqtada al-Sadr held a strong centralist position, as was true of the followers of Jaaf-ari and then Maliki, the two Shiite prime ministers who assumed power in 2005 and 2006, respectively.

58. Visser, *A Responsible End*, 63.

59. Sistani fatwa, October 13, 2005.

60. Sistani statement on Iraqi elections, December 10, 2005.

61. Bassem Mroue, "Iraq Closing Borders Ahead of Election," Agence France Presse, De-cember 11, 2005, as quoted in Visser, "Sistani, the United States and Politics in Iraq," 19.

62. The proposal was made in an op-ed: Joseph R. Biden Jr. and Leslie H. Gelb, "Unity Through Autonomy in Iraq," *New York Times,* May 1, 2006. See also Visser, *A Responsi-ble End,* 250.

63. See Alex Berenson, "Iraq's Shiites Insist on Democracy. Washington Cringes," *New York Times,* November 30, 2003.

64. Edward Wong, "Leading Shiite Clerics Pushing Islamic Constitution in Iraq," *New York Times,* February 6, 2005.

65. For the latest version of the Iraqi constitution, access the following: www.iraqination ality.gov.iq/attach/iraqi_constitution.pdf.

66. Article 2 of Egypt's 1971 Constitution recognized that "the principles of Islamic Sharia are a main source of legislation." The article was amended in 1981, following the May 22, 1980, referendum to "the principles of Islamic Sharia are *the* main source of legisla-tion" (emphasis added). See Nathan J. Brown, *Constitutions in a Nonconstitutional World: Arab Basic Laws and the Prospects for Accountable Government* (New York: SUNY Press, 2002), 180–84. Brown outlines the various Supreme Constitutional Court rulings and their interpretations of Article 2 over the years. It is also generally the case that some of these re-gime gestures to amend the constitution and increase their own Islamic credentials tended to follow legitimacy crises or major exogenous or endogenous shocks to their systems. In the case of Egypt, President Sadat had signed a peace deal with Israel in 1979 that was not well received by neighboring Arab countries. Egypt, formerly the headquarters of the Arab League, saw its membership suspended, until its reinstatement in 1989. Domestically, Sadat wanted to appeal to members of the Muslim Brotherhood, given their widespread popularity, in a bid to regain legitimacy following this unpopular deal. In discussions with Yusuf al-Qaradawi, for-merly a leader and member of the organization, Qaradawi wondered whether the proposed changes to the constitution were an attempt to co-opt the voices of the Islamists. At that time, Sadat also offered Qaradawi a position in the ministry, which he declined, expressing an in-terest in retaining his autonomy. Sadat, in reaction to domestic and regional unrest, attempted to gain moral authority and offer a symbolic gesture to Islam with his proposed amendment. The amendment to the constitution did not save him. He was assassinated by members of the Egyptian Islamic Jihad on October 6, 1981. As it turned out, the amendment would not have a great impact on legislation. Instead, broader policy issues, such as peace deals and US for-eign policy, not the constitution, would shape the political behavior of Egyptians.

67. See Noah Feldman and Roman Martinez, "Constitutional Politics and Text in the New Iraq: An Experiment in Islamic Democracy," *Fordham Law Review* 75, no. 2 (2006): 902–05. The authors offer a detailed account of the changes from the TAL to the permanent

constitution, caused by pressure from people whom they referred to as the "leading Shiʻi cler-ics," or negotiations that reflected the stronger hands of the "Shiʻi Islamist parties." Despite some of the generalized language on Islamists used, Feldman and Martinez do an excellent job analyzing the enhancements in the constitutional language with changes in words such as "respect" for "guarantee" of rights. The authors also help to contextualize the debates about Islam as a "fundamental" source of legislation rather than just "a source of legisla-tion." However, the broader problem I am addressing here is the care that is needed to undo the broader "Shiite bloc" terminology that we use to discuss these issues and the power and action attached to these groups. It's important to distinguish the "Islamism" of Sistani from those who, although they may have religious ideas, may not have the credentials to engage in jurisprudence. However, they do have political power and the space to legislate.

68. Shak Hanish, "The Role of Islam in the Making of the New Iraqi Constitution," *Digest of Middle East Studies* 16, no. 1 (2007): 30–41.

69. See Haider Hamoudi, "Notes in Defense of the Iraqi Constitution," *University of Pennsylvania Journal of Law and Social Change* 14, no. 4 (2011): 395–97. Hamoudi ac-knowledged that praise for the constitution was tantamount to "academic heresy" in some circles. But he was equally surprised that many people with whom he shared his ideas had a deep knowledge of Iraq but seemed to be vulnerable to groupthink. He heard repeated cri-tiques about the inability of the central government to tax, that the regions were on the verge of gaining independence, and that the provisions were vague. Some had hoped that future amendments would provide some clarity.

70. Sistani response to *Washington Post* questions, June 20, 2003.

71. Sistani response to *Japan Times* questions, July 28, 2003.

72. Sistani response to *Polish Weekly* questions, September 26, 2003.

73. Sistani's position first appeared in the "democratic fatwa," June 26, 2003. He offered similar statements during the constitution-writing process.

74. Sistani response to *Indian Pioneer* questions, August 14, 2003. He repeated this exact phrase on several other occasions.

75. Sistani response to *Fox News* questions, October 23, 2003.

76. Sistani response to *Washington Post* questions, October 23, 2003. Sistani offered an almost identical response to *Al-Youm,* November 9, 2003.

77. Sistani response to *Al-Zaman* questions, August 15, 2003.

78. Sistani response to *Al-Maktabeh,* February 12, 2004. Sistani's response to *Der Spiegel* questions is similar, February 15, 2004.

79. Babak Rahimi, "Ayatollah Sistani and the Democratization of Post-Baʻathist Iraq," *United States Institute of Peace Special Report* 187 (June 2007): 8–9.

80. For the language on the Universal Declaration of Human Rights, see the United Na-tions website: www.un.org/en/universal-declaration-human-rights.

81. Mark Juergensmeyer, *The New Cold War? Religious Nationalism Confronts the Sec-ular State* (Berkeley: University of California Press, 1994).

82. Sistani response to *Japanese Times* questions, July 28, 2003.

3. Sistani, a Guide Only

1. Sistani's written response to AFP Baghdad questions, August 21, 2005, quoted in "Sistani: Iraq Could Face 'Partition' Without Reform," al-Arabiya.net, http://english.alara biya.net/en/News/middle-east/2015/08/21/Iraq-could-face-partition-without-reform.html.

2. Juan Cole, "An Apocalyptic Day in Iraq," *Information Clearing House,* February 22, 2006, www.informationclearinghouse.info/article12020.htm.

3. Sistani statement on the visit of designated Prime Minister Maliki to his Eminence, Sistani, April 27, 2006.

4. See the full *Human Development Report* here: www.iq.undp.org/content/iraq/en/home/countryinfo.html.

5. Sistani statement on the visit of designated Prime Minister Maliki to his Eminence, April 27, 2006.

6. Sistani statement on the visit of Prime Minister Maliki to his Eminence, September 1, 2006.

7. Reported by Matthew Sherman, as quoted by Dexter Filkins, "What We Left Behind: An Increasingly Authoritarian Leader, a Return of Sectarian Violence, and a Nation Worried for Its Future," *New Yorker,* April 28, 2014.

8. Mariam Karouny, "Iraq's SCIRI Party to Change Platform: Officials," Reuters, May 11, 2007, www.reuters.com/article/us-iraq-party-idUSYAT15330920070511.

9. Sistani fatwa, January 19, 2009.

10. Sistani, as quoted in "Iraq's Shi'i Clerics Refuse to Intervene in Talks to Form Government," in *al-Hayat* website, London, in Arabic, March 27, 2010, accessed on BBC Monitoring Middle East, www.lexisnexis.com.peach.conncoll.edu:2048/lnacui2api/api/version1/getDocCui?lni=7Y3P-2GK1-2R51-748F&csi=270944,270077,11059,8411&hl=t&hv=t&hnsd=f&hns=t&hgn=t&oc=00240&perma=true.

11. Sistani, as quoted in "Iraqi Shi'i Cleric Al-Sistani Rejects Rule of 'Sectarian' Majority," report by al-Sharqiyah Television, Dubai, in Arabic, May 30, 2009, accessed on BBC Monitoring Middle East, www.lexisnexis.com.peach.conncoll.edu:2048/lnacui2api/api/version1/getDocCui?lni=7VTG-V7N1-2R51-700H&csi=270944,270077,11059,8411&hl=t&hv=t&hnsd=f&hns=t&hgn=t&oc=00240&perma=true.

12. Muhannad al-Ghazi, "Iraq's Jaafari Law Would Violate Human Rights," *Al-Monitor,* November 21, 2013.

13. The cleric and spiritual leader of the Islamic Virtue Party (al-Fadhila), Muhammad al-Yacoubi, was among the main supporters of the Jaafari personal status law.

14. Reidar Visser, *A Responsible End? The United States and the Iraqi Transition, 2005–2010* (Charlottesville, VA: Just World Books, 2010), 94.

15. See Nicola Pratt, *Democracy and Authoritarianism in the Arab World* (Boulder, CO: Lynne Rienner, 2007).

16. See Filkins, "What We Left Behind." Hashimi flew to the Kurdish region, where he received protection. Back in Baghdad, he was convicted and sentenced to death in absentia. Filkins details several more ways in which Maliki abused power.

17. Ibid.

18. Sistani statement about the protests that took place on Friday, February 12, 2011, dated February 22, 2011.

19. Sistani statement on the meeting with Iraqi General Abboud Qanbar, October 16, 2010, www1.alforattv.net/modules/news/article.php?storyid=48359. Qanbar was an Iraqi general who was appointed by Maliki in 2007 as commander of the Baghdad Operational Command, which placed him in charge of all security forces in Baghdad. He was charged with securing the country's capital. Qanbar had also served under Saddam Hussein during the war with Iran from 1980 to 1988. He is known for his refusal to intervene during the 1991 Shiite uprising in the South.

20. Sistani delivered his message to the parliamentarian through his representative, Sheikh Abd al-Mahdi al-Karbalai on January 11, 2013, www1.alforattv.net/modules/news/article.php?storyid=84537.

21. See the UN report on Kobler's meeting with Sistani: www.uniraq.org/index.php?option=com_k2&view=item&id=202:srsg-martin-kobler-meets-with-grand-ayatollah-sistani-in-najaf&Itemid=605&lang=en.

22. One of the interesting developments during this time period is the criticism of Sistani from within the government. A prominent figure from the State of Law Coalition, Maliki's bloc, said that the Sistani did not have "any power to criticize the government's work and object to its failure in management." He added that many shared his opinion but did not openly declare it. There was also some speculation at the time about whether Sistani's representatives would be arrested by Maliki's forces because of the content of their sermons. See Ali Mamouri, "Tensions Mount Between Iraqi Government, Najaf," *Al-Monitor,* August 22, 2013.

23. See Ali Mamouri, "What Is Sistani's Position on the Iraqi Elections?" *Al-Monitor,* March 13, 2014.

24. See Ali Mamouri, "Sistani Calls on Iraqi Voters to 'Choose Wisely,'" *Al-Monitor,* April 15, 2014.

25. See Loveday Morris, "A Letter from Sistani Turned the Tide Against Iraqi Leader," *Washington Post,* August 13, 2014.

26. Charles Davis, "The Iraq War Never Ended: An Interview with Anand Gopal," *Telesur,* April 23, 2016, https://www.juancole.com/2016/07/never-ended-interview.html.

27. Laila Alhamad, "Venues of Engagement," in *Political Participation in the Middle East,* ed. Ellen Lust-Okar and Saloua Zerhouni (Boulder, CO: Lynne Rienner, 2008), 40.

28. Mustafa Habib, "Did Ayatollah Sistani Just Save Iraq from Iran-Backed Militias by Pushing Government Reforms?" niqash.org, August 14, 2015, https://www.juancole.com/2015/08/ayatollah-militias-pushing.html.

29. Sistani fatwa, August 7, 2015.

30. Friday sermon delivered by Najaf representative Sayyid Ahmad al-Safi, August 7, 2015. The full transcript can be found at www.najafpulse.net/tags/friday-sermon.

31. Ibid. For a discussion on the protests, see "Iraqis Protest at Government Corruption," Belfast Telegraph Online, August 8, 2015, www.lexisnexis.com.peach.conncoll.edu:2048/lnacui2api/api/version1/getDocCui?lni=5GMJ-JRJ1-F021-608S&csi=270944,270077,11059,8411&hl=t&hv=t&hnsd=f&hns=t&hgn=t&oc=00240&perma=true.

32. Mohamad Bazzi, "Commentary: The 'Bad Boy' Cleric Poised to Be Iraq's Next Kingmaker," Reuters, May 3, 2016, www.reuters.com/article/us-mideast-iraq-commentary-idUSKCN0XT1SJ.

33. Ali Mamouri, "Will the Shiite Alliance in Iraq Continue to Survive?" *Al-Monitor,* April 6, 2016.

34. See Ali Mamouri, "Muqtada al-Sadr, Chameleon of Iraq's Politics," *Al-Monitor,* May 4, 2016.

35. Anand Gopal, "The Hell After ISIS," *Atlantic,* May 2016, https://www.theatlantic.com/magazine/archive/2016/05/the-hell-after-isis/476391.

36. Haider Hamoudi, "Navigating the Najaf Mantra with the Four Grand Ayatollahs," *Daily Star* (Beirut), November 5, 2009.

4. Quietists Turned Activists?

1. See, for example, Susan Sachs, "The Cleric Spoiling U.S. Plans," *New York Times,* January 18, 2004; Larry Kaplow, "Iraq's Most Influential Man Gets Pulled Back into Politics," June 24, 2014, npr.org, www.npr.org/sections/parallels/2014/06/24/325169087/iraqs-most-influential-man-gets-pulled-back-into-politics; Martin Chulov, "Shia Leaders in Two Countries Struggle for Control Over Iraqi State," *Guardian,* April 15, 2016.

2. Thomas Friedman, "A Nobel for Sistani," *New York Times,* March 20, 2005.

3. Noah Feldman, "The Democratic Fatwa: Islam and Democracy in the Realm of Constitutional Politics," *Oklahoma Law Review* 58, no. 1 (2005): 1–9.

4. Reidar Visser, "Sistani, the United States and Politics in Iraq: From Quietism to Machiavellianism?" (Working Paper 700, Norwegian Institute of International Affairs, March 2006). Visser did not make this argument but refuted the "Machiavellian" claim. See Christopher Dickey, "Make or Break," *Newsweek*, November 9, 2004. For a sample of a journalist's coverage of the confusion surrounding Sistani's new political role, see also Edward Wong, "The Struggle for Iraq: Iraq's Path Hinges on Words of Enigmatic Cleric," *New York Times*, January 25, 2004.

5. Regarding suspicions of the clerics from within Iraq, see Adnan Hussein, "Najaf Seminary Plays Role in Iraqi Opposition," *Al-Monitor*, August 19, 2013.

6. Jillian Schwedler, "Can Islamists Become Moderates?" *World Politics* 63, no. 2 (2011): 350, 351. Schwedler reviews the "inclusion-moderation thesis," which argues that groups become moderates as a result of their inclusion in pluralist political processes. She demonstrates that "moderate" is typically used synonymously with "protodemocratic" or describes groups that "work within the system."

7. Visser, "Sistani, the United States and Politics in Iraq," 5–6, 13–14.

8. Sistani response to *Washington Post* questions, June 20, 2003.

9. Sistani response to Associated Press questions, October 16, 2003.

10. I borrow this concept from Robert Lee, *Religion and Politics in the Middle East: Identity, Ideology, Institutions, and Attitudes* (Boulder, CO: Westview, 2013). Lee argues that in the short term, religion drives political behavior in the region but that over the long term, we see that political context tends to shape and bend religious positions. Lee does not discuss Iraq or the role of nonstate actors such as the ayatollahs; instead, his argument is a broader critique of modernization theory and its assumptions about a linear path to development, especially with regard to measurements such as secularism. His case studies, in which he emphasizes state use of religion, include Egypt, Israel, Saudi Arabia, and Iran. His thesis is useful, so I have modified and expanded it for my case study.

11. See Linda Walbridge, "The Counterreformation: Becoming a Marja' in the Modern World," in *The Most Learned of the Shi'a: The Institution of the Marja' Taqlid*, ed. by Linda Walbridge (Oxford and New York: Oxford University Press, 2001), 237; Faleh A. Jabar, *The Shiite Movement in Iraq* (London: Saqi, 2003), 273; and Muntazra Nazir, "Democracy, Islam, and Insurgency in Iraq," *Pakistan Horizon* 59, no. 3 (2006): 56.

12. See Robert Gleave, "Conceptions of Authority in Iraqi Shi'ism: Baqir al-Hakim, Ha'iri and Sistani on *Ijtihad, Taqlid* and *Marja'iyya*," *Theory, Culture and Society* 24, no. 2 (2007): 64.

13. Soren Schmidt, "The Role of Religion in Politics: The Case of Shia-Islamism in Iraq," *Nordic Journal of Religion and Society* 22, no. 2 (2000): 123–43.

14. Juan Cole, "The Decline of Grand Ayatollah Sistani's Influence in 2006–2007," *Die Friendens-Warte* 82, nos. 2–3 (2007): 67–83.

15. See Mohamad Bazzi, "The Sistani Factor: How a Struggle Within Shiism Will Shape the Future of Iraq," *Boston Review*, August 12, 2014.

16. It should also be noted that the binary comparison was also justified from within the clerical class. Ayatollah Muhammad Sadiq al-Sadr had strongly condemned Sistani and other "quietist" Shiite leaders for not speaking out against Ba'ath oppression. Sadr developed the theory of the "silent jurisprudent" as a contrast to the "speaking jurisprudent," in which he argued that the ayatollahs had a religious duty to speak out against tyranny. See Juan Cole, "The United States and Shi'ite Religious Factions in Post-Ba'thist Iraq," *Middle East Journal* 57, no. 4 (2003): 550–53.

17. See, for example, Seyyed Vali Reza Nasr, "Iraq: The First Arab Shia State," *Missouri Review* 29, no. 2 (2006): 132–53.

18. The concept of *velayat-e faqih* was first developed by Sheikh Ahmed al-Niraqi, a scholar from Kashan, Iran, who died in 1820. A chapter in his book *Awaid al-Ayyam* titled "Velayat-e Faqih" detailed the theory of Islamic governance. Khomeini was influenced by Niraqi's work as he developed his theory of government.

19. Augustus Richard Norton, "Al-Najaf: Its Resurgence as a Religious and University Center," *Middle East Policy* 18, no. 1 (2011): 132–45.

20. T. M. Aziz, "The Role of Muhammad Baqir al-Sadr in Shii Political Activism in Iraq from 1958–1980," *International Journal of Middle East Studies* 25, no. 2 (1993): 207–22.

21. John Walbridge, "Muhammad Baqir al-Sadr: The Search for New Foundations," in Walbridge, *The Most Learned of the Shi'a*, 131–39.

22. Talib Aziz, "Baqir al-Sadr's Quest for the Marja'iyya," in Walbridge, *The Most Learned of the Shi'a*, 140–48.

23. Chibli Mallat, *The Renewal of Islamic Law: Muhammad Baqer as-Sadr, Najaf and the Shi'i International* (Cambridge, UK: Cambridge University Press, 1993).

24. Norton, "Al-Najaf."

25. See Martin Walker, "The Making of Modern Iraq," *Wilson Quarterly* 27, no. 2 (2003): 29–40.

26. Juan Cole, "The United States and Shi'ite Religious Factions in Post-Ba'thist Iraq," *Middle East Journal* 57, no. 4 (2003): 552.

27. Ayatollah Kazem al-Haeri is an Iraqi ayatollah, but he is not included in the Najaf *hawza* because he did not return to Iraq after 2003, as did Muhammad Baqir al-Hakim.

28. Haeri statement, July 2002. For a full list of his fatwas and statements, see his website: www.alhaeri.org.

29. Hakim statement, May 14, 2001. Hakim was among the most vocal and prolific ayatollahs in opposition to Saddam Hussein. His website is still managed after his death: www.al-hakim.com.

30. Naomi Klein, "Of Course the White House Fears Free Elections in Iraq," *Guardian*, January 23, 2004.

31. Eric Schmitt, "U.S. Officials Say a Theocratic Iraq Is Unlikely," *New York Times*, February 7, 2005.

32. Hakim was not included as part of the *hawza* before he returned to Iraq in 2003, but statements made by Sistani about him, especially after his death, included him as a "peer" and therefore part of the *hawza*.

33. Ali Akbar Dareinia, "Top Iraqi Opposition Leader Returns Home," Associated Press, May 10, 2003.

34. Ibid.

35. "Top Shiite Cleric Draws Huge Crowds; Returned Exile Urges Peaceful Change Under Islam, Rejects U.S. Control," Associated Press, May 13, 2003.

36. "Shiite Leader Calls for Democracy: Iraqi Ayatollah Had Advocated Islamic Regime," Associated Press, May 14, 2003.

37. Tony Walker, "Meet an Alternative to Saddam Hussein," *Australian Financial Review*, February 22, 2003. Prior to his death, Ayatollah Baqir al-Hakim encouraged his brother Abd al-Aziz to participate in the Iraqi Governing Council despite his misgivings about the occupation. He reasoned that participation was important in order to avoid the historical mistakes that allowed Shiites to be disenfranchised. In a December 3, 2003, interview with PBS, Aziz made some of SCIRI's positions clear: "We don't want an Islamic government. We want a constitutional government that preserves the rights of everybody. . . . To respect Islam is one thing, and to establish an Islamic government is something else." See the interview at www.pbs.org/wgbh/pages/frontline/shows/beyond/interviews/hakim.html. Therefore, even if

Ayatollah Hakim had accepted the invitation to take on a political role, it could have been in the form of a consultative council, in the way that he encouraged his brother months later.

38. SCIRI, by contrast, had proposed some ideas that violated Iraq's unity, as discussed in chapter 2.

39. Leonard Doyle, "Exiled Ayatollah Mohammed Baqir al Hakim Combines Anti-American Sentiments with a Desire to See Saddam Hussein Toppled," *Independent* (London), October 26, 2002.

40. Muhammad Baqir al-Hakim, 'Aqidiatuna *wa ru'yatuna al-siyasiyah*, (Beirut: Dar al-Muhajjah al-Bayda, 2009), 18. This book was republished in 2009. The first publication date is not clear. It does not appear on any of the websites dedicated to Hakim, nor does the publisher mention the original publication date in the introduction to the reprinted edition. From the context of the mentions of Khamenei, who came to power in 1989, as well as the current events discussions, it appears to have been written in the mid-1990s. I have used chapters from the book extensively in this section on Hakim to explain his political vision.

41. Ibid.

42. Ibid., 29.

43. Ibid., 35.

44. Ibid., 39.

45. Ibid., 43.

46. Ibid., 45–46.

47. Ibid., 49.

48. Ibid., 87.

49. Ibid., 106.

50. Gleave, "Conceptions of Authority in Iraqi Shi'ism," 71.

51. Soraya Sarhaddi Nelson, "Prominent Exiled Cleric Wants Government Role," *Saint Paul Pioneer Press,* May 11, 2003. "Islam on America's terms" was the term Khomeini used to describe the anti-Soviet mujahideen in Afghanistan.

52. See Ali Akbar Dareini, "Shiite Leader Calls for Coalition to Leave," Associated Press, May 12, 2003.

53. In 2008 Khalil al-Khafaji organized a seminar titled "The Legacy of His Eminence al-Hakim." Khafaji presented a study on Ayatollah Hakim's life. It is divided into two chapters, one that traces Hakim's life up to 1980, when he left Iraq. The second chapter is devoted to Hakim's political life through 2003, the year of his death. The text of the seminar can be found on the website dedicated to Hakim, http://al-hakim.com/?p=1002.

54. For a detailed discussion, see Faleh A. Jabar, "The Constitution of Iraq: Religious and Ethnic Relations," Micro Study, Minority Rights and Conflict Prevention. Minority Rights Group International, December 16, 2006. The report can be accessed at http://minori tyrights.org/wp-content/uploads/old-site-downloads/download-97-The-Constitution-of-Iraq-Religious-and-Ethnic-Relations.pdf.

55. Ayatollah Hussain Ali Montazeri was one such critic. Montazeri was supposed to be next in line to Khomeini as leader of the Islamic Republic, but after he criticized several of Khomeini's decisions, Khomeini stripped him of that designation. In exchanges, Montazeri warned Sistani of the potential dangers of Khomeini-style government for Iraq. See Babak Rahimi, "Democratic Authority, Public Islam and Shi'i Jurisprudence in Iran and Iraq: Hussain Ali Montazeri and Ali Sistani," *International Political Science Review* 33, no. 2 (2012): 194–208.

56. Sistani statement, "Referendums on public property, Sunni mosques, and other issues," April 20, 2003.

57. Sistani response to *New York Times* questions, May 3, 2003.

58. Sistani response to *Washington Post* questions, June 26, 2003.

59. These remarks were delivered during Sistani's June 26, 2003 fatwa.

60. Sistani offered similar responses on at least two occasions: see *Washington Post* questions, June 26, 2003; *Asahi* questions, July 28, 2003.

61. See Ali Mamouri, "Qom, Najaf Differ on Approaches to Tolerance," *Al-Monitor,* January 24, 2014.

62. See the discussion of Sistani's views of the *marja'iyya* in Gleave, "Conceptions of Authority in Iraqi Shi'ism."

63. Sistani offered similar responses to questions from *Asahi* and *New York Times,* July 28, 2003.

64. Sistani offered slightly different responses to a question about the most suitable form of government for Iraq. See his reply to Associated Press, May 3, 2003; *Washington Post,* June 26, 2003; *Los Angeles Times,* July 2, 2003; *Polish Weekly,* September 26, 2003.

65. See selected statements in John Ehrenberg, J. Patrice McSherry, Jose Sanchez, and Caroleen Marji Sayej, *The Iraq Papers* (Oxford and New York: Oxford University Press, 2010), 320–22.

66. Visser, "Sistani, the United States and Politics in Iraq," 16.

67. Ibid., 27.

68. Cole, "The Decline of Grand Ayatollah Sistani's Influence," 67.

69. Sistani response to Associated Press questions, October 16, 2003.

70. Sistani response to *Al-Maktabeh* questions, February 12, 2004.

71. Sistani statement on the visit of designated Prime Minister Maliki to his Eminence, April 27, 2006.

72. Sistani statement on the visit of Prime Minister Maliki to his Eminence, September 1, 2006.

73. Sistani statement on the visit of designated Prime Minister Maliki to his Eminence, April 27, 2006.

74. Bruce E. Moon argues that post-authoritarian transitions to democracy can take as long as fifty years to consolidate. See "Long Time Coming: Prospects for Democracy in Iraq," *International Security* 33, no. 4 (2009): 115–48.

75. Sistani response to *New York Times* questions, May 3, 2003.

76. Sistani's position, as relayed through his son, Muhammad Rida, June 23, 2003.

77. Muhammad Rida's response to Reuters questions, June 23, 2003.

78. Sistani response to *New York Times* questions, May 3, 2003.

79. Aziz Alwan and Caroline Alexander, "Clerical Battle for Iraq Streets Tests Limit of Iran's Power," *Bloomberg Business,* June 10, 2015, https://www.bloomberg.com/news/articles/2015-06-10/clerical-battle-for-iraqi-streets-tests-limits-of-iranian-power.

80. See Paul McGeough, "The Struggle to Succeed Grand Ayatollah Ali Sistani," *Foreign Affairs,* May 23, 2012, https://www.foreignaffairs.com/articles/middle-east/2012-05-23/struggle-succeed-grand-ayatollah-ali-sistani.

81. Haider Hamoudi, "Navigating the Najaf Mantra with the Four Grand Ayatollahs," *Daily Star* (Beirut), November 5, 2009.

82. Fayyad statement, "A Word of Guidance to the Beloved People of Iraq," June 21, 2003.

83. Muhammad Ishaq al-Fayyad, *Types of Government,* www.alfayadh.com/site/index.php?show=pages&id=46.

84. Ibid., 5.

85. Ibid., 15.

86. Ibid., 27.

87. Ibid., 42.

88. Ibid., 60.

89. Ibid., 65.

90. For one study of how the Western media portray Islam, which supports some of Fayyad's arguments, see Owais Arshad, Varun Setlur, and Usaid Siddiqui, *Are Muslims Collectively Responsible? A Sentiment Analysis of the* New York Times, 2015, http://static1.squarespace.com/static/558067a3e4b0cb2f81614c38/t/564d7b91e4b082df3a4e291e/1447918481058/nytandislam_study.pdf.

91. Juan Cole, "Grand Ayatollah Ishaq Fayyad's Fatwa in Favor of the Constitution," *Informed Comment*, September 26, 2005, https://www.juancole.com/2005/09/grand-ayatollah-ishaq-fayyads-fatwa-in.html.

92. Fayyad, "*Bayan* on the *hawza* of Najaf," June 18. 2008.

93. Ibid.

94. Fayyad, *bayan* delivered to *Asahi*, June 4, 2007, www.alfayadh.com/site/index.php?show=news&action=article&id=36.

95. Ibid.

96. Edward Wong, "Leading Shiite Clerics Pushing Islamic Constitution in Iraq," *New York Times*, February 6, 2005.

97. Fayyad, statement, Al-Sharqiyah TV, Dubai, July 14, 2008, accessed on BBC Monitoring Middle East, www.lexisnexis.com.peach.conncoll.edu:2048/lnacui2api/api/version1/getDocCui?lni=4T0D-JDM0-TX34-N1KV&csi=270944,270077,11059,8411&hl=t&hv=t&hnsd=f&hns=t&hgn=t&oc=00240&perma=true.

98. Fayyad response to questions from *Asahi*, June 2007.

99. Jack Watling, "The Shia Power Brokers of the New Iraq," *Atlantic*, September 11, 2016, https://www.theatlantic.com/international/archive/2016/10/iraq-shia-isis-sistani-shrine/505520.

100. Bashir al-Najafi, *Najaf the Pioneer for Hawzas Around the World* (Najaf, Iraq: al-Anwar Foundation, 2008), 7.

101. Bashir al-Najafi, "Speech in Memory of Khomeini," May 30, 2012, www.alnajafy.com/list/mainnews-1-444-789.html.

102. David Rieff, "The Shiite Surge," *New York Times*, February 1, 2004.

103. William Booth, "Awaiting the Word from the Shiite Clerics: The Devout and U.S. Seek Signals from Authorities," *Washington Post*, May 15, 2003.

104. Alissa J. Rubin, "Clerics in an Iraqi Religious Center Are Silent on a Turbulent Election Next Door," *New York Times*, June 23, 2009.

105. Fadil Rashad, "Ayatollah al-Najafi's Son: Paris Seeks Shi'i Religious Authorities' Mediation in the Iranian Nuclear Crisis," *Al-Hayat*, June 24, 2010, accessed on BBC Monitoring Middle East, www.lexisnexis.com.peach.conncoll.edu:2048/lnacui2api/api/version1/getDocCui?lni=7YSX-0M20-Y9M2-Y37F&csi=270944,270077,11059,8411&hl=t&hv=t&hnsd=f&hns=t&hgn=t&oc=00240&perma=true.

106. Fadil Rashad, "Al Najaf Leaves US Troop Extension Decision up to Representatives of Iraqi People in Parliament," *Al-Hayat*, April 26, 2011, accessed on BBC Monitoring Middle East, www.lexisnexis.com.peach.conncoll.edu:2048/lnacui2api/api/version1/getDocCui?lni=52PW-SWW1-JC8S-C51M&csi=270944,270077,11059,8411&hl=t&hv=t&hnsd=f&hns=t&hgn=t&oc=00240&perma=true.

107. Najafi, as quoted in "Iraqi TV Reports on Expected Cabinet Reshuffle, Reconciliation Conference," Al-Sharqiyah TV, Baghdad, December 16, 2006, accessed on BBC Monitoring Middle East, www.lexisnexis.com.peach.conncoll.edu:2048/lnacui2api/api/version1/getDocCui?lni=4MKD-6X60-TX34-N1VP&csi=270944,270077,11059,8411&hl=t&hv=t&hnsd=f&hns=t&hgn=t&oc=00240&perma=true.

108. Fadil Rashad, "Shi'i Religious Authority Abides by Neutrality in Negotiations to Form the Government," *Al-Hayat*, March 27, 2010, accessed on BBC Monitoring Middle East, www.lexisnexis.com.peach.conncoll.edu:2048/lnacui2api/api/version1/getDocCui?lni=7Y3 P-2GK1-2R51-748F&csi=270944,270077,11059,8411&hl=t&hv=t&hnsd=f&hns=t&hgn=t&oc=00240&perma=true.

109. Edward Wong, "Shiite Coalition Strained as Iraq Elections Near; Fissures Grow in Conservative Grouping," *International Herald Tribune*, December 9, 2005.

110. Kirk Semple, "Suspects Still at Large in Iraqi Torture Case," *New York Times*, November 8, 2006.

111. "Final Results of Iraqi Provincial Elections in Around Three Weeks," Al-Iraqiyah TV, Baghdad, February 2, 2009, accessed on BBC Monitoring Middle East, www.lexis nexis.com.peach.conncoll.edu:2048/lnacui2api/api/version1/getDocCui?lni=4VHR-FPV 0-TX34-N07R&csi=270944,270077,11059,8411&hl=t&hv=t&hnsd=f&hns=t&hgn=t&oc =00240&perma=true.

112. BBC Monitoring headlines, quotations from Iraqi press, *Al-Bayinah*, Baghdad, March 8, 2011, accessed on BBC Monitoring Middle East, www.lexisnexis.com.peach. conncoll.edu:2048/lnacui2api/api/version1/getDocCui?lni=52BF-6WN1-JC8S-C22B&csi=2 70944,270077,11059,8411&hl=t&hv=t&hnsd=f&hns=t&hgn=t&oc=00240&perma=true.

113. "Al-Iraqiyah List Supports Iraqi Vice-President Abd al-Mahdi for Premier," Al-Sharqiyah TV, Dubai, October 20, 2010, accessed on BBC Monitoring Middle East, www. lexisnexis.com.peach.conncoll.edu:2048/lnacui2api/api/version1/getDocCui?lni=518V-385 1-JC8S-C15F&csi=270944,270077,11059,8411&hl=t&hv=t&hnsd=f&hns=t&hgn=t&oc= 00240&perma=true.

114. "Cleric Urges Iraq Poll Neutrality," Aljazeera.net, February 27, 2010, accessed on BBC Monitoring Middle East, www.lexisnexis.com.peach.conncoll.edu:2048/lnacui2api/api/ version1/getDocCui?lni=7XWS-77B0-YBWY-S0WG&csi=270944,270077,11059,8411&hl =t&hv=t&hnsd=f&hns=t&hgn=t&oc=00240&perma=true.

115. "Iraqi Shi'i Cleric Warns Against "Re-electing Advocates of Sectarianism," Al-Sharqiyah TV, Dubai, February 26, 2010, accessed on BBC Monitoring Middle East, www.lexisne xis.com.peach.conncoll.edu:2048/lnacui2api/api/version1/getDocCui?lni=7XWG-X680-Y9M2-Y20S&csi=270944,270077,11059,8411&hl=t&hv=t&hnsd=f&hns=t&hgn=t&oc=00240& perma=true.

116. Mushreq Abbas, "Shi'i Parties Return from Iran with an Agreement to Support al-Maliki," *Al-Hayat*, February 2, 2013, accessed on BBC Monitoring Middle East, www. lexisnexis.com.peach.conncoll.edu:2048/lnacui2api/api/version1/getDocCui?lni=57N8-W9K 1-DYRV-33VN&csi=270944,270077,11059,8411&hl=t&hv=t&hnsd=f&hns=t&hgn=t&oc =00240&perma=true.

117. BBC Monitoring Headlines, quotations from Iraqi press, *Sawt al-Iraq*, Baghdad, April 11, 2013, accessed on BBC Monitoring Middle East, www.lexisnexis.com.peach. conncoll.edu:2048/lnacui2api/api/version1/getDocCui?lni=585J-3D91-DYRV-32TJ&csi=27 0944,270077,11059,8411&hl=t&hv=t&hnsd=f&hns=t&hgn=t&oc=00240&perma=true.

118. "Bashir al-Najafi Participates in the Parliamentary Elections," National Iraqi News Agency, April 30, 2014, accessed on BBC Monitoring Middle East, www.lexisnexis.com.peach. conncoll.edu:2048/lnacui2api/api/version1/getDocCui?lni=5C3G-YW01-F11P-X2V6& csi=270944,270077,11059,8411&hl=t&hv=t&hnsd=f&hns=t&hgn=t&oc=00240&per ma=true.

119. The video is online at https://www.youtube.com/watch?v=5WcrvtxySz8.

120. Steven Lee Myers, "Iraqi Cleric Avoids Using His Power to Sway Voters," *New York Times*, March 3, 2010.

121. "Iraq Bill Sparks Fury Over Child Marriage Claims," *Daily Pak Banker,* March 19, 2014, accessed on BBC Monitoring Middle East, www.lexisnexis.com.peach.conncoll.edu: 2048/lnacui2api/api/version1/getDocCui?lni=5BSG-RVR1-DXCW-D1CB&csi=270944,270 077,11059,8411&hl=t&hv=t&hnsd=f&hns=t&hgn=t&oc=00240&perma=true.

122. "Iraqi Justice Minister Presses Shiite Personal Status Law," *Legal Monitor Worldwide,* March 4, 2014, accessed on BBC Monitoring Middle East, www.lexisnexis.com.peach. conncoll.edu:2048/lnacui2api/api/version1/getDocCui?lni=5BNB-T9V1-JDJN-62BT&csi=2 70944,270077,11059,8411&hl=t&hv=t&hnsd=f&hns=t&hgn=t&oc=00240&perma=true.

123. Statement by Najafi, Al-Hayat website, London, March 27, 2010, accessed on BBC Monitoring Middle East, www.lexisnexis.com.peach.conncoll.edu:2048/lnacui2api/api/ver sion1/getDocCui?lni=7Y3P-2GK1-2R51-748F&csi=270944,270077,11059,8411&hl=t&hv =t&hnsd=f&hns=t&hgn=t&oc=00240&perma=true.

5. Local and Regional Sectarian Narratives

1. See the discussion in chapter 1 on the competition among new social actors and how identities were reshaped after 2003.

2. By "construct," I refer to the range of works within social constructionism for which the understanding of the world forms the basis for shared assumptions about reality. The social construct forms an idea that would be widely accepted as natural but may not represent a reality shared by those in the society. It would be an "invention" or "artificial creation" of that society. Thinkers such as Jurgen Habermas and Michel Foucault wrote about power dynamics and how they are reproduced in order to dominate subordinate cultures. Accordingly, discourses are a powerful tool in the process in which language eventually does not mirror reality; it constitutes or creates reality. See Gail T. Fairhurst and David Grant, "The Social Construction of Leadership: A Sailing Guide," *Management Communication Quarterly* 24, no. 2 (2010): 171–210.

3. For a discussion on civil wars and their impact on states, see James D. Fearon, "Iraq's Civil War," *Foreign Affairs,* March/April 2007.

4. For a list of collapsed states, see Robert Olson, "Iraq, an Example of a Collapsed State," *Global Policy Forum,* February 21, 2008, https://www.globalpolicy.org/component/content/article/173/30484.html.

5. See Rajiv Chandrasekaran, *Imperial Life in the Emerald City: Inside Iraq's Green Zone* (New York: Vintage, 2010).

6. Reidar Visser, "Ethnicity, Federalism, and the Idea of Sectarian Citizenship in Iraq: A Critique," *International Review of the Red Cross* 89, no. 868 (2007): 809–22.

7. See Martin Walker, "The Making of Modern Iraq," *Wilson Quarterly* 27, no. 2 (2003): 29–40.

8. Joseph R. Biden Jr. and Leslie H. Gelb, "Unity Through Autonomy in Iraq," *New York Times,* May 1, 2006. In this article the authors lay out a plan for the establishment of three autonomous regions in Iraq based on the notion that things were "already heading toward partition."

9. An analysis of the "best comprehensive survey of the Modern Middle East history" describes Iraq as follows: "The British officials who determined the boundaries of the post-Ottoman Arab world were at their most arbitrary in the case of the new state of Iraq. The Ottomans had administered the Mesopotamian region as three separate and very distinct provinces." Quoted in William Cleveland, *A History of the Modern Middle East,* 3rd ed. (Boulder, CO: Westview, 2012), 204; *The Middle East,* 11th ed. (Washington, DC: Congressional Quarterly, 2007), 264, casually describes Iraqis as having "difficulty accepting the

concept of an Iraqi nation" because they "readily identified with ancient local orientations." Examples abound.

10. See Peter Galbraith's *The End of Iraq: How American Incompetence Created a War Without End* (New York: Simon & Schuster, 2007); Liam Anderson and Gareth R. V. Stansfield, *The Future of Iraq: Dictatorship, Democracy or Division?* (New York: Palgrave, 2004); For pundits, see Tim Sebastian, anchor of *HARDtalk*, BBC World News, as referenced in Reidar Visser, *A Responsible End? The United States and the Iraqi Transition, 2005–2010* (Charlottesville, VA: Just World Books, 2010), 22.

11. Sami Zubaida, "The Fragments Imagine the Nation: The Case of Iraq," *International Journal of Middle East Studies* 34, no. 2 (2002): 202–15.

12. Visser worked extensively in British archives of Basra that dated to the 1920s, focusing on the Basra separatist movement. His other sources included archives at the Public Record Office at Kew in London, where he accessed the Ottoman and early British Mandate Period; Visser also gained access to newspapers such as *Times of Mesopotamia* through the Library of Congress.

13. Yael Tamir, "The Enigma of Nationalism," *World Politics* 47, no. 3 (1995): 418–40. This review article offers an extensive analysis of Benedict Anderson's *Imagined Communities: Reflections on the Origin and Spread of Nationalism* (New York: Verso, 1983).

14. Reidar Visser, "Historical Myths of a Divided Iraq," *Survival: Global Politics and Strategy* 50, no. 2 (2008): 95–106. Visser writes extensively on this topic; see also *Basra, the Failed Gulf State: Separatism and Nationalism in Southern Iraq* (Berlin: Lit Verlag, 2005), 62–63.

15. Other scholars and historians such as Eugene Rogan and James Gelvin offer careful analyses of Arabs during the Ottoman and post-Ottoman period. See Eugene Rogan, *The Arabs* (New York: Basic, 2011), and *The Fall of the Ottomans: The Great War in the Middle East* (New York: Basic, 2015). See also James Gelvin, "The League of Nations and the Question of National Identity in the Fertile Crescent," *World Affairs* 158, no. 1 (1995): 35–43.

16. As discussed in chapter 2, the sectarian model was premised first on the idea of the Transitional Administrative Law (TAL), the temporary constitution that laid the foundation for federalism in the permanent constitution. It also designated a collective presidency, based on a predetermined ethno-sectarian structure. It had a council that consisted of three people: a Kurd, a Sunni Arab, and an Arab Shiite.

17. John Ehrenberg, J. Patrice McSherry, Jose R. Sanchez, and Caroleen Marji Sayej, eds., *The Iraq Papers* (Oxford and New York: Oxford University Press, 2010), 253.

18. Ibid., 257.

19. Declaration of the Shia of Iraq, July 2002. This document declared "loyalty to Iraq" rather than loyalty to any sect or national or religious affiliation. It reflected the voices of a range of Shiites. See www.iraqishia.com/Docs/Declaration.htm.

20. Ibid.

21. Ibid.

22. See Abbas Kelidar, "States Without Foundations: The Political Evolution of State and Society in the Arab East," *Journal of Contemporary History* 28, no. 2 (1993): 315–38; Bernard Lewis, "The Roots of Muslim Rage," *Atlantic*, September 1990, https://www.theatlantic.com/magazine/archive/1990/09/the-roots-of-muslim-rage/304643.

23. Roger Owen, "The Middle East in the Eighteenth Century—An 'Islamic' Society in Decline?" *British Journal of Middle Eastern Studies* 3, no. 2 (1976): 110–17.

24. Sistani response to *New York Times* question, May 3, 2003.

25. Sistani response to Reuters questions, April 20, 2003.

26. Sistani response to *Le Nouvel Observateur*, August 29, 2003.

27. Sistani statement, "The martyrdom of His Eminence Ayatollah al-Sayyid Muhammad Baqir al-Hakim," August 30, 2003.

28. Sistani response to *Indian Pioneer* questions, August 14, 2003.

29. Sistani statement, "Sadrist Movement asks his Eminence al-Sayyid Sistani about threats from al-Zarqawi," September 25, 2005.

30. Sistani response to *Der Spiegel* questions, February 15, 2004.

31. Sistani statement, "Referendums on public property, Sunni mosques, and other issues," April 20, 2003.

32. Sistani response to *New York Times* questions, July 28, 2003.

33. Sistani response to *Al-Youm* questions, November 9, 2003.

34. Sistani response to *Kzata Hiebaurcha al-Bulenah* questions, August 25, 2003.

35. Sistani response to *Washington Post* questions, October 23, 2003.

36. Sistani statement, "A Message to the Iraqi people about sectarian sedition," July 18, 2006.

37. Ibid.

38. Ibid.

39. Sistani statement, "Referendum on the fate of officials from the previous regime," May 15, 2003.

40. Sistani statement, "A Letter to Egyptian president Hosni Mubarak on his comments on Shiite loyalty," April 8, 2006.

41. Sistani statement, "A Referendum on the temporary government formed by the United Nations," June 2, 2004.

42. Sistani statement, "A Message to the Iraqi people on sectarian sedition," July 18, 2006.

43. In 2006 there were 29,451 civilian deaths, and June was the deadliest month, with 3,298 deaths. This is a significant increase when compared to 16,593 deaths in 2005. For the statistics, see https://www.iraqbodycount.org/database.

44. Sistani statement, "A Message to the Iraqi people on sectarian sedition," July 18, 2006.

45. Sistani response to *New York Times* questions, July 28, 2003.

46. Ibid.

47. Sistani response to CNN.net questions, January 5, 2004.

48. Sistani statement on the visit of designated Prime Minister Maliki to his Eminence, April 27, 2006.

49. Sistani response to *Polish Weekly* questions, September 30, 2003.

50. Sistani response to Associated Press questions, October 16, 2003.

51. Sistani statement, "A message to the Iraqi people about sectarian sedition," July 18, 2006.

52. Sistani response to *Le Nouvel Observateur* questions, August 29, 2003.

53. Sistani response to Associated Press questions, May 3, 2003.

54. Sistani statement, "The martyrdom of his Eminence Ayatollah al-Sayyid Muhammad Baqir al-Hakim," August 30, 2003.

55. Juan Cole makes a similar argument in order to distinguish why the Wahhabis in Saudi Arabia are associated with extremism when compared to the Wahhabis in Qatar. For Cole the explanatory variable is foreign intervention. Saudi Arabia's relationship with the United States made it susceptible to the rise of homegrown extremism. See Cole, *Engaging the Muslim World* (New York: Palgrave Macmillan, 2010, chapter 2), for a fuller discussion of this connection.

56. In a separate statement on the explosion in Karbala, Sistani reiterated the need for security, the responsibility of occupation forces to control borders, and the need for Iraqis to be cautious about the motivations of those who want to sow sedition among Iraqis. Sistani, "Statement on the explosions of 10th al-Muharram in Karbala," March 1, 2004.

57. Sistani response to *Washington Post* questions, October 23, 2003.

58. Sistani statement, "Sadrist Movement asks his Eminence al-Sayyid Sistani about threats from al-Zarqawi," September 25, 2005.

59. Sistani statement, "A Message to the Iraqi people about sectarian sedition," July 18, 2006.

60. Ibid.

61. Ibid.

62. Ibid.

63. Ibid.

64. Sistani response to *Foresight* questions, October 7, 2006.

65. Sistani statement on protests, February 21, 2011.

66. Dexter Filkins, "What We Left Behind: An Increasingly Authoritarian Leader, a Return of Sectarian Violence, and a Nation Worried for Its Future," *New Yorker,* April 28, 2014.

67. Ibid.

68. Sistani statement, "A speech on the current situation in Iraq," delivered by his representative Sheikh abd al-Mahdi al-Karbalai, June 11, 2014.

69. Sistani fatwa on ISIS, June 13, 2014. This fatwa received widespread media coverage. Many translations of the fatwa are available, along with extensive commentary on Sistani's specific use of terms to rally support for the cause.

70. The PMF at that time was composed of various actors. It also united existing militias and operated outside of the Iraqi regular armed forces. It was composed of a range of parties, some with ties to groups in Iran. It was also evident that the PMF was responsible for sectarian attacks and that its modus operandi had shifted. Many observers believed that it was imperative that the militia be folded back into the armed services.

71. Ayatollah Saeed al-Hakim, *Directive to the Iraqi People* (Cairo: Dar al-Hilal, 2003), 3. The book is available online at www.alhakeem.com/arabic/lib.

72. Ibid., 3.

73. Ibid., 7.

74. Ibid., 7.

75. Ibid., 8.

76. Ibid., 8.

77. Ibid., 11.

78. Ibid., 11.

79. See Lisa Wedeen, *Ambiguities of Domination: Politics, Rhetoric and Symbols in Contemporary Syria* (Chicago: University of Chicago Press, 1999). This book explores why Syrians never took the steps from individual to collective transgressions against the brutality of a bankrupt regime. Arguing against the scholarship which assumed that Syrians complied because they believed the regime was legitimate, Wedeen demonstrated that their compliance was reflective of their own need to survive.

80. Hakim, undated fatwa on the difference between Sunnis and Shiites, www.alhakeem. com/arabic/pages/quesans/listgroup.php?AllGroup.

81. Fayyad statement, "A word of guidance to the beloved people of Iraq," June 21, 2003.

82. Fayyad, as quoted in "Iraqi Shi'i cleric calls for elections regardless of security situation," *Al-Adalah,* Baghdad, October 12, 2004, http://0-www.lexisnexis.com.helin.uri.edu/lnacui2api/api/version1/getDocCui?lni=4DJ9-FPN0-00KJ-D3XX&csi=10962,153459,1534 47&hl=t&hv=t&hnsd=f&hns=t&hgn=t&oc=00240&perma=true. See also Juan Cole, "Sadrists to Boycott Elections: Daraji," *Informed Comment,* September 28, 2004, https://www.juancole.com/2004/09/sadrists-to-boycott-elections-daraji.html.

83. See Dalal Saoud, "Najaf Imams Call for Confronting Coalition," United Press International, April 4, 2003, https://www.upi.com/Defense-News/2003/04/04/Najaf-imams-call-for-confronting-coalition/59301049478688.

84. Edward Said was a professor of English, history, and comparative literature at Columbia University. His book *Orientalism* explores the power dynamic between the Orient and the Occident. Said talked about the ways in the which the West defined the East through its sense of superiority in order to colonize and subjugate its populace.

85. Fayyad statement, "A word of guidance to the beloved people of Iraq," June 21, 2003.

86. Ibid.

87. Ibid.

88. Ibid.

89. Ibid.

90. Fayyad *bayan*, "Statement on the success of the elections," April 1, 2005.

91. Fayyad statement to Prime Minister Jaafari urging him to sever state sponsorship of terrorism, September 26, 2005.

92. Ibid.

93. Fayyad statement, "A message to Iraqi Prime Minister Maliki to offer guidance and solutions to problems in the country," December 30, 2006.

94. Ibid.

95. Fayyad statement to Prime Minister Jaafari urging him to sever state sponsorship of terrorism, September 26, 2005.

96. Fayyad response to *Asahi* questions, June 4, 2007.

97. Ibid.

98. For the statistics, see the UN Refugee Agency (UNHCR): www.unhcr.org/461f7cb92. pdf. I also conducted fieldwork among Iraqi refugees in Jordan in the summer of 2010. I interviewed dozens of families, and one question I asked of all of them was "Would you ever return to Iraq?" All my interviewees responded that they would never return to Iraq, regardless of the circumstances.

99. Fayyad response to *Asahi* questions, June 4, 2007.

100. Ibid.

101. Sistani, "A letter to Egyptian president Hosni Mubarak on his comments on Shiite loyalty," April 8, 2006.

102. Ibid.

103. Ibid.

104. Sistani response to Associated Press questions, May 3, 2003.

105. According to a Human Rights Watch report, civilians were tried in military court. The report, titled "Bahrain: Set Aside Martial Law Death Sentences" (Human Rights Watch Report, May 2, 2011), can be found at https://www.hrw.org/news/2011/05/02/bahrain-set-aside-martial-law-death-sentences. For a discussion of protests, see "Bahrain's Shias Demand Reform at Mass Rally," Al-Jazeera online, March 9, 2012, www.aljazeera.com/news/middle east/2012/03/201239144334860869.html.

106. BBC News aired a special on the crisis, "Bahrain's Forgotten Spring," BBC News, *Our World,* March 18, 2012, www.bbc.co.uk/programmes/b01dms66.

107. Fayyad *bayan,* "The Situation in Bahrain," March 16, 2011.

108. Ibid.

109. "Larijani Meets with Iraqi Speaker, Clerics on Syria, Palestinians," *Al-Monitor,* November 29, 2012. This article was translated from Arabic into English, *Al-Zaman,* November 28, 2012. The original article can be found at https://www.azzaman.com/?p=19692.

110. Sistani statement, "A letter to Prime Minister Nouri al-Maliki on the falsification of documents under the name of his Eminence, Al-Sayyid al-Sistani," September 5, 2006.

111. Sistani, "A statement from the office of his Eminence on Islamic unity and the rejection of sectarian strife," February 3, 2007.

112. Ibid.

113. See Amatzia Baram, "Neo-Tribalism in Iraq: Saddam Hussein's Tribal Policies 1991–1996," *International Journal of Middle East Studies* 29, no. 1 (1997): 1–31.

Conclusion

1. Jack Watling, "The Shia Power Brokers of the New Iraq," *Atlantic,* September 11, 2016, https://www.theatlantic.com/international/archive/2016/10/iraq-shia-isis-sistani-shrine/505520.

2. Hayder al-Khoei, "Post-Sistani Iraq, Iran, and the Future of Shia Islam," *War on the Rocks,* September 8, 2016, https://warontherocks.com/2016/09/post-sistani-iraq-iran-and-the-future-of-shia-islam.

3. Abbas Kadhim, "The *Hawza* Under Siege: A Study in the Ba'th Party Archive" (Occasional Paper 1, Institute for Iraqi Studies, Boston University, June 2013).

4. Edward Wong, "Leading Shiite Clerics Pushing Islamic Constitution in Iraq," *New York Times,* February 6, 2005.

5. See Jillian Schwedler, "Can Islamists Become Moderates? Rethinking the Inclusion-Moderation Hypothesis," *World Politics* 63, no. 2 (2011): 347–41.

6. Noah Feldman, "A Lesson for Newt Gingrich: What Shariah Is (And Isn't)," *New York Times,* July 15, 2016.

7. Shadi Hamid, "Donald Trump and the Authoritarian Temptation," *Atlantic,* May 6, 2016, https://www.theatlantic.com/international/archive/2016/05/trump-president-illiberal-democracy/481494.

8. Nathan Brown, *Arguing Islam After the Revival of Arab Politics* (Oxford and New York: Oxford University Press, 2016).

9. Nathan Brown, "Rethinking Religion and Politics: Where the Fault Lines Lie in the Arab World," memo prepared for the Islam and International Order Workshop, April 29–30, 2015.

10. Ali Mamouri, "Shiite Political Differences Widen Gap Between Najaf, Qom," *Al-Monitor,* February 27, 2017.

REFERENCES

Ahram, Ariel I. "Symbolic Frames: Identity and Legitimacy in Iraqi Islamist Discourse." *Rhetoric and Public Affairs* 11, no. 1 (2008): 113–32.

Albrecht, Holger. "The Nature of Political Participation. In Lust-Okar and Zerhouni, *Political Participation*, 15–32.

Al-Fayyad. *Kitab anwa' al hukumeh*. December 2005.

Al-Hakim, Muhammad Baqir. *'Aqidiatuna wa ru'yatuna al-siyasiyah*. Beirut: Dar al-Muhajjah al-Bayda, 2009.

Al-Hakim, Muhammad Saeed. *Risala Tawjihiyya ila al-sha'ab al-Iraqi*. Cairo: Dar al-Hilal, 2003.

Alhamad, Laila. "Formal and Informal Venues of Engagement." In Lust-Okar and Zerhouni, *Political Participation*, 33–47.

Al-Khalil, Samir. *The Republic of Fear: The Inside Story of Saddam's Iraq*. New York: Pantheon, 1990.

Al-Khoei, Hayder. "Post-Sistani Iraq, Iran, and the Future of Shia Islam." *War on the Rocks*, September 8, 2016, https://warontherocks.com/2016/09/post-sistani-iraq-iran-and-the-future-of-shia-islam.

Allawi, Ali. *The Occupation of Iraq: Winning the War, Losing the Peace*. New Haven, CT: Yale University Press, 2008.

Al-Najafi, Bashir Hussein. *Najaf the Pioneer for Hawzas Around the World*. Najaf, Iraq: Al-Anwar Foundation, 2008.

Anderson, Benedict. *Imagined Communities: Reflections on the Origin and Spread of Nationalism*. New York: Verso, 1983.

Anderson, Liam, and Gareth R. V. Stansfield. *The Future of Iraq: Dictatorship, Democracy or Division?* New York: Palgrave, 2004.

Arato, Andrew. *Constitution Making Under Occupation: The Politics of Imposed Revolution in Iraq*. New York: Columbia University Press, 2009.

Arshad, Owais, Varun Setlur, and Usaid Siddiqui. *Are Muslims Collectively Responsible? A Sentiment Analysis of the* New York Times. 2015, http://static1.squarespace.com/static/558067a3e4b0cb2f81614c38/t/564d7b91e4b082df3a4e291e/1447918481058/nytandislam_study.pdf.

Aziz, T. M. "The Role of Muhammad Baqir al-Sadr in Shii Political Activism in Iraq from 1958–1980." *International Journal of Middle East Studies* 25, no. 2 (1993): 207–22.

Aziz, Talib. "Baqir al-Sadr's Quest for the Marja 'iya." In Walbridge, *The Most Learned of the Shi'a*, 140–48.

Baram, Amatzia. "Neo-Tribalism in Iraq: Saddam Hussein's Tribal Policies 1991–1996." *International Journal of Middle East Studies* 29, no. 1 (1997): 1–31.

——. "Religious Extremism and Ecumenical Tendencies in Modern Iraqi Shiism." In *The Sunna and Shi'a in History: Division and Ecumenism in the Muslim Middle East*, edited by Ofra Bengio and Meir Litvak, 105–23. New York: Palgrave, 2011.

Barrett, Richard. *The Islamic State*. Soufan Group, November 2014, www.soufangroup.com/the-islamic-state.

Bauman, Zygmunt. *Globalization: The Human Consequences*. New York: Columbia University Press, 1998.

Bazzi, Mohamad. "The Sistani Factor: How a Struggle Within Shiism Will Shape the Future of Iraq." *Boston Review*, August 12, 2014, http://bostonreview.net/world/mohamad-bazzi-sistani-factor-isis-shiism-iraq.

Bengio, Ofra. *Saddam's Word: Political Discourse in Iraq*. Oxford and New York: Oxford University Press, 1998.

Benraad, Myriam. "Iraq's Tribal 'Sahwa': Its Rise and Fall." *Middle East Policy Council* 18, no. 1 (2011): 121–31.

Brown, Nathan J. *Arguing Islam After the Revival of Arab Politics*. Oxford and New York: Oxford University Press, 2016.

——. *Constitutions in a Nonconstitutional World: Arab Basic Laws and the Prospects for Accountable Government*. New York: SUNY Press, 2002.

——. "Rethinking Religion and Politics: Where the Fault Lines Lie in the Arab World." Memo prepared for the Islam and International Order Workshop, April 29–30, 2015.

Cammett, Melani. *Compassionate Communalism*. Ithaca, NY: Cornell University Press, 2014.

Chandrasekaran, Rajiv. *Imperial Life in the Emerald City: Inside Iraq's Green Zone*. New York: Vintage, 2010.

Childress, Sarah. "Ryan Crocker: Our National Security . . . Is at Stake Right Now." *PBS Frontline*, July 29, 2014, www.pbs.org/wgbh/frontline/article/ryan-crocker-our-national-security-is-at-stake-right-now.

Cleveland, William. *A History of the Modern Middle East.* 3rd ed. Boulder, CO: Westview, 2012.

Cohen, Youssef. *The Manipulation of Consent: The State and Working Class Consciousness in Brazil.* Pittsburgh, PA: University of Pittsburgh Press, 1989.

Cole, Juan. "An Apocalyptic Day in Iraq." *Information Clearing House,* February 22, 2006, www.informationclearinghouse.info/article12020.htm.

——. "The Decline of Grand Ayatollah Sistani's Influence in 2006–2007." *Die Friendens-Warte* 82, nos. 2–3 (2007): 67–83.

——. *Engaging the Muslim World.* New York: Palgrave Macmillan, 2010.

——. "Federalism Issue Bedevils Constitution." *Informed Comment,* August 11, 2005, https://www.juancole.com/2005/08/federalism-issue-bedevils-constitution.html.

——. "Grand Ayatollah Ishaq Fayyad's Fatwa in Favor of the Constitution." *Informed Comment,* September 26, 2005, https://www.juancole.com/2005/09/grand-ayatollah-ishaq-fayyads-fatwa-in.html.

——. "Sadrists to Boycott Elections: Daraji." *Informed Comment,* September 28, 2004, https://www.juancole.com/2004/09/sadrists-to-boycott-elections-daraji.html.

——. "The United States and Shi'ite Religious Factions in Post-Ba'thist Iraq." *Middle East Journal* 57, no. 4 (2003): 543–66.

Davis, Charles. "The Iraq War Never Ended: An Interview with Anand Gopal." *Telesur,* April 23, 2016, https://www.juancole.com/2016/04/the-iraq-war-never-ended-an-interview-with-anand-gopal.html.

Ehrenberg, John, J. Patrice McSherry, Jose R. Sanchez, and Caroleen Marji Sayej, eds. *The Iraq Papers.* Oxford and New York: Oxford University Press, 2010.

Fairhurst, Gail T., and David Grant. "The Social Construction of Leadership: A Sailing Guide." *Management Communication Quarterly* 24, no. 2 (2010): 171–210.

Feldman, Noah. "The Democratic Fatwa: Islam and Democracy in the Realm of Constitutional Politics." *Oklahoma Law Review* 58, no. 1 (2005): 1–9.

Feldman, Noah, and Roman Martinez. "Constitutional Politics and Text in the New Iraq: An Experiment in Islamic Democracy." *Fordham Law Review* 75, no. 2 (2006): 883–920.

Galbraith, Peter W. *The End of Iraq: How American Incompetence Created a War Without End.* New York: Simon & Schuster, 2007.

Gelvin, James. "The League of Nations and the Question of National Identity in the Fertile Crescent." *World Affairs* 158, no. 1 (1995): 35–43.

Giddens, Anthony. *Runaway World: How Globalization Is Re-shaping Our Lives.* London: Routledge, 2000.

Gleave, Robert. "Conceptions of Authority in Iraqi Shi'ism: Baqir al-Hakim, Ha'iri and Sistani on *Ijtihad, Taqlid and Marja'iyya.*" *Theory, Culture and Society* 24, no. 2 (2007): 59–78.

Gopal, Anand. "The Hell After ISIS." *Atlantic,* May 2016, https://www.theatlantic.com/magazine/archive/2016/05/the-hell-after-isis/476391.

Habib, Mustafa. "Did Ayatollah Sistani Just Save Iraq from Iran-Backed Militias by Pushing Gov't Reforms?" *niqash.org,* August 14, 2015, https://www.juancole.com/2015/08/ayatollah-militias-pushing.html.

Hallaq, Wael. "Was the Gate of Ijtihad Closed?" *International Journal of Middle East Studies* 16, no. 1 (1984): 3–41.

Hamid, Shadi. "Donald Trump and the Authoritarian Temptation." *Atlantic*, May 6, 2016, https://www.theatlantic.com/international/archive/2016/05/trump-president-illiberal-democracy/481494.

Hamoudi, Haider. "Notes in Defense of the Iraqi Constitution." *University of Pennsylvania Journal of Law and Social Change* 14, no. 4 (2011): 395–410.

Hanish, Shak. "The Role of Islam in the Making of the New Iraqi Constitution." *Digest of Middle East Studies* 16, no. 1 (2007): 30–41.

Howorth, Jolyon. "France: Defender of International Legitimacy." In *The Iraq War: Causes and Consequences,* edited by Rick Fawn and Raymond Hinnebusch, 49–60. Boulder, CO: Lynne Rienner, 2008.

Jabar, Faleh A. "The Constitution of Iraq: Religious and Ethnic Relations." Micro Study, Minority Rights and Conflict Prevention. Minority Rights Group International, December 16, 2006.

Joseph, Edward P., and Michael E. O'Hanlan. "The Case for Soft Partition in Iraq." Analysis Paper Number 12. Washington, DC: Saban Center for Middle East Policy at the Brookings Institution, June 2007.

Juergensmeyer, Mark. *The New Cold War? Religious Nationalism Confronts the Secular State.* Berkeley: University of California Press, 1994.

Kadhim, Abbas. "The *Hawza* Under Siege: A Study in the Ba'th Party Archive." Occasional Paper 1, Institute for Iraqi Studies, Boston University, June 2013.

Katzman, Kenneth. "The Kurds in Post-Saddam Iraq." Congressional Research Service, October 1, 2010, https://fas.org/sgp/crs/mideast/RS22079.pdf.

Keddie, Nikki R. *Modern Iran: Roots and Results of Revolution.* New Haven, CT: Yale University Press, 2003.

Kelidar, Abbas. "States Without Foundations: The Political Evolution of State and Society in the Arab East." *Journal of Contemporary History* 28, no. 2 (1993): 315–38.

Khalaji, Mehdi. *The Last Marja: Sistani and the End of Traditional Religious Authority in Shiism.* Policy Focus #59. Washington, DC: Washington Institute for Near East Policy, 2006.

Lee, Robert. *Religion and Politics in the Middle East: Identity, Ideology, Institutions, and Attitudes.* Boulder, CO: Westview, 2013.

Lewis, Bernard. "The Roots of Muslim Rage." *Atlantic*, September 1990, https://www.theatlantic.com/magazine/archive/1990/09/the-roots-of-muslim-rage/304643.

Lust-Okar, Ellen, and Saloua Zerhouni, eds. *Political Participation in the Middle East.* Boulder, CO: Lynne Rienner, 2008.

Lynch, Marc. *The Arab Uprising: The Unfinished Revolutions of the New Middle East.* New York: PublicAffairs, 2013.

Makiya, Kanan. *The Rope: A Novel.* New York: Pantheon, 2016.

Mallat, Chibli. *The Renewal of Islamic Law: Muhammad Baqer as-Sadr, Najaf and the Shi'i International.* Cambridge, UK: Cambridge University Press, 1993.

McGeough, Paul. "The Struggle to Succeed Grand Ayatollah Ali Sistani." *Foreign Affairs,* May 23, 2012, https://www.foreignaffairs.com/articles/middle-east/2012-05-23/struggle-succeed-grand-ayatollah-ali-sistani.

Moon, Bruce E. "Long Time Coming: Prospects for Democracy in Iraq." *International Security* 33, no. 4 (2009): 115–48.

Nakash, Yitzhak. *Reaching for Power: The Shi'a in the Modern Arab World.* Princeton, NJ: Princeton University Press, 2006.

——. *The Shi'is of Iraq.* Princeton, NJ: Princeton University Press, 1994.

Nasr, Seyyed Vali Reza. "Iraq: The First Arab Shia State." *Missouri Review* 29, no. 2 (2006): 132–53.

——. *The Shia Revival: How Conflicts Within Islam Will Shape the Future.* New York: W.W. Norton, 2006.

Nazir, Muntazra. "Democracy, Islam and Insurgency in Iraq." *Pakistan Horizon* 59, no. 3 (2006): 47–65.

Norton, Augustus Richard. "Al-Najaf: Its Resurgence as a Religious and University Center." *Middle East Policy* 18, no. 1 (2011): 132–45.

Olson, Robert. "Iraq: An Example of a Collapsed State." *Global Policy Forum,* February 21, 2008, https://www.globalpolicy.org/component/content/article/173/30484.html.

Owen, Roger. "The Middle East in the Eighteenth Century—An 'Islamic' Society in Decline?" *British Journal of Middle Eastern Studies* 3, no. 2 (1976): 110–17.

Peled, Yoav. "Restoring Ethnic Democracy: The Or Commission and Palestinian Citizenship in Israel," *Citizenship Studies* 9, no. 1 (2005): 89–105.

Plattner, Marc. "Liberalism and Democracy: Can't Have One Without the Other." *Foreign Affairs* 77, no. 2 (1998): 171–80.

Pratt, Nicola. *Democracy and Authoritarianism in the Arab World.* Boulder, CO: Lynne Rienner, 2007.

Rahimi, Babak. "Ayatollah Sistani and the Democratization of Post-Ba'athist Iraq." *United States Institute of Peace Special Report* 187 (June 2007): 1–24.

——. "Democratic Authority, Public Islam, and Shi'i Jurisprudence in Iran and Iraq: Hussain Ali Montazeri and Ali Sistani." *International Political Science Review* 33, no. 2 (2012): 194–208.

Rogan, Eugene. *The Arabs.* New York: Basic, 2011.

——. *The Fall of the Ottomans: The Great War in the Middle East.* New York: Basic, 2015.

Said, Edward W. *Orientalism.* New York: Pantheon, 1978.

Schmidt, Soren. "The Role of Religion in Politics. The Case of Shia-Islamism in Iraq." *Nordic Journal of Religion and Society* 22, no. 2 (2009): 123–43.

Schwedler, Jillian. "Can Islamists Become Moderates? Rethinking the Inclusion-Moderation Hypothesis." *World Politics* 63, no. 2 (2011): 347–76.

Snow, David A., and Robert D. Benford. "Master Frames and Cycles of Protest." In *Frontiers in Social Movement Theory,* edited by Aldon D. Morris and Carol McClurg Mueller, 133–55. New Haven, CT: Yale University Press, 1992.

Tamir, Yael. "The Enigma of Nationalism." *World Politics* 47, no. 3 (1995): 418–40.

Taylor, Charles. *Varieties of Religion Today: William James Revisited.* Cambridge, MA: Harvard University Press, 2002.

Visser, Reidar. *Basra, the Failed Gulf State: Separatism and Nationalism in Southern Iraq.* Berlin: Lit Verlag, 2005.

——. "Ethnicity, Federalism, and the Idea of Sectarian Citizenship in Iraq: A Critique." *International Review of the Red Cross* 89, no. 868 (2007): 809–22.

——. "Historical Myths of a Divided Iraq." *Survival: Global Politics and Strategy* 50, no. 2 (2008): 95–106.

——. *A Responsible End? The United States and the Iraqi Transition, 2005–2010.* Charlottesville, VA: Just World Books, 2010.

——. "Sistani, the United States and Politics in Iraq: From Quietism to Machiavellianism?" Working Paper 700, Norwegian Institute of International Affairs, March 2006.

Volpi, Frederic, and Bryan S. Turner. "Making Islamic Authority Matter." *Theory, Culture and Society* 24, no. 2 (2007): 1–19.

Walbridge, John. "Muhammad-Baqir al-Sadr: The Search for New Foundations." In Linda S. Walbridge, *The Most Learned of the Shi'a*, 131–39.

Walbridge, Linda, ed. *The Most Learned of the Shi'a: The Institution of the Marja' Taqlid.* Oxford and New York: Oxford University Press, 2001.

Walker, Martin. "The Making of Modern Iraq." *Wilson Quarterly* 27, no. 2 (2003): 29–40.

Walker, Tony. "Meet an Alternative to Saddam Hussein." *Australian Financial Review,* February 22, 2003.

Watling, Jack. "The Shia Power Brokers of the New Iraq." *Atlantic,* September 11, 2016, https://www.theatlantic.com/international/archive/2016/10/iraq-shia-isis-sistani-shrine/505520.

Wedeen, Lisa. *Ambiguities of Domination: Politics, Rhetoric and Symbols in Contemporary Syria.* Chicago: University of Chicago Press, 1999.

Wictorowicz, Quintan, and Suha Taji Farouki. "Islamic NGOs and Muslim Politics: A Case from Jordan." *Third World Quarterly* 21, no. 4 (2000): 685–99.

Zakaria, Fareed. "Islam, Democracy, and Constitutional Liberalism." *Political Science Quarterly* 119, no. 1 (2004): 1–20.

Zubaida, Sami. "The Fragments Imagine the Nation: The Case of Iraq." *International Journal of Middle East Studies* 34, no. 2 (2002): 205–15.

——. "Islamic Reformation?" *Open Democracy,* January 5, 2016, https://www.open democracy.net/north-africa-west-asia/sami-zubaida/islamic-reformation.

INDEX

CPSIA information can be obtained
at www.ICGtesting.com
Printed in the USA
LVOW12*1300030418

572123LV00005B/14/P